THE POLITICAL CONTEXT OF LAW

A possible caricature of Thomas Weyland, chief justice of the Bench 1278–89, in a contemporary report. See p. 39 and note 37.

THE POLITICAL CONTEXT OF LAW

PROCEEDINGS OF THE
SEVENTH BRITISH LEGAL
HISTORY CONFERENCE
CANTERBURY 1985

EDITED BY
RICHARD EALES
AND DAVID SULLIVAN

THE HAMBLEDON PRESS
LONDON AND RONCEVERTE

Published by The Hambledon Press 1987

102 Gloucester Avenue, London NW1 8HX (U.K.)

309 Greenbrier Avenue, Ronceverte,
West Virginia 24970 (U.S.A.)

ISBN 0 907628 84 2

British Library Cataloguing in Publication Data

The political context of law: essays on legal history
1. Law – England
I. Eales, Richard II. Sullivan, David.
344.2 KD532

Library of Congress Cataloging-in-Publication Data

British Legal History Conference (7th: 1985:
University of Kent at Canterbury)
The political context of law.

Includes index.
1. Law – Great Britain – History and criticism – Congresses.
2. Law and politics – Congresses.
I. Eales, R. G.
II. Sullivan, David.
III. Title.
KD606.B743 1985 349.41 87–88
344.1

Typeset by Vitaset, Paddock Wood, Kent
Printed and Bound in Great Britain by
WBC Bristol and Maesteg

Contents

Preface

The Seventh British Legal History Conference was held in Canterbury, at the University of Kent, from 9 to 12 July 1985. Well over a hundred historians attended, the majority from Britain and North America, but with representatives also from Holland, Austria, Germany, Sweden, Poland and Japan. Thirty papers were delivered at the conference, on a wide range of subjects. Of these some were discussions of work in progress not yet ready for publication, and some were committed to publication elsewhere. Others again, while valuable contributions to the conference and of high quality, were felt to be too peripheral to British legal history for publication here. Of the remainder a good selection appears below, and we hope it will convey something of the range and vitality of the meetings and the discussion provoked, besides providing contributions to many areas of research.

As organizers of the 1985 conference we should like to thank Prof. A. W. B. Simpson and Mr. J. N. Adams of the University of Kent, and Dr. R. Virgoe of the University of East Anglia for their help and advice. As editors of this volume we should like to thank the contributors for their co-operation, and Martin Sheppard for agreeing to publish it, and for handling the subsequent arrangements with courtesy and patience.

Richard Eales
David Sullivan

Canterbury 1986

List of Contributors

Dafydd Jenkins is Emeritus Professor of Legal History and Welsh Law, University College, Aberystwyth.

Hector MacQueen is Lecturer in Scots Law, University of Edinburgh.

Paul Brand is a legal historian working in London.

Edward Powell is Fellow and Director of Studies in History, Downing College, Cambridge.

Amanda Bevan is Assistant Keeper at the Public Records Office.

R. J. Schoeck is Professor at the University of Colorado, Boulder.

Norman L. Jones is Associate Professor of History, Utah State University.

W. M. Bartel is Professor at the Jagellonian University, Cracow.

John McEldowney is Lecturer in Law, University of Warwick.

Hamar Foster is Associate Professor of Law, University of Victoria, British Columbia.

G. R. Rubin is Lecturer in Law, University of Kent, Canterbury.

A. D. E. Lewis is Lecturer in Law, University College, London.

The British Legal History Conference

The first British Legal History Conference was held in 1972 at Aberystwyth, on the initiative of Professor Dafydd Jenkins. Since then there have been meetings at London/Cambridge (1974 and 1975), Edinburgh (1977), Birmingham (1979), Bristol (1981) and Norwich (1983), and the Conference has established itself as a leading forum for the discussion of the subject.

Proceedings of the first six Conferences have been published as follows:

Legal History Studies 1972, ed. D. Jenkins, University of Wales Press, Cardiff 1975

Legal Records and the Historian, ed. J. H. Baker, Royal Historical Society, London 1978

Law-making and Law-makers in British History, ed. A. Harding, Royal Historical Society, London 1980

Law, Litigants and the Legal Profession, ed. E. W. Ives and A. H. Manchester, Royal Historical Society, London 1983

Law and Social Change, ed. J. Guy, Royal Historical Society, London 1984

Custom, Courts and Counsel, ed. A. Kiralfy, M. Slatter and R. Virgoe, in *Journal of Legal History* v, 1984, and as a separate volume, Frank Cass, London 1985

Introduction

Richard Eales

The study of British legal history, and in particular the history of the English common law, has long been regarded by those who take it seriously as a demanding vocation. An ability to understand and interpret the thought processes of *both* lawyers and historians, now or in the past, is not easily come by. Thus G. R. Elton, discussing reasons for the longevity of Maitland's reputation, and above all for the durability of his conclusions,[1] suggested as a contributory cause the fact that 'In his own line, he has never until very recently had numerous successors able to take up his questions and his sources, and able to develop his themes beyond the point to which he had taken them'. Legal historians 'of quality' are so rare indeed, that 'For a time it seemed as though only one of rank was to be permitted to each generation', though now it is possible to name 'a dozen who have really learned to the ends of the spectrum together'. (It is to be hoped that this number is sufficient to save the rest from destruction).

Clearly, there is much to be said for such a view. The skills required to accomplish tasks like those Maitland imposed on himself[2] are not, and never have been, common. But there is another side to the picture: the expansion of legal history studies in the last generation, of which the British Legal History Conferences and the volumes to which they have given rise are a small symptom. Elton concedes that 'of late the great revival of legal history has at last picked up the message and inspiration of Maitland'. We have been told so often in recent years that legal history has 'come of age'[3] that it seems reasonable to ask what is the proof of majority. Part of the answer undoubtedly lies with those leading scholars who have had the

[1] G. R. Elton, *F. W. Maitland*, London 1985, quotations at 34, 36. As a breezily-written and opinionated paean for Maitland's scholarship and caution, this book is not without dramatic irony, but it contains acute observations on Maitland's methods and approach.

[2] Or their modern equivalents, like S. E. Thorne's formidable re-editing of *Bracton: On the Laws and Customs of England*, Cambridge, Mass. 1968 and 1977.

[3] Perhaps the best evidence of this will be provided when there is no longer the need to keep saying so.

independence of mind and range of vision to challenge some of the old orthodoxies. But equally important is the sheer quantity of useful research now being done. If it is hard to operate satisfactorily on both sides of the frontier between law and history, and it is, then the way forward still lies in free trade and the abolition of border restrictions, rather than in issuing passports to a few exceptional figures who can satisfy demanding requirements for dual nationality.

The recent expansion of output, added to the cumulative achievement of Selden Society editors and others over the years, has now made a wider range of legal sources, and guidance on how to interpret them, available to non-legal historians.[4] In return legal historians have been encouraged to acquire more catholic tastes: research is chronologically wider spread and there is more interest in the broad context of social, economic and political forces within which law operates. It helps to recognize that not all the methodological problems of the legal historian are unique. Historians of science or medicine have to balance a teleological view of the past, as the process leading to the current state of knowledge, with a more properly historical concern for all the conditions prevailing at any one period. Historians of art have to set an 'internalized' analysis of the evolution of styles and techniques from artist to artist against an awareness of external forces like patronage. Lawyers have evolved their own complex methods of appropriating and applying the past to resolve contemporary problems, but that does not mean that studying their history is impossible or even, perhaps, quite so formidably difficult as has sometimes been thought.

Nevertheless, there remain great difficulties to be overcome in relating the study of law to such abstractions as social change. 'Internalized' legal history, ranging over evolving institutions, procedures and doctrines, as well as the personnel and interests of the legal profession, already presents complex issues of analysis and interpretation, before taking into account growing literacy, the long term effects of the Black Death, or anything similar. The inter-action of law and society has been an almost infinitely diverse mutual process, and general syntheses of its operation are still a long way off, even for short time spans. It is possible to isolate the most obvious variables (is change sudden or gradual, does it occur from within the legal system or is it imposed from without, and so on) and use them as

[4] Though much remains to be done. J. H. Baker, introduction to *Legal Records and the Historian*, London 1978, 1-6, is a judicious survey of some of the problems.

criteria for classifying events,[5] but only as a preliminary signposting operation.

But if, so far, awareness of a wider context for legal history has tended to produce more problems rather than more solutions, it might at least be credited with helping to displace nineteenth-century constitutional theories which tended to link the study of law with a particular set of assumptions about the development of the state. The link was epxressed in what is sometimes called 'old-fashioned political history': a story of national events and national institutions which assumes *a priori* that these are always and in every period the phenomena of greatest importance. The title of this book is not intended as a plea for a return to 'old-fashioned political history,'[6] but reflects the concern of many of the contributors with ways in which political pressures and constraints have influenced law and legal decisions. Politics is taken here in a broad sense, to include mechanisms of patronage and local power, and the value system which underpinned social status, not just the operation of national governments, and the struggle to control or influence them. Many of the papers published below demonstrate that the study of political contexts of this kind can lead the way, through particular cases, to more general explanations of legal change.[7]

One obvious link lies in the career ambitions and attitudes of men connected with the law, so far as they can be recovered by biographical study. Biography presents special problems for the medievalist, but Dr. Brand's paper on Edward I's chief justice Thomas Weyland shows just how much can be done with expert handling of the available sources. In defending Weyland's reputation from many of the accusations made against him, Brand clears the way for an understanding of what really lay behind Edward I's 'disgrace of the judges' in 1289-90, and also for a wider comparative study of the medieval judiciary.[8] In the realm of the history of ideas, Professor Schoeck's study of Christopher St. German takes up some questions about the sources and argument of *Doctor and Student* raised by the

[5] J. A. Guy, introduction to *Law and Social Change*, London 1984, 1-8.

[6] Frequently a misnomer in any case: political history has shown as much capacity to renew itself from within and question its own presuppositions as any other branch of the discipline, if not more.

[7] Which does not mean, of course, that the contributors share any common methodology, or would necessarily subscribe to these remarks.

[8] See P. Brand, 'Edward I and the judges: the "state trials" of 1289-1293' in *Thirteenth-Century England I*, ed. P. R. Coss and S. D. Lloyd, Woodbridge 1986, 31-40.

modern editor of the treatise.[9] He shows that further inquiry into these issues helps to tie St. German's legal thought even more closely to his evolving political position. Professor Jones's paper on usury in the Elizabethan exchequer stands, as he shows, at the centre of many concerns of early modern historians. *Inter alia*, the wide range of cases discussed illuminates the motives and attitudes towards the law of those who were caught up in the operation of the usury statutes: all the way from low-life informers to courtiers profiting by political patronage.

More institutional studies may also have a political and indeed a human dimension. Defined administrative procedures frequently rest on tacit assumptions about the attitudes and loyalties of those who operate them. Dr. Powell's lucid and convincing re-assessment of criminal law enforcement in fourteenth-century England shows how the balance between central and local authority was preserved, as much by influence and the personnel of the commissions as by repeated redefinitions of jurisdiction. His conclusions will be of importance for the social history of crime and for the study of the gentry and local politics in late-medieval England. Dr. Bevan's consideration of the assize system in the 1530s fills in what now looks like a significant gap in previous accounts of the enforcement of the Reformation. By implication, her paper also raises the general question of how far early modern governments were equipped to enforce treason laws as a check on the expression of political dissent.

In recent times, disputes between law officers and political advisers to governments have become all too familiar. Dr. Rubin acutely diagnoses the causes of a long-running disagreement of this kind, over the issue of contingency planning for a military emergency, in the thirty years up to 1914. The attitudes shown by lawyers and military authorities in the course of their exchanges are revealing about the assumptions which lay behind law-making and law enforcement in this area. Dr. McEldowney focuses attention on another debate: one that was at its height in the 1820s and 1830s, over the appointment of sheriffs in Ireland. Again a gap was perceived between theory and practice, with the additional complication that much of the theory was derived from debatable interpretations of medieval statutes.

A subsidiary theme in this volume is that of the influence of English, or British, law on other legal systems. Influence ranges from

[9] *Doctor and Student*, ed. T. F. T. Plucknett and J. L. Barton, Selden Soc. xci, 1974.

direct imposition, by colonization or conquest, down to selective borrowings and awareness of parallel developments. Professor Bartel's paper, for instance, shows how English legal writings of the late eighteenth century, by Blackstone as well as Bentham, were disseminated through France and widely read on the continent, but with only limited practical effects. Professor Foster's paper on frontier 'lawlessness' compares the literature on America, Canada and New Zealand to show how a common legal inheritance could develop in different ways, and that law and order could be competing rather than convergent demands. Both Professor Jenkins and Mr. MacQueen consider, among other apsects of their subjects, the influence of the expansive kingdom of England on its Celtic neighbours in the middle ages. In his survey of the Welsh lawbooks, Professor Jenkins summarizes a great deal of work, much of it based on his own impressive documentary research, into the origins, chronological development and uses of these texts. By taking up the suggestion that the lawbooks were codified, at least in part, as a reaction to English 'legal imperialism' he has also thrown down a challenge to political historians, who must ask themselves how this tallies with the policies of English kings towards Wales, and where the Marcher lordships fit into the picture. Mr. MacQueen's discussion of the early history of the brieve of right charts a clear path through some confusing problems and directs attention, by implication, to English influence over Scots law exerted during the generally peaceful period which preceded the outbreak of the Wars of Independence in the 1290s.[10] Mr. Lewis's paper on the *nolo* plea also turns on a comparative study. He looks at the origins of an almost forgotten feature of English law and shows elegantly how it found a new role in American practice.

[10] K. J. Stringer, *Earl David of Huntingdon 1152-1219*, Edinburgh 1985, ch. 9 is a recent study of this delicate political balance and how it was sustained.

Abbreviations

All [other] references are given in full at their first occurrence in each paper, thereafter abbreviated.

B.I.H.R.	*Bulletin of the Institute of Historical Research*
BL	British Library
D.N.B.	*Dictionary of National Biography*, (63 vols., 1885-1901)
E.H.R.	*English Historical Review*
ER	*English Reports*
Foedera	*Rymer's Foedera, 1066-1383,* ed. A. Clarke et al., 4 vols, 1816-1869
P.R.O.	Public Record Office
Rot. Parl	*Rotuli Parliamentorum*, 6 vols., 1783

Manuscript sources in the P.R.O. are cited under P.R.O. class headings as follows:

C	Chancery
CAB	Cabinet Papers
CP	Common Pleas
DL	Duchy of Lancaster
E	Exchequer
JUST	Justices Itinerant
KB	King's Bench
SC	Special Collections
TS	Treasury Solicitor Papers
WO	War Office Papers

1

The Lawbooks of Medieval Wales

Dafydd Jenkins

Students of Welsh history have long recognised that the lawbooks of medieval Wales are a valuable historical source, but until fairly recently the use made of this source has been insufficiently critical, though for this the historians are not wholly to blame. There has been a tendency to take the texts at their face value, to accept their accounts of historical facts as true, and to assume that the social background indicated is that of one period. In particular, historians have allowed themselves to be misled by the use of *Cyfraith Hywel Dda*, 'the Law of Hywel the Good', as a name for the whole body of medieval Welsh law. Hywel died as ruler of nearly all Wales in 949 or 950, and it has all too often been assumed that any statement found in any Welsh law text is true for tenth-century Wales.

For this rather naive use of the material, the specialists in Welsh law must take most of the blame, since they have been slow to respond to a challenge given them by Maitland, ninety years ago:

> Until the day comes . . . when those who are skilled in Celtic philology will have sorted that miscellaneous mass which we know as the Ancient Laws of Wales, the materials which will be at the service of investigators will be of an extremely dangerous and unsatisfactory kind . . . We seem almost entitled to say that it is improbable *a priori* that the Welsh Laws, even in their purest form, represent to us the life of the people as it was being lived, really and truly lived, at any one time. We seem almost bound to frame some theory of development which will mark some rules as new and others as old.[1]

In the last thirty years or so, however, we have seen just such a theory of development taking ever clearer shape, as the result of an exciting inter-disciplinary collaboration of philologists, historians, geographers, palaeographers, archaeologists, and even students of forestry and falconry.

There is still plenty to be done, but the more scientific cultivation of

[1] F. W. Maitland, *Collected Papers*, vol. 3, ed. H. A. L. Fisher, Cambridge 1911, 3-4. The paper was first published in 1895.

the field is now beginning to yield a crop of publications which show the hybrid vigour resulting from the combination of the law texts and other sources. The lawbooks are, for instance, obviously relevant to Dr. David Stephenson's *The Governance of Gwynedd*,[2] for some of the most important of them were written in that part of Wales during the century with which the book is most concerned. But the lawbooks also cast their light both backward and forward from the twelfth and thirteenth centuries. In Dr. Wendy Davies's *Wales in the Early Middle Ages*,[3] as in her other papers, comparison of passages from the lawbooks with documents which may derive from earlier centuries indicates how far the later medieval material has its roots in a much earlier age. On the other hand, Professor R. R. Davies, in a number of detailed papers, and particularly in his *Lordship and Society in the March of Wales, 1282-1400*,[4] uses the lawbook material for comparison with the record evidence from areas which were strongly affected by Anglo-Norman ideas and practices, and (in effect) underlines Maitland's warning that the lawbooks do not give an instantaneous picture of any moment in Welsh social history.

Indeed, the historians have been doing so much for us that the greatest danger may now be that their work will be held up for want of adequately-edited texts. For the production of these, what we most need are more workers who combine some training in law with some competence in medieval Welsh, which is not a very difficult language. For anyone who can easily read modern Welsh, the ability to read medieval Welsh can be acquired in a matter of days, and students who have no knowledge of Welsh can learn to read medieval Welsh far more quickly than they can learn to understand modern colloquial Welsh.

Maitland, of course, did not read medieval Welsh, but his two papers (of 1881 and 1895) show an insight seldom equalled since, and never surpassed: he did not only see what the conditions of satisfactory study would be, but was able to clarify some obscurities from his wide knowledge of other legal material. He worked with the translation in the then current edition of the Welsh law texts, the Record Commission's *Ancient Laws and Institutes of Wales* of 1841, edited by Aneurin Owen and issued in two forms, namely in one folio volume and in two octavo volumes. This was certainly the finest

[2] D. Stephenson, *The Governance of Gwynedd*, Cardiff 1984.

[3] W. Davies, *Wales in the Early Middle Ages*, Leicester 1982.

[4] R. R. Davies, *Lordship and Society in the March of Wales, 1282-1400*, Oxford 1978.

production of the older Welsh scholarship, and compares favourably with its English contemporary, Thorpe's *Ancient Laws of England*; it was immeasurably better than the parallel Irish collection. Its translation is on the whole reliable, though often weak in its understanding of legal technicalities; but we are now very conscious of the defects of the edition, which stem from its failure to make the relation of the printed text to the manuscripts clear enough. It is usually possible to determine whether a particular passage occurs in a particular manuscript; it is sometimes possible to learn that passages occur in a different order in different manuscripts; it is never possible to determine exactly what any particular manuscript contained and in what order. The whole body of the material has been shared between the two volumes in a way which conceals the structure of the manuscripts: Volume I contains three texts which Owen called Codes and which we now call Redactions; Volume II contains (apart from three Latin texts) material in Welsh which Owen called 'Anomalous Laws', though they are in fact anomalous only as not falling tidily into the pattern of the Redactions. Later editors (including myself) have followed the same rather doubtful practice of isolating the Redaction from the associated material.[5]

The lawbooks are the only substantial source of information for the indigenous law of Wales: we have no law reports, and from courts of native jurisdiction no records to speak of. Since some Welsh law was still applied in many parts of Wales under non-Welsh rule between 1282 and 1536, we can make cautious use of court records from marcher lordships and from the (English) Principality, while extents and surveys from this period give us a check on the land law; but all this evidence has to be subjected to a discount for the lapse of time and the change of circumstances from the age of our most important lawbooks, the thirteenth century.

Welsh medieval legal material first appeared in print in a bilingual Protestant pamphlet published in 1550, which used the evidence of a lawbook in support of the argument that the marriage of the clergy was approved by the Pope in the mid-tenth century; our interest, however, is not in that argument but in an introductory quotation

[5] In defence of the separation of *Llyfr Colan* and *Damweiniau Colan* it can be said that the first presents a unique text, whereas the second has a text which has counterparts in other manuscripts, and it was at one time intended to edit the text from all the manuscripts. A rather similar argument would apply to the texts printed in *Ancient Laws*; Owen's greatest fault was that he did not indicate clearly the make-up of any manuscript.

from the lawbook (which in fact undermines the argument). The English version of the passage is inaccurate, so it is here translated afresh: 'Here is a lawbook which Hywel the Good made at the White House on Taf, though there be in it other things, being good laws which wise men made both before that and after that'.[6]

On this quotation three propositions can be rested. First comes the obvious warning that we must not assume, as has so often been done, that a statement in a Welsh law manuscript gives a true picture of tenth-century Wales because Welsh law was the Law of Hywel and Hywel lived in the tenth century. We have also to remember that a statement in a manuscript of (say) the thirteenth century cannot be taken at its face value as reflecting thirteenth-century conditions, and here Maitland has been before us:

> Some Welsh lawyer has collected things new and old. Possibly he was bound to copy down some rules that were well-nigh but not quite obsolete when he copied them. In 1819 an English lawyer who wished to make a complete statement of English law would have been bound to speak of trial by battle as of one of the methods by which lawsuits could be decided. We know well from our own history how apt were the lawyers of past ages to fuse the old with the new, to borrow rules from the most varied sources, without telling us whether those rules were practicable or impracticable, living or dead, imported novelties or obsolescent survivals of a forgotten age.[7]

This leads to the second proposition, which is that nearly all our surviving medieval law manuscripts were put together for practising or teaching lawyers, each of whom wanted as much useful material as possible in the little book which formed his working library. The result is that every manuscript differs in content at least slightly from every other, though (as we shall see later) groups of manuscripts have so much in common that they must be related to one another and to older prototypes. In a Welsh manuscript there is a great likelihood that there will have been added to the basic redaction a fair amount (often a great deal) of miscellaneous material – whether tucked in at appropriate points in the basic text or added at the end. This is only a variant on what Maitland said, in a paper published as early as 1881:

> There seems really very little ground for doubt that the bulk of Mr. Owen's three codes . . . was at one time law in Wales, or at least was thought to be law. This qualification we add because it is very apparent

[6] *Ban wedy i Dynny*, 1550, Aii. Reprint in *Yny lhyvyr hwn*, Bangor and London 1902.

[7] Maitland, *Collected Papers*, vol. 3, 4.

that a large part of these masses of law is neither law made by any 'sovereign one or many' (to use Austin's phrase), nor yet 'judge-made' law, nor yet again a mere record of popular customs. It is lawyer-made law, glossators' law, text-writers' law.[8]

In a recent paper Professor Alan Harding has expressed disagreement with my view of the lawbooks as prepared for practitioners' use: 'I cannot see *Regiam Majestatem* or the books of Welsh law, any more than the *Sachsenspiegel*, as practitioners' manuals for use in court'.[9] He goes on to make a valid point to which I shall refer later, but it seems to me that whereas my view refers to the manuscripts as we have them, Harding is thinking of the Redactions which lie behind the individual manuscripts.

The third proposition is a much less positive one about King Hywel. Did Hywel really have anything to do with the law? The three Redactions have a prologue giving an account of what Hywel is supposed to have done, and it is significant that they call him 'king of all Wales'. Medieval Wales was not a single centralised state, but a collection of independent lands, each having a ruler who claimed regal status (rather like medieval Germany, but without a co-ordinating Emperor). From time to time one ruler would gain control of several kingdoms in a sort of personal union, which would break up at his death. Yet there seems to have been (in theory, at least) unity of law though there was no political unity, and even the theory must surely have been established under a ruler who had authority over a large part of Wales. Hywel is really the only king who had authority over enough of the country, under peaceful enough conditions, to make a co-ordination of law possible.

According to the prologues, Hywel convened a representative assembly from all his dominions, and after the existing law had been examined and revised, a new lawbook was written and solemnly promulgated with Hywel's authority. To this basic account many manuscripts have added more and more incredible details; and most of the manuscripts say that the assembly met at *Y Tŷ Gwyn*, 'the White House', on Taf in Dyfed, i.e. Whitland.

Twentieth-century scholarship has looked critically at the prologues, but Hywel's connection with the law is accepted as virtually certain, and his convening of a representative assembly as

[8] Maitland, *Collected Papers*, vol. 1, 202.

[9] A. Harding, 'Regiam Majestatem amongst Medieval Law-Books', *Juridical Review*, 1984. See also A. Harding, 'Legislators, Lawyers and Law-books', in *Lawyers and Laymen*, ed. T. M. Charles-Edwards et al., Cardiff 1986, 237-57.

probable.[10] We are more doubtful about Whitland as the meeting place, because of the references in some manuscripts to a *Llyfr y Tŷ Gwyn*, 'Book of the White House' or 'Whitland Book'. There is no suggestion that those who referred to it thought of it as the original Hywelian text, and it must surely have been a manuscript at (or from) Whitland Abbey.[11] This Whitland book seems to have been in Latin, and was probably written in the twelfth century, and some years ago there was a strong tendency to believe that the Hywelian Assembly was placed at Whitland because of the Whitland manuscript.[12] More recently the case for Whitland as a centre of importance in earlier centuries has seemed to be stronger, and we are at least ready to suspend disbelief in Whitland as the meeting place of an assembly convened by Hywel. Perhaps we were not on wholly sound ground when we recently inaugurated an impressive memorial to Hywel at Whitland; but even if Hywel never went to Whitland at all, we can say with complete assurance that there was a time when someone at Whitland knew as much about the Law of Hywel as anyone in Wales.

We can now turn to the manuscripts. About forty of these were written before 1536: so they were written for use rather than out of antiquarian interest. Five of them are in Latin, and with them we shall not be much concerned, except to point out that the Welsh Blegywryd Redaction is basically a translation of the Latin Redaction D. The Latin Redactions have been excellently edited by the late Dr. H. D. Emanuel.[13] The rest of the medieval manuscripts are in Welsh, and at a very rough guess, they would give us a total body of perhaps six thousand different sentences: 'sentence' is an extremely vague entity, but as a rough measure of the size of a text, the number of sentences will serve.

The largest single manuscript, so far as my information goes, is BL Additional 22,356 (the *S* of *Ancient Laws*), which contains 2,546

[10] See J. G. Edwards, *Hywel Dda and the Welsh Lawbooks*, Bangor 1929, reprinted in *Celtic Law Papers*, ed. D. Jenkins, Brussels 1973; and 'Studies in the Welsh Laws since 1928', *Welsh History Review* i, 1963, Special Number 1-17. See also D. A. Binchy, 'The Pseudo-historical Prologue to the Senchas Már', *Studia Celtica* x/xi, 1975/6, 1-28.

[11] The abbey, which became the mother of the Cistercian houses of western and northern Wales, was founded by a Norman in 1140 at another site; it moved to its final site about 1150, and soon gained the patronage of the Welsh princes, and especially of the Lord Rhys.

[12] *Llyfr Colan*, ed. D. Jenkins, Cardiff 1963, xxxi-xxxii; *Carmarthenshire Antiquary* xviii, 1982, 26 note 5.

[13] *The Latin Texts of the Welsh Laws*, ed. H. D. Emanuel, Cardiff 1967.

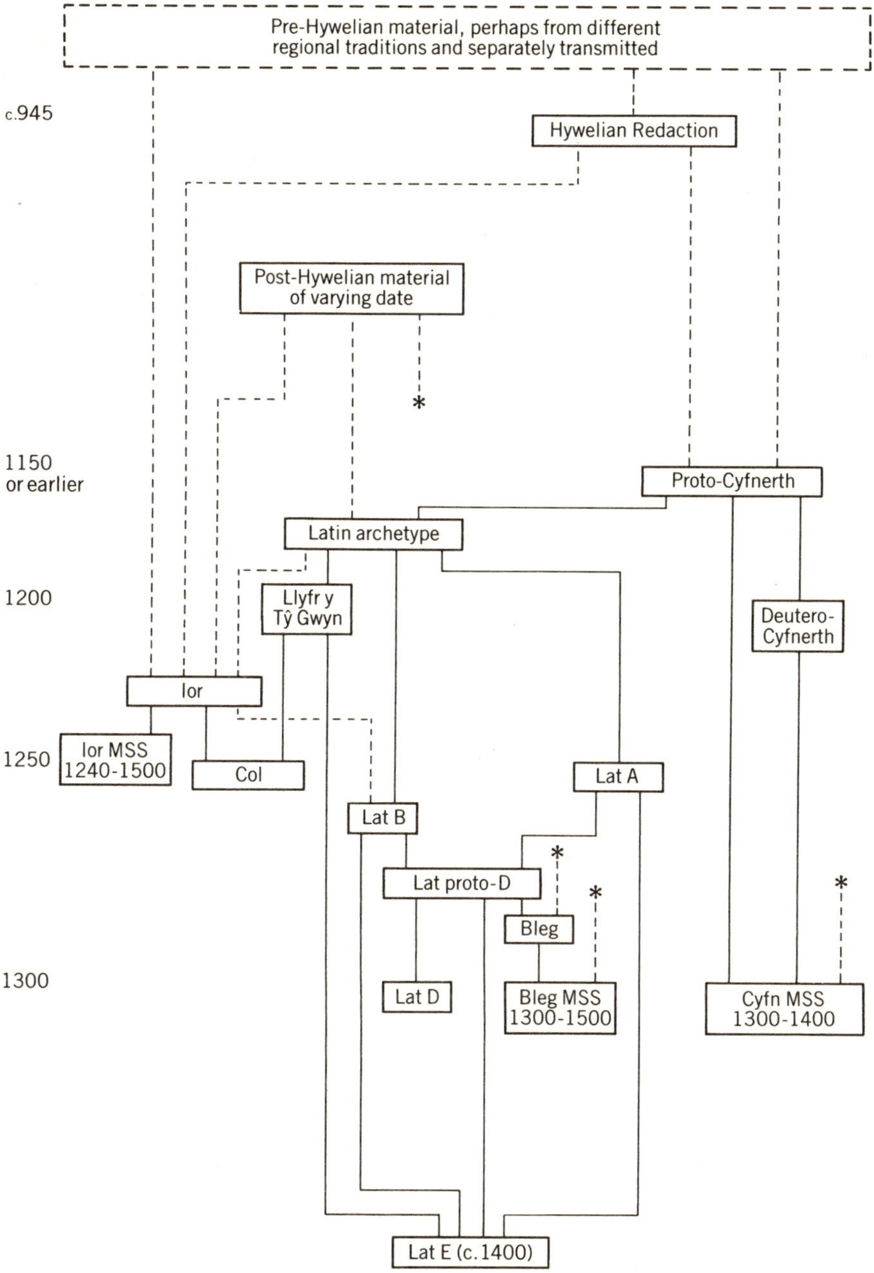
Pre-Hywelian material, perhaps from different regional traditions and separately transmitted
c.945
Hywelian Redaction
Post-Hywelian material of varying date
*
1150 or earlier
Proto-Cyfnerth
Latin archetype
1200
Llyfr y Tŷ Gwyn
Deutero-Cyfnerth
Ior
1250
Ior MSS 1240-1500
Col
Lat A
Lat B
*
Lat proto-D
*
*
Bleg
1300
Lat D
Bleg MSS 1300-1500
Cyfn MSS 1300-1400
Lat E (c.1400)

sentences and about 70,000 words; most manuscripts seem to have between 1,000 and 1,500 sentences. Of those 6,000 sentences, probably rather more than half are to be found somewhere in tractates – a tractate being defined as a more or less orderly collection of material on a single subject; 'more or less orderly' because on examination many tractates seem to lack logical arrangement. It is sometimes possible to show that a tractate has a well-ordered core, though it has become untidy by the haphazard addition of sentences.

Like sentences, tractates vary greatly in length. At one end of the scale we have the Laws of Court, which in *Ancient Laws* fills forty-three chapters and nearly forty pages; this can be divided into sub-tractates, each of which deals with one officer of the court, or with some particular aspect of its organisation. At the other end of the scale we can take the tractate on Wounding an Animal in the same text – a single chapter filling almost exactly one page. This particular little tractate is also a model of order, in great contrast with such a tractate as that on *Galanas* (i.e. Homicide and Blood-feud).

Sentences tend to coalesce in tractates, and tractates in turn tend to coalesce in Redactions. A few of the manuscripts seem to be unorganised collections of tractates and loose sentences, but the great majority of the manuscripts have as their first item a version of one of three Redactions, though nearly all have a 'tail' of miscellaneous material. Tails vary greatly in length, and in some manuscripts are longer than the body to which they are attached: in that longest manuscript the Redaction comprises 1,233 sentences and the Tail the remaining 1,313. And if we cannot say that the Tail wags the Redaction, it is certainly true that much of the important material is in the Tail. It is there that we expect to find the statements of law which the compiler took in as likely to be of practical use to him; but additional material is often slipped in to the tractates of the Redaction, and indeed between tractates, as well as forming the Tail.

This additional material is perhaps the strongest evidence for the view that our manuscripts were compiled for the use of practitioners. Their small size is another piece of evidence: while there are some large-page volumes which may have been made for monastic or aristocratic libraries or for judges on the bench, the great majority of the surviving manuscripts are pocket editions of about the size of a modern paperback or smaller: they would go comfortably into a modern pocket, or into the sleeve of a gown. Moreover it is clear enough that much of the content even of the Redactions is not a statement of legal rules promulgated by authority: thus we find time and again a discussion of the form, 'Some say [that the rule of law is this]; others say [that it is the other]'; the compiler then says, not (as a modern text-writer would) 'the better view is', but 'we say' or 'the law says'. And very occasionally we find an opinion attributed to a named man, whose reputation was evidently high: there are two or three citations of Iorwerth ap Madog (who can be identified as living in the first half of the thirteenth century),[14] but the most stimulating citation is that of Goronwy ap Moriddig, found in Latin and Welsh manuscripts of the late thirteenth century: 'Goronwy ap Moriddig used to say that a man was not bound to pay anything to another man for lying with his wife while she approved the act; and if the act is manifest, the wife is bound to pay his *sarhaed* to her husband, or her husband may freely repudiate her'.[15] In this passage 'used to say' translates the Latin and Welsh imperfects, *dicebat* and *dywedai*; and here we seem to have the kind of reminiscence that is found in the manuscripts in which an English common lawyer would record (among many other potentially useful things) something that had been said over dinner. 'In . . . assembling the material for their working books the lawyers of medieval Wales were like the members of the Inns of Court in the sixteenth and seventeenth centuries, as they have been revealed to us by the work of J. H. Baker, E. W. Ives, and others'.[16]

However important the Tail may have been in practice, the core of the typical law manuscript is a version of one of the Redactions. Their existence has been recognised at least since the publication of *Ancient Laws*; as Owen put it: '. . . it appeared that there were three distinct forms of laws existing, . . . Upon further research these three independent codes were found to belong respectively to Venedotia or North Wales, Dimetia or South Wales, and one adapted to Gwent or South-east Wales'.[17]

Owen therefore called the Redactions the Venedotian, Dimetian, and Gwentian Codes, but twentieth-century scholarship (beginning with A. W. Wade-Evans in 1909)[18] has rejected his nomenclature.

[14] For Iorwerth ap Madog see *Celtic Law Papers*, 123-33.

[15] *The Latin Texts of the Welsh Laws*, 345. 33 = *Llyfr Blegywryd*, ed. S. J. Williams and J. E. Powell, Cardiff 1942, 67. 1. Goronwy ap Moriddig seems to be the man of that name who gave evidence at St Asaph in 1274 about legal procedure as he had seen it in the 1230s: O. E. Jones, 'Llyfr Coch Asaph', unpublished M.A. thesis, University of Wales 1968, 72-3, 173.

[16] *Tijdschrift voor Rechtsgeschiedenis* xlix, 1981, 325. The law recorded in the Welsh books is of course very different from that of the Inns of Court.

[17] *Ancient Laws and Institutes of Wales*, vol. 1, ed. A. Owen, 1841, viii.

[18] *Welsh Medieval Law*, ed. A. W. Wade-Evans, Oxford 1909, vii-xii.

The Redactions are digests rather than codes, and there is no sufficient ground for the implication that they were intended to be exclusively appicable to particular regions. Though more neutral names might be desirable, there has now come to be general acceptance of the labels Iorwerth Redaction (with the abbreviation Ior), Blegywryd Redaction (Bleg), and Cyfnerth Redaction (Cyfn) for the Venedotian, Dimetian, and Gwentian Codes respectively, and it has been generally agreed since the 1950s that the three Redactions represent (however roughly) different stages in sophisticated development: Cyfnerth is the earliest and crudest form; Blegywryd is related to Cyfnerth but shows substantial ecclesiastical influence; Iorwerth is by far the most sophisticated: it must have first come into existence in the thirteenth century, not very long before its oldest surviving manuscripts were written. It contains the kernel of the classical law.[19]

If we look at the earliest surviving manuscripts, we shall be led (as Aneurin Owen was) to think of the Iorwerth Redaction as northern and the Blegywryd Redaction as southern. The Cyfnerth manuscripts are less definitely placeable, but the textual resemblance to Blegywryd leads to the association of Cyfnerth with Blegywryd – so that some scholars now speak of 'northern' and 'southern' Redactions, and it has been suggested that in the pre-Hywelian era there were separate northern and southern traditions. Both traditions would be represented in each of the Redactions, but in different proportions: each would have a kernel drawn from its own tradition, with borrowings from the other. It may well be true that there were different pre-Hywelian traditions in different parts of Wales, but there is no positive evidence of this, and it is to be expected that any such differences would be masked by the later development of the Redactions. The provenance of the surviving manuscripts is evidence only for regional popularity in the period when they were written: it is poor evidence for regional origin of any part of the material, especially when we remember that all Welsh lawbooks were treated as admissible authority throughout Wales. We ought not to be very sceptical about the statement in the prologue to Book III of the Iorwerth Redaction:

> And this book was gathered together by Iorwerth ap Madog from the book of Cyfnerth ap Morgenau and the book of Gwair ap Rhufawn and

[19] See T. Jones Pierce, *Medieval Welsh Society*, ed. J. Beverley Smith, Cardiff 1972, 294-5. The paper was first published in 1952.

> the book of Goronwy ap Moriddig [and the old book of the White House], and besides that from the best books that he found also in Gwynedd and Powys and Deheubarth. And this book is called 'the Test Book', that is to say the Three Columns of Law, and the Value of Wild and Tame, and what pertains to that.[20]

This is the more likely to be true since Cyfnerth ap Morgenau was a first cousin of Iorwerth's grandfather[21] and Goronwy ap Moriddig was still alive when the statement was written.

In point of construction, the Redactions seem to show a deliberate attempt at pattern, though the pattern is often obscured by untidy additions in the individual manuscripts. According to one prologue, Hywel 'commanded [the laws] to be written in three parts: the first the law of his daily court; the second the law of the country; the third of the usage of each one of them'[22] – and all three Redactions have a quite clearly marked first part (which it is natural to call Book I), dealing with the Laws of Court. Book II deals with the Laws of Country, and in some manuscripts is introduced with a flourish: 'Thus far by the permission of God we have treated of the laws of a court; now by the help of the glorious Lord Jesus Christ we will set out the laws of a country'.[23] But no text makes any proclamation under the patronage of the Holy Ghost of a Book III dealing with usage, though some Blegywryd manuscripts do seem to have gathered together material on legal procedure at the end of the Redaction. We shall see that the Iorwerth Redaction has a clearly-marked Book III, constructed with a quite different purpose and called *Llyfr Prawf Ynaid*, 'the Justices' Test Book'.

As things stand, we do not yet know enough to write an authoritative account of the relation of the Redactions, but a working hypothesis can be presented here as a commentary on the provisional stemma printed above (page 7). The stemma has been simplified in order to reduce confusion, and because of the simplification it does less than justice to the cross-fertilisation between Redactions which the manuscripts show.

We start with pre-Hywelian material, about which we can say little more than that it surely existed and was not all taken into the Hywelian book: some statements which first appear in a single

[20] *Ancient Laws*, vol. 1, 218. The bracketed mention of the old book of the White House is found only in two manuscripts, neither from the thirteenth century.
[21] For Cyfnerth and Morgenau see *Celtic Law Papers*, 123-33.
[22] *Latin Texts*, 316. 15-17 = *Llyfr Blegywryd*, 1. 22.
[23] *Welsh Medieval Law*, 36. 21.

manuscript (and sometimes in a manuscript known to be relatively late) have such an archaic air that they must go back beyond Hywel's time. Some of this archaic material is in the form of proverb or triad, and may have circulated orally before being written down for the first time at a relatively late date, but other material is likely to have been in writing before Hywel's time.[24] It must be remembered that legal documents were being written in Welsh by the ninth century at the latest.[25] It is probable, but unproveable, that at this stage there were different regional traditions. It also seems probable that the Hywelian Book had only a limited scope: on the one hand, if we adopt the hypothesis that the Hywelian Book cannot have contained more than the common core of the common cores of the three Redactions, it would be quite short; and on the other hand it is *a priori* likely enough that the King who stimulated the co-ordination of the law would have taken care to have the matters which most concerned him recorded, and would have troubled less about other matters.

On both these grounds it can be argued that the Hywelian Book included the Laws of Court, the Three Columns of Law, and the Value of Wild and Tame, but not much more. The Laws of Court deal with the rights of members of the royal entourage, and in particular with the support which the peripatetic court could claim from the local community; the provisions for commutation of the obligation of support, which appear in other parts of the texts, are a later addition. The Three Columns of Law are the Nine Abetments of Homicide, of Theft, and of Fire; they are of obvious interest to the King because they are a source of income. Thus, whereas the principal act of homicide is only a tort (having begun as the occasion of a blood-feud, which came to be terminated by financial compensation), the abetments are crimes, for which no compensation is paid to the victim's kin, but only a financial penalty to the King. The value of the stolen property affects the punishment for theft; so it was in the royal interest to have the values of animals, the most important potential stolen property, clearly set out.

Between this Hywelian Book and our earliest manuscripts there is a gap of nearly three centuries. (It now seems likely that the oldest Welsh manuscript, MS. *C* of Ior, and the oldest Latin manuscript, Peniarth 28, were written about 1240: Pen 28 is certainly later than the

[24] Binchy, 'Prologue', 1 note 4.

[25] D. Jenkins and M. E. Owen, 'The Welsh Marginalia in the Lichfield Gospels', *Cambridge Medieval Celtic Studies* v, 1983, 37-66; vii, 1984, 91-120.

late twelfth century, to which it was previously ascribed.)[26] How can this gap be filled? I think we can safely say that Proto-Cyfnerth must have existed about 1150 or soon after, and that the development which eventually produced the Blegywryd Redaction began in the next quarter-century. Here I take up Alan Harding's suggestion that 'the Welsh law-books [were] a reaction, perhaps, to the growing dominance of Henry II and his laws', but as 'a repudiation, rather than a product, of legal imperialism'.[27] I think they were a repudiation because of the political strength of Rhys ap Gruffudd, 'the Lord Rhys', who was the leading ruler in South Wales from about 1155, and was given a special status by Henry II in 1172, with the title Justiciar of South Wales. Dr. A. D. Carr has recently suggested that it might 'seem more appropriate to commemorate the laws of the Lord Rhys, perhaps at Cardigan, than the laws of Hywel Dda at Whitland'.[28]

I certainly follow Harding in recognising the significance of Henry II's legal imperialism, but I cannot go all the way with his earlier statement that: 'The story of King Hywel the Good's promulgation of laws for all Wales . . . is not an historical description of legal unity but a myth of political unification'[29] – at least if the implication is that the myth came into existence only in the time of Henry II, and that seems to me (and to Dr. Carr) unlikely for more than one reason. For one thing, the lawbooks have references to an earlier ruler than the Lord Rhys as having altered the rules of Hywel's Law. This was Bleddyn ap Cynfyn, who ruled much of Wales from 1063 to 1075, from the starting-point of a kingdom in Powys; it could be argued that Proto-Cyfnerth arose in Powys in the time of Bleddyn, in an earlier reflection of the political climate, though this idea will need detailed examination.

Wherever Proto-Cyfnerth arose, it seems to have left descendants in south and north. The stemma sufficiently indicates the Latin development: it ought probably to display a second Deutero-Cyfnerth, for there are two lineages of Cyfnerth manuscripts, one being southern or perhaps south-eastern (and omitted from the stemma as being closely parallel to the Latin-Blegywryd lineage). The Deutero-Cyfnerth shown on the stemma is a northern edition: it

26 See Daniel Huws, 'Leges Howelda at Canterbury', *National Library of Wales Journal* xix, 1976, 340-44.

27 Harding, 'Regiam Majestatem', 111.

28 A. D. Carr, *A Look at Hywel's Law*, Whitland 1985, 11.

29 Harding, 'Regiam Majestatem', 110.

is evidenced by manuscripts with prefaces attributing the composition of the book to Morgenau and his son Cyfnerth, who lived in Arfon at the end of the twelfth century.[30] This Deutero-Cyfnerth has left no northern progeny: in my view this is because it became obsolete in Gwynedd when juristic learning took a great leap forward in the early thirteenth century under the favourable conditions created by the political power of Llywelyn ab Iorwerth, 'the Great ', who died in 1240 after extending his authority from Gwynedd over most of Wales.

This leap produced the Iorwerth Redaction, which owes its name to respect for Iorwerth ap Madog ap Rhawd, who was mentioned earlier as being cited as an authority. Exactly how much Iorwerth did for the Redaction we can hardly say: he surely gave it its final form by adding to it the tractates on the Value of Inanimate Property, on Co-operative Ploughing, and on Cattle Trespass, as appendices to the Justices' Test Book. (The Test Book was so called because it contained the material which was said to be the minimum knowledge required for appointment as a judge.) We are less sure that it was he, rather than an earlier redactor, who put together the basic Justices' Test Book, comprising the Three Columns of Law and the Value of Wild and Tame; but the Redactor who created the Test Book also gave the whole Redaction its form, since he removed the basic Test Book from its place in the Law of the Country. The result is that Book II of the Iorwerth Redaction is very different from that of the Blegywryd and Cyfnerth Redactions, in which the Three Columns come first and give the Book its shape; in Ior the Laws of the Country are a miscellany of tractates on Women, Contract, Land Law, etc., and much of the material has no parallel in Bleg and Cyfn. The Iorwerth Redactor, as the Test Book prologue indicates, took his material wherever he could find it; he certainly added a great deal to the bare bones of the Three Columns of Law, by way of rules relating to the principal offences rather than the abetments.

This gathering together of material from different sources is yet more clearly seen in *Llyfr Colan* (Col), which is a revised edition of the Iorwerth Redaction found only in the thirteenth-century manuscript Peniarth 30, and taking its name from that given to the manuscript in the seventeenth century because it was written in two columns. The material falls into two nearly equal parts, though the manuscript makes no distinction between them. The second part is a disorderly

[30] Note 17 above.

Tail which has been published under the name *Damweinau Colan*[31]; for most of it, this manuscript provides the earliest version. In the first part published as *Llyfr Colan*,[32] material taken from the Iorwerth Redaction is partly re-worded (usually more clearly and concisely) and partly corrected, while to it is added much other material, perhaps all derived from a single source in Latin. That source was not one of the extant Latin texts, but may have been the 'Whitland Book' itself or a copy of it. Comparison of the Col text with that of the Iorwerth Redaction gives the earliest positive evidence of cross-fertilisation between the Redactions, and leads to the question whether any other systems of non-Roman medieval law have quite as variable a collection of practitioners' books.

Bibliographical Note

The three Welsh Redactions have been published in twentieth-century English translations:

- Cyfn in *Welsh Medieval Law*, ed. A. W. Wade-Evans, Oxford 1909, reprinted Aalen 1979.
- Bleg in *The Laws of Hywel Dda (the Book of Blegywryd)*, tr. Melville Richards, Liverpool 1954. This is a translation of the text of *Cyfreithiau Hywel Dda yn ôl Llyfr Blegywryd*, ed. S. J. Williams and J. E. Powell, Cardiff 1942, which is based on three manuscripts.
- Ior (with substantial selections from other texts) in *The Law of Hywel Dda: Law Texts from Medieval Wales*, ed. D. Jenkins, Llandysul 1986.

For material from the second volume of *Ancient Laws* not translated in any of these, only the *Ancient Laws* translation is available. The five Latin Redactions are published in *The Latin Texts of the Welsh Laws*, ed. H. D. Emanuel, Cardiff 1967, without translation either of the Latin or of the many passages in Welsh which are embedded in the Latin. Latin Redaction A is available in an English translation by I. F. Fletcher (Aberystwyth, forthcoming).

[31] *Damweiniau Colan*, ed. D. Jenkins, Aberystwyth 1973.
[32] Note 12 above.

2

The Brieve of Right Re-Visited

Hector MacQueen

By the later medieval period there had developed in Scotland a system of forms of action commenced by royal writ or brieve which was very much based on that found in contemporary England. This was especially true of actions for the recovery of land. There were three main forms of action for this purpose in Scotland, the brieves of *dissasine, mortancestor* and right. I have written elsewhere about each of these, concentrating mainly on the period after 1300;[1] in this paper, I will examine some aspects of the history of the brieve of right before 1300.

David Sellar has recently argued persuasively that trial by combat was still competent on the brieve of right in the mid-fourteenth century. Indeed he said that combat might still be generally competent today, never having been formally abolished in Scotland, and was somewhat astonished when, a few months after the appearance of his article, that argument was taken up on behalf of two accused in the High Court of Justiciary at Edinburgh.[2] Mr. Sellar's conclusions *inter alia* refute my earlier view that cases on the brieve of right were always determined by an assize and I accept his correction. But I would still hold that combats on the brieve of right were most unusual in the fourteenth century and that in particular the case on which he based his discussion was quite exceptional.[3] However the fact that combat was competent at all is surely a most important indication, to be taken along with other points of procedure on the brieve (for example, the tenant's four *essonzies* or excuses before he

[1] 'The Brieve of Right in Scots law', *Journal of Legal History* iii, 1982; 'Dissasine and Mortancestor in Scots law', *ibid.* iv, 1983.

[2] 'Courtesy, Battle and the Brieve of Right 1368 – a story continued', in *Miscellany Two*, Stair Soc. xxxv, 1984. On the recent combat case see my 'Desuetude, the *Cessante* Maxim and Trial by Combat in Scots law', *Journal of Legal History* vii, 1986.

[3] In later medieval law combat was only competent if no other proof were available. In the case of 1368 discussed by Mr. Sellar the issue was a claim of courtesy and the question whether a child had been still-born or heard to cry before its death, a matter upon which an ordinary proof may have been impossible.

needed to answer the claim against him), that its history goes back well beyond 1300, the approximate date for the earliest direct evidence of its form and use.

This early evidence mostly takes the form of styles for the brieve and comment thereupon in treatises and registers of brieves, and they suggest that the brieve of right was quite distinct in content from the original English writ of right. The latter was directed to the lord of whom the demandant claimed to hold the disputed lands and commanded him to do full right in the matter or else the sheriff would. By contrast the Scottish brieve was addressed straight to the sheriff and commanded him to cause the pursuer to have full right of lands of which he was being unjustly deforced by the defender. Moreover, the resulting litigation would go through entirely in the sheriff's court, whereas in England the sheriff only acted on the lord's default and, if the tenant opted to put himself on the grand assize, the case would be heard before the royal justices. But default by the lord seems to have been common in the thirteenth century, so it looks as though the Scottish brieve was merely less cumbersome in bringing actions of right before an assize in the King's court. Indeed, some derivations from the English writ are plainly to be discerned, in the formula of 'full right' and the accusation of 'deforcement' against the defender.

However, one important point of difference is that in all the Scottish formularies the bearer of the brieve (that is, the pursuer) is said to be one who claims to hold, not of a lord, but of the King: in other words, to be a tenant-in-chief. In England the tenant-in-chief did not use the classical writ of right to regain lands. Instead, at any rate after Magna Carta in 1215,[4] he used a writ called the *precipe in capite*; and it is significant that elements of the Scottish brieve of right can be seen to derive from this writ also, namely, the statement mentioned above that the demandant holds in chief of the King, and secondly, that the claim arises out of heritable right.

The interest of this lies in the fact that the *precipe in capite* was not originally described as a writ of right, even though it was a means of recovering full right in land. According to Maitland, 'in course of time the term "Writ of Right" gains a somewhat extended sense and is used so as to include the *precipe in capite*' because by both writs the

[4] Prior to 1215 there was a writ *precipe quod reddat* available to tenants-in-chief and others, but clause 34 of Magna Carta prevented its use by the latter. See further below, 20-21.

demandant sought full proprietary right.[5] Maitland did not supply references or a precise chronology for this development. In the first half of the thirteenth century his statement seems to be substantiated only by *Bracton's* description of the *precipe in capite* as the writ of right for one who ought to hold of the King in chief.[6] By contrast in the *Early Registers of Writs* spanning the period 1227 (or earlier) to c. 1320 the writ of right and the *precipe in capite* are always distinguished from each other: first because only tenants-in-chief could use the *precipe* and secondly because of the technicalities of sealing the writ in chancery. The *precipe* was sent out 'close' – that is, it was so folded and sealed that it could not be read without first breaking the seal – while the writ of right was a letter patent, readable without breaking the seal. In none of these early registers is the *precipe in capite* called a writ of right.[7] Nor does it appear to be so described in treatises such as *Brevia Placitata* and *Novae Narrationes*. When these works and others such as *Britton* refer to the writ of right they appear to be concerned only with the writ addressed to the lord's court.[8] I have not conducted an extensive search of court records, but the earliest references to the *precipe in capite* as a writ of right known to me in such material are of date 1276 and 1277.[9] When we reach the Year Books at the end of the thirteenth and the beginning of the fourteenth centuries we can find several examples of the *precipe in capite* being called a writ of right; but

[5] F. W. Maitland, *The Forms of Action at Common Law*, ed. A. H. Chaytor and W. J. Whittaker, Cambridge 1936, 19. See also his 'History of the Register of Original Writs', *Harvard Law Review* iii, 1889-90, 110 note 1.

[6] *Bracton: On the Laws and Customs of England*, vol 4, ed. G. E. Woodbine and S. E. Thorne, Harvard 1977, 49 (f. 328 b). For the date of *Bracton* see *ibid.*, vol 3, introduction, xiii-lii. That the substantive law underlying the two writs was the same was recognised in Judicium Essoniorum, a tract possibly dating in part from the 1220s and 1230s: see *Four Thirteenth Century Law Tracts*, ed. G. E. Woodbine, New Haven 1910, 116 and 132-3. I owe this reference and the note on its date to Dr. P. A. Brand.

[7] *Early Registers of Writs*, ed. E. de Haas and G. D. G. Hall, Selden Soc. lxxxvii, 1970 (henceforth *ERW*), 1-2, 18, 33, 108, 113. For an argument that the earliest of the registers is dateable to 1210 not 1227 see P. A. Brand, 'Ireland and the Literature of the Early Common Law', *Irish Jurist* xvi, 1981.

[8] *Brevia Placitata*, ed. G. J. Turner, Selden Soc. lxvi, 1947, 11, 53, 86, 163; *Novae Narrationes*, ed. E. Shanks and S. F. C. Milsom, Selden Soc. lxxx, 1963, 41 (B 38 A); *Britton*, ed. F. M. Nichols, vol. 2, Oxford 1865, 326-44.

[9] Cambridge Univ. Lib. Ms. Dd. 7. 14, ff. 403b-404a; CP 40/19, m. 20. I am most grateful to Dr. P. A. Brand for these references. For the earlier period I have consulted the *Curia Regis Rolls* (under index references to writs *de recto, precipe* and *precipe in capite*); see also *Roll of the Shropshire Eyre of 1256*, ed. A. Harding, Selden Soc. xcvi, 1980, no. 128, and *Bracton's Note Book*, ed. F. W. Maitland, London 1887, nos. 10, 212, 1436.

it is noticeable that this usage is found in the reports rather than in the official records.[10]

There are yet other writs in the registers which, although basically in the *precipe* form, are called writs *de recto*. These do not appear in the very earliest registers; the first is in the Luffield register of the 1260s. In these writs B is commanded to render land to A or else answer before the King's justices. But there is no statement that the land in question is held of the King; instead there is a clause tacked on at the end of the writ saying that the lord has remitted his court to the King.[11] Such a clause had been made necessary in 1215 by clause 34 of Magna Carta, which laid down that *precipe* writs should not be issued if there was a lord with jurisdiction. Thus *precipe* writs had always to be shown to meet this provision, and to say that lands were held of the King or that the lord had remitted his court did just that.[12] The only distinction between the two writs lay in these phrases, yet the *precipe quia dominus remisit curiam suam* was known officially as a writ of right; this, I would tentatively suggest, being because it was established as a writ of course later than the *precipe in capite*, at a date when the wider use of the term 'writ of right' had become customary.

It might therefore be suggested that this wide use of the term writ of right became established quite well on in the thirteenth century, perhaps chiefly influenced by *Bracton* and the recognition that each of the various writs related to the same body of substantive law. The suggestion gains support from provisions in the Statute of Wales of 1284, which gave a number of writs to be available thenceforth to the English King's Welsh subjects. Although these included *novel disseisin* and *mort d'ancestor*, there is no sign of writs of right or of the *precipe in capite*. Instead the Welsh were to have what the statute called the *breve commune* or the general writ.[13] This took the form of the *precipe quod reddat*, the writ found in *Glanvill* and used in England prior to Magna Carta to enable any dispossessed land-holder, regardless of whether or not he held in chief, to recover his property before the King's justices.[14] It was the use of this writ which clause 34 of Magna Carta

[10] The earliest yearbook reference I have noted is *20 and 21 Edward I 1292-1293*, Rolls Series 1866, 378-9. For others see e.g. *6 Edward II 1313*, Selden Soc. xliii, 1926, 6-9; *8 Edward II 1314-15*, Selden Soc. xli, 1924, 172-4; *10 Edward II 1316-17*, Selden Soc. liv, 1935, 104-5; *12 Edward II 1318*, Selden Soc. lxv, 1946, 103-6 and 115-6. See also *The Eyre of Northamptonshire 1329-1330*, vol. 2, Selden Soc. xcviii, 1982, 523.

[11] *ERW*, 36 (no. 8), 113 (no. 23).

[12] M. T. Clanchy, 'Magna Carta, Clause Thirty Four', *E.H.R.* lxxix, 1964.

[13] *Statutes of the Realm*, vol. 1, London 1810, 60 (12 Edward I c. 6).

[14] See Clanchy, 543-5.

sought to restrict in 1215 but of course that had no application to Wales. The point of interest for us has recently been demonstrated by L. B. Smith: the writ was referred to in the courts as the '*breve de recto*' of the laws of Wales.[15]

We can now return to the later medieval Scottish brieve of right and state some conclusions. It seems hybrid in form, a combination of the English writ of right and the *precipe in capite*. In many ways it is more like the latter; a significant point may be that the brieve of right was also sent out of the King's writing office as a letter close.[16] Nevertheless the Scottish brieve takes the official title '*de recto*'. It is hard to resist the inference that the brieve is a form of the latter part of the thirteenth century, getting its title because it is to be the way in which full proprietary right, as distinct from the lesser rights protected by the brieves of *dissasine* and *mortancestor*, may be reclaimed.

Discussing the rule requiring brieves to compel a man to answer for his lands, T. M. Cooper commented that 'so far as has been noted there are no examples in the Scottish records of the period of a brieve of right addressed to a baron'.[17] This would hardly be surprising if the brieve of right was, as the styles suggest, confined to cases involving tenants-in-chief. However there are cases on record in which action was begun in a franchise court by a royal brieve. In none of them are we told that the writ was a brieve of right or that it commanded the lord in question to do right, but in examining each of the cases it is worth bearing in mind the argument of Professor Harding, that the twelfth century royal protection might be enforced by orders '*facere rectum*', and, in addition, a document of 1165 or 1166 in which it is stated that actions against the men of Holyrood Abbey should be begun by a request to the abbot to do full right (*plenum rectum*); if he fails to do so, then the sheriff and the justice will do it instead.[18] This sounds exactly like the early English writ of right.

15 L. B. Smith, 'The Statute of Wales 1284', *Welsh History Review* x, 1980-81, 141-4.

16 See A. A. M. Duncan, 'The *Acta* of Robert I', *Scottish Historical Review* xxxii, 1953, 8, commenting on a brieve sewn to the rolls of Aberdeen burgh court in 1317 and published in *Early Records of the Burgh of Aberdeen, 1317, 1398-1407*, ed. W. C. Dickinson, Scottish History Society 3rd series xlix, 1957, 7-8.

17 *Regiam Majestatem and Quoniam Attachiamenta*, ed. T. M. Cooper, Stair Soc. xi, 1947, 213.

18 A. Harding, 'The Medieval Brieves of Protection and the Development of the Common Law', *Juridical Review* xi, 1966, 119, 126; *Regesta Regum Scottorum II: The Acts of William I 1165-1214*, ed. G. W. S. Barrow, Edinburgh 1971, no. 39.

All our Scottish cases come however from the thirteenth century. The earliest of them is, to judge from the witness list to the document in which it is recorded, datable to the 1230s. The document notes a quit-claim to the monks of Durham serving God at Coldingham made by Matthew of Houberne for certain lands in Coldingham 'of which he had impleaded the prior and convent of Coldingham by brieve of the lord king in the court of the same prior of Coldingham'. The witness list is headed by the sheriff of Berwick, William de Lindsay; was he there to do right had the prior refused to do so?[19] A second, less explicit, case may be the quit-claim by Michael of Auchencrow to the prior and convent of Coldingham of half a carrucate in Old Cambus 'which he claimed by brieve of the lord king'.[20] It is not stated in which court the claim was made, but the witnesses to the quit-claim are the suitors of the prior's court in the 1240s. Yet another case from the prior's court is the one in which Bertram son of Henry of Ulvestoun impleaded his cousin Waldeve Kokes for two oxgangs of land in Nether Ayton 'by letters of the lord king'. Again we are not told to which court these letters were addressed, but the eventual settlement was reached 'in the full court of the lord prior of Coldingham at Ayton'. The name of the sheriff of Berwick is second in the list of witnesses to the compromise.[21]

Moving from Berwickshire we must go to the Lennox for our final case, which was part of a well-known litigation in thirteenth-century Scottish legal history, the so-called Monachkenneran dispute. This arose in the 1230s out of the activities of one Dougal, a younger brother of the earl of Lennox and rector of the church at Kilpatrick on the north bank of the Clyde estuary. The church had been granted to Paisley Abbey by the earl of Lennox but Dougal alienated the lands attached to it without the abbey's authority. The abbey recovered the lands in a series of actions before papal judges delegate, but allowed Dougal to retain his position as rector for life. He died in 1270, and in the following year his three grand-nieces were served as his co-heirs. Thereafter these ladies, together with their husbands, raised actions by royal letters in the earl's court against Paisley Abbey, claiming rights in some of the lands attached to the church of Kilpatrick. The abbey bought off their claims for substantial sums. What was the nature of the claim against the abbey? As we have seen, the lands were

[19] J. Raine, *The History and Antiquities of North Durham*, London 1852, appendix, no. 296.

[20] Raine, appendix, no. 91.

[21] W. Fraser, *The Stirlings of Keir*, Edinburgh 1858, 197-8.

held of the earl of Lennox, so that a dispute about them naturally fell within the jurisdiction of his court. Grand-nieces could not have used the brieve of *mortancestor*, since they were outwith the degrees of relationship for the form of action. It seems very possible that the 'royal letters' took the form of a brieve along the lines of the English writ of right.[22]

We may therefore tentatively suppose that in thirteenth-century Scotland there was a brieve available to those who claimed to hold of a subject-superior rather than of the Crown and which would have been addressed to the superior's court. There is no direct warrant for calling this a brieve of right, or for suggesting that it commanded the addressee to do right or else the sheriff would. However, given what we know about the extent of English influence on the early development of the Scottish system of brieves, it seems likely that this particular brieve bore some resemblance to the classical English writ of right.

Clearly the brieve had disappeared by the time the earliest surviving formularies were written, at the start of the fourteenth century. But this does not mean that the man who held of a subject-superior had lost a remedy for the recovery of his lands. *Regiam Majestatem*, an early fourteenth-century text, gives a form for the statement of claim to be made on a brieve of right, and by this the pursuer is made to claim to hold 'heritably of the lord king or (in the alternative) of another lord'.[23] Thus it would seem that, despite its own statement about holding of the King, the brieve of right was available to the sub-tenant by the time this part of *Regiam* was written. Perhaps we can now begin to see the course of development. The brieve of right which is found in the formularies looks like a fusion of the English *precipe in capite* and *breve de recto*. Is this more or less exactly what it was, except that it was the original Scottish versions of those two writs, borrowed at some earlier period, which were fused into a single writ for general use in the recovery of land? If the normal procedure on a brieve addressed to a subject-superior's court was in any event for the case to be transferred to the sheriff, as the English

[22] For the three quit-claims see *Registrum Monasterii de Passelet*, Maitland Club, 1832: New Club, 1877, 180, 192 and 198, and for the earlier history of the Monachkenneran dispute, 157-70. Before 1318 a person could only sue by brieve of mortancestor in virtue of a claim through parents, uncles, aunts and siblings: see MacQueen, 'Dissasine and Mortancestor', 32.

[23] *Regiam Majestatem*, I, 9. I have used the edition of *Regiam* in *The Acts of the Parliaments of Scotland* ed. T. Thomson and C. Innes, vol. 1, Edinburgh 1814, 597-641.

parallel would suggest, then this would have been a sensible rationalisation greatly reducing the amount of time used up in pleas of right. Moreover, such thinking – the channelling of a number of actions into a single remedy – reflects that which went into the Statute of Wales and its *breve commune*. There was nothing in Scots law comparable to clause 34 of Magna Carta, protecting the feudal jurisdictions and giving rise to a confusing multiplicity of writs, and so there was freedom to rationalise the structure as law and practice developed in the course of the thirteenth century. Perhaps, finally, it was this freedom of action which explains why, in Scotland as in post-conquest Wales,[24] no equivalent of the writs of entry emerged and the single action '*de recto*' could stand alone in their place.

[24] See Smith, 141-4. It is, of course, not the case that Magna Carta was the sole reason for the emergence of writs of entry; see now R. C. Palmer, 'The Origins of Property in England', *Law and History Review* iii, 1985, 24-46.

Appendix: Forms of Writs

SCOTLAND

Brieve of Right
The king to the sheriff. We command that you cause N, the bearer of the presents, to have full right of four carrucates in your bailiary which he claims to hold of us heritably, rendering therefor to us twenty silver shillings annually and giving such forinsec service and aid as pertains to the service of half a knight; of which carrucates of land R unjustly deforces him, as he says; acting thereupon so that we do not hear any complaint of default of right.

ENGLAND

Writ of Right
The king to N. I command you to do full right without delay to R in respect of two carrucates of land in Middleton which he claims to hold of you and which W is withholding from him. If you do not do it the sheriff will that I may hear no further complaint for default of right in this matter.

Precipe in Capite
The king to the sheriff. Command B that justly and without delay he render to A ten acres of land which he claims to be his right and inheritance and to hold of us in chief and whereof he complains that the aforesaid B deforces him; and if he does not do it then summon the aforesaid B to be before our justices at Westminster to show why he has not done this.

Writ of Right quia dominus remisit curiam suam
The king to the sheriff. Command B that justly and without delay he render to A ten acres of land which he claims to be his right and inheritance and whereof he complains that the said B unjustly deforces him. And if he does not do it then summon the said B to be before our justices at Westminster to show why he has not done this; because the chief lord of that fee has remitted to us his court thereof.

[The forms are derived from the *Register of Brieves*, ed. T. M. Cooper, Stair Soc. x, 1946, and *Early Registers of Writs* ed. E. de Haas and G. D. G. Hall, Selden Soc. lxxxvii, 1970.]

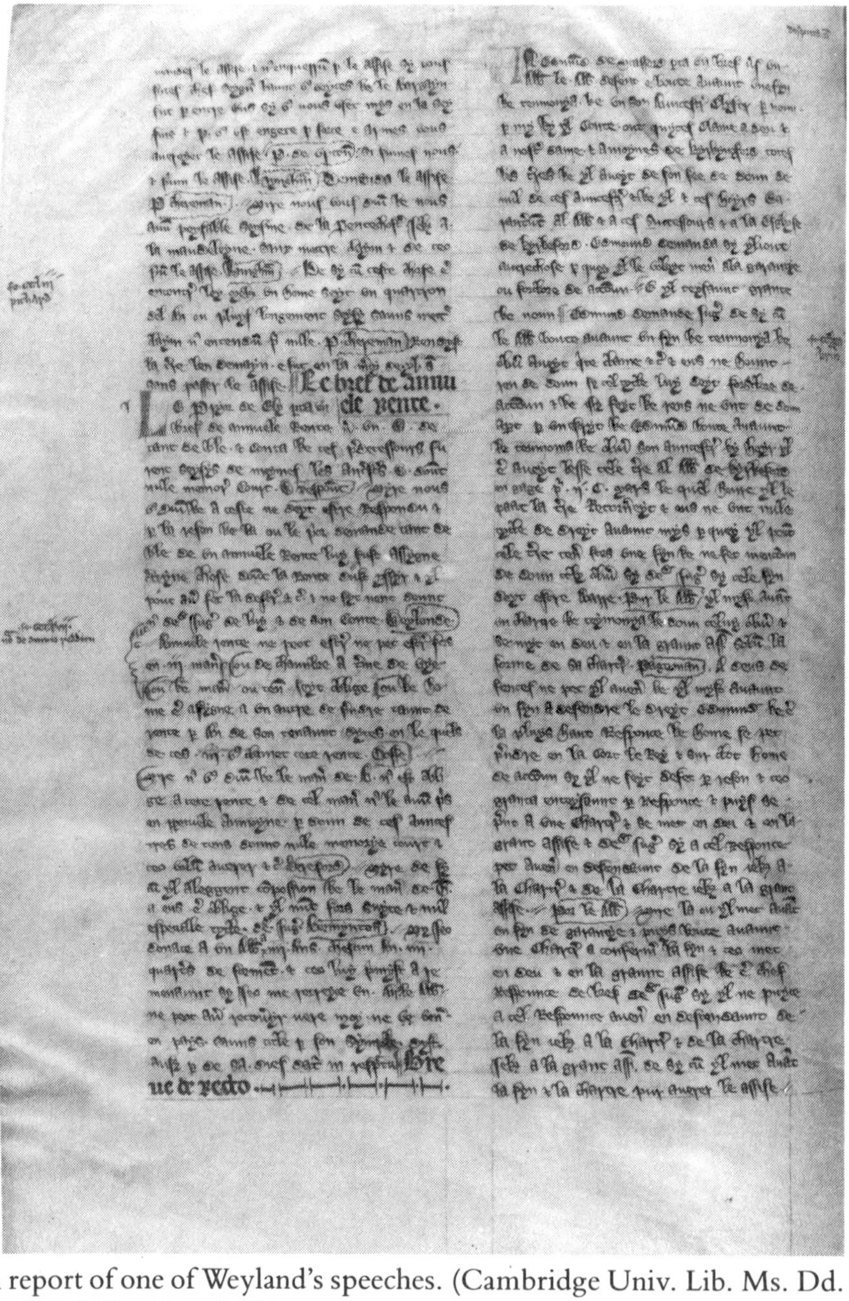

A report of one of Weyland's speeches. (Cambridge Univ. Lib. Ms. Dd. 7. 14, ff.239b-240a, 370b)

3

Chief Justice and Felon: The Career of Thomas Weyland

Paul Brand

On 20 February 1290, at a special gaol delivery session held at the Tower of London, Thomas Weyland took an oath of abjuration, promising to leave England and not to return to it nor to enter any of Edward I's other territories without special permission from the King. He was assigned Dover as his port of embarkation and given nine days to reach it. Despite the time of year, Weyland, like other abjurors, had to make his journey barefoot and without any covering for his head. He was assigned specific places to reach each day en route to Dover but he was not allowed to leave the highway when he reached them to take shelter for the night. The places assigned are, as might be expected, all on Watling Street, the main route from London to Dover; and the stages assigned to each day of the journey were fairly easy ones. The furthest Weyland was expected to travel in any one day was about nine miles. We are told that he was in a weak condition when starting out and that he was deliberately given an easy journey for this reason.

Just under nine months before this enforced winter walk, Thomas Weyland had still been in office as one of the most senior of Edward I's judges. In Trinity term 1289 Weyland had presided over the Bench at Westminster, the main royal court for the hearing of civil litigation, as its chief justice, and as late as 18 July 1289 was still sitting as an assize justice at Waltham Cross in Hertfordshire. How had this dramatic downfall come about? And who was Thomas Weyland? What were his origins and background? What do we know about his career as a royal justice? And what happened to him after his downfall?

This paper on the life and career of Thomas Weyland is part of a much larger long-term study of the Edwardian judiciary as a whole. For most of its history the common law has been the product of a complex interaction between lawyers, judges, and the world outside the court room. One essential preliminary to the understanding of that interaction in any period of its history is the accumulation of reliable information about the judges: to see from what social class or group they were drawn; what kind of experience and training they had acquired prior to their appointment; how they actually functioned within their courts; what the norms of judicial behaviour were both in theory and in practice; what was the status enjoyed by members of the judiciary; what were the terms on which they held their posts.

The reign of Edward I (1272-1307) is the first period in which we can begin to give satisfactory answers to many of these questions. It is the first period for which we possess detailed information about what was actually said and done in the King's courts in the form of unofficial reports of cases heard there, written in the Anglo-Norman French that was the language used by judges and lawyers. For earlier periods we possess only the formal and often summary reports of litigation contained in the Latin plea-roll enrolments, the official record of business done in the court, which are much less informative. We can, for the first time, in Edward's reign begin to see in detail the ways in which the common law was being shaped and developed and the contribution which was being made to that process by individual judges. It is also the first period for which relevant sources survive in sufficient quantity to make it possible for us to acquire detailed information on the background of all the members of the higher judiciary. Comparatively little work has, however, been done on the judges of Edward I, and scholars who have worked on them have generally used only a small part of the surviving sources relevant to such a study.[1]

Thomas Weyland, for example, has attracted the attention of a small number of scholars. In the mid-nineteenth century his life was briefly reviewed by Lord Campbell as part of his series of *Lives of the Chief Justices of England*, and Edward Foss similarly gave a short account of it in his comprehensive prosopographical work, *The Judges of England*. Thomas Weyland was also sufficiently well-known (or, rather, notorious) for T. F. Tout at the end of the nineteenth century to have written a fresh account of his life for the *Dictionary of National Biography*. Much more recently, his life and career have again been

[1] The only comprehensive study of the justices of Edward I is that contained in the third volume of Edward Foss's *The Judges of England* published in 1851. G. O. Sayles, writing in 1936, noted that 'The lives of the judges as set forth in the pages of Foss clamour for re-editing and amplification, but the task is formidable and not likely to be faced for many years': *Select Cases in the Court of King's Bench*, vol. 1, ed. G. O. Sayles, Selden Soc. lv, 1936, xlix. The only general study of any kind devoted to the Edwardian justices published since then has been that by Sayles himself in the same volume. This was, however, confined to King's Bench justices and was intended only to provide a 'skeleton outline' of their careers.

discussed by Professor Anne Spitzer.[2] Each of these scholars, however, used only such materials bearing on the life and career of Thomas Weyland as were already in print. They made no use of the extensive material relevant to both which survives in manuscript in the Public Record Office, nor of the many unprinted Year Book reports of cases heard in the Bench during the period of his chief justiceship, sources of major importance for our knowledge of Thomas Weyland's life and career.

Using these new sources, I will demonstrate that Weyland's origins and early career were not as supposed by earlier biographers; make a fresh appraisal of his work as a royal justice; and show the need for a major revision of the hitherto accepted view as to the chronology and causes of his dramatic downfall in 1289. I will also hope to demonstrate the need for a reassessment of the traditional view of Thomas Weyland as a clearly and notoriously corrupt justice and conclude by filling in some of the hitherto unknown details of just what happened to him after his disgrace.

1

Tout's biographical note on Thomas Weyland in the *Dictionary of National Biography* asserts that he was born into a 'respectable' Norfolk gentry family, which drew its name from 'Weyland, a wood near Watton, which [also] gives its name to a Norfolk hundred' and that he was probably a younger son of William de Weyland, escheator of England south of the Trent in the early 1260s and a justice of the Bench in 1272-3. In fact, Thomas Weyland was the third son of Herbert and Beatrice Weyland and William Weyland was an elder brother, and there is no reason to suppose that either of his parents belonged to the gentry.[3] Herbert Weyland certainly did not come from the Norfolk gentry family of Weyland, for no such family existed at this time. He was probably from a local peasant family.[4] Thomas's mother, Beatrice, was one of six daughters and coheiresses of Stephen of Witnesham, who had been a minor landholder in

[2] J. Campbell, *The Lives of the Chief Justices of England*, vol. 1, London 1849, 77-78; Foss, vol. 2, 170-2; T. F. Tout in the *D.N.B.* sub Weyland; Anne L. Spitzer, 'The Legal Careers of Thomas Weyland and Gilbert of Thornton', *Journal of Legal History* vi, 1985, 62-83.

[3] F. Blomefield, *An Essay towards a Topographical History of the County of Norfolk*, vol. 6, London 1807, 173 note 4; *Cal. Fine Rolls, 1272-1307*, 22; CP 25(1)/214/27, no. 24; E 159/34, m. 4d.; *Cal. Fine Rolls, 1272-1307*, 21.

Witnesham, a Suffolk village some four miles north-east of Ipswich, and in two other neighbouring villages, Westerfield and Akenham.[5] The family surname of Weyland is not toponymic in origin but is probably derived from the personal name Wayland. It was only as Thomas and his brothers began to rise in the world that they began to add the locative 'de' to their name, perhaps with the deliberate intention of suggesting that it was a toponymic and thus disguising the lowliness of their origins.

The comparative obscurity of Weyland's beginnings is typical of a majority of the higher judiciary of the reign of Edward I. Of the thirty-eight men who served as justices of the Bench or King's Bench during his reign only five seem to have come from knightly or baronial families.[6] Most justices, like Weyland, came from the ranks of the lower free tenantry; and at least one senior royal justice, Ellis of Sutton, a justice of King's Bench from 1285 to 1287, was of servile birth.[7] Thomas Weyland is a typical figure in another sense, too. No less than five of the twenty-five Bench justices of the reign of Edward I came from his home county of Suffolk, more than from any other county.[8]

[4] The authority vouched by Tout for his statement that the manor of Oxburgh in Norfolk had been in the possession of the Weyland family in the early thirteenth century is the Black Book of the Exchequer, as printed by Walter Rye in *Norfolk Antiquarian Miscellany*, vol. 1, Norwich 1877. This, however, contains extracts from an account of an aid collected in 20 Edward III (1346-7). The manor only passed into the possession of members of the Weyland family around 1270 when the future chancellor Robert Burnell settled it on Thomas's elder brother William, William's illegitimate son Nicholas and Nicholas's wife Juliana: KB 27/49, m. 21. For the earlier history of the manor see Blomefield, vol. 6, 168-71. The manor continued to be held by the descendants of Nicholas.

[5] CP 25(1)/213/16, no. 78; CP 25(1)/213/18, no. 30.

[6] Of the justices of the Bench, Gilbert of Preston (chief justice in 1273) was the eldest son and inherited the lands of a Northamptonshire knightly family which can be traced back to the time of Domesday Book; John of Cobham (justice 1273-5) was the eldest son and inherited the lands of a former Bench justice who had become a member of the Kent gentry; John de Lovetot (justice 1275-89) was the younger son of one of the coheirs of the Huntingdonshire barony of Southoe. Of the justices of King's Bench Walter of Hopton (justice 1274-8) was probably the eldest son and inherited the lands of a Shropshire knightly family; Robert Malet (justice 1290-5) was the eldest son and inherited the lands of a minor Buckinghamshire knightly family. Fuller details and references will be found in my forthcoming study of the judges of Edward I.

[7] Ellis was manumitted in 1269 by the archbishop of York at the request of Gilbert of Preston: *Register of William Wickwane*, ed. W. Brown, Surtees Soc. cxiv, 1907, 334.

[8] His brother William Weyland; John of Mettingham; William of Gisleham and Hervey of Stanton. No other county produced more than two.

Thomas Weyland was born in, or not long before, the year 1230.[9] Little has so far come to light about the first forty years or so of his life, the period prior to his first appointment as a royal justice at the very end of Henry III's reign. During this time he must have been accumulating the experience that rendered him eligible for appointment as a royal justice, but it is not clear what the nature of that experience was.

Foss states that Thomas Weyland had been 'brought up to the study of the law . . .' and that he owed his initial appointment as a royal justice in 1272 to the eminence he had by then obtained in the legal profession.[10] This appears to have been no more than guess-work on Foss's part, a conjecture for which he cites no evidence and which seems to have been based on an error made by Dugdale. The latter deduced from a writ of 1275 ordering that Weyland be paid his expenses that he was at that time a King's serjeant, and thus a leading member of the legal profession. In fact, the payment was one made to him for his services as a justice of the Bench not as a King's serjeant, and there is no evidence that Thomas Weyland was ever a serjeant, still less a King's serjeant.[11] It is possible to identify many, if not all, of the Bench serjeants of the latter part of the reign of Henry III. Thomas Weyland is not one of them. In any case, at the time of Weyland's initial appointment as a royal justice (in 1272), the serjeants of the Bench had not yet become a significant source of justices. The first justices to be appointed from their ranks seem to have been Richard of Boyland and Alan of Walkingham, who became justices in eyre in 1279; and it was only in and after 1290 that Bench serjeants began to be appointed as justices of the Bench itself and of the court of King's Bench.[12]

Service as a clerk in one of the King's courts was certainly seen at this time as one good way of acquiring the expertise in law and legal procedure needed in a royal justice; and many of the men appointed as

[9] In Easter term 1251 he acted as the attorney of his eldest brother John for the making of a final concord: CP 25(1)/214/22, no. 72. It seems probable that all attorneys were required to be of age.

[10] D. Crook, *Records of the General Eyre*, P.R.O. Handbooks 20, 1982, 134, 140, 141; *Select Cases . . . King's Bench*, vol. 1, cxxxv.

[11] The *liberate* was for twenty pounds 'in subvencionem expensarum suarum quas fecit in servicio regis': C62/51, m. 2.

[12] The bench serjeants appointed as justices of the Bench were Robert of Hartforth (Hertford) (1291-4); William of Gisleham (1290-3); William of Barford (Bereford) (1292, 1294-1326); and William Howard (1297-1308). The only Bench serjeant appointed a justice of King's Bench was Gilbert of Thornton (1290-4) but William of Ormsby had been an eyre serjeant.

royal justices during Edward I's reign can be shown to have been promoted from the ranks of these clerks.[13] Thomas's eldest brother John was just such a clerk. From the frequency of references to his minor property transactions on the plea rolls and his frequent use of final concords it seems clear that he was a clerk of one or more of the justices of the Bench from at least 1244 onwards and by the time of his death (in either 1259 or 1260) he had become sufficiently senior to enter the King's own service.[14] His career had brought him a degree of material prosperity as well, allowing him to make several purchases of land in his own area of Suffolk and at least one major acquisition, the Suffolk manor of Brandeston, for which he paid in excess of one hundred pounds.[15] Thomas Weyland may have followed him into clerical service in the courts. Such clerks were normally in clerical orders and it is known that at some fairly early period in his life Thomas was ordained a subdeacon.[16] But there is no positive evidence that Thomas Weyland was ever a court clerk and the balance of probabilities seems to be against this, for as early as the 1250s he was in a position to spend sums much larger than those available to his brother on property acquisition. In 1256 he paid one hundred marks to purchase the Suffolk manor of Chillesford and only three years later he was able to pay a further three hundred marks to buy another Suffolk manor, that of Blaxhall.[17] By the mid-1260s, moreover, he had in effect laicised himself. It was at this time that he married his first wife Anne; and by 1270, at the latest, he had received the honour of a knighthood, a status incompatible with clerical orders.[18]

The other main career pattern typical of a substantial number of Edwardian judges was service to one or more of the great magnates as

[13] Examples from the justices of the Bench include Ralph de Hengham (1273-4, 1301-8); Roger of Leicester (1276-89); William of Brompton (1278-89); Ellis of Beckingham (1285-1307); Lambert of Threekingham (1300-1316); Henry the Marshal of Guildford (1305-6); and Harvey of Stanton (1306-13). King's Bench justices who had once been clerks include Ralph de Hengham (1274-90); Martin of Littlebury (1273-4); Walter of Wimborne (1276-89); and Ellis of Sutton (1285-7). Fuller details and references will be included in my study of Edwardian justices.

[14] KB26/133, m. 5d; BL Additional Charter 5898; KB26/160, mm. 35d, 39d, 54; *Cal. Charter Rolls*, ii, 20-21.

[15] Above note 14; CP 25(1)/214/20, no. 23; CP 25(1)/214/22, no. 72; CP 25(1)/214/21, no. 17; CP 25(1)/214/23, no. 28; CP 25(1)/214/26, no. 3 etc.

[16] *Registrum Epistolarum fratris Johannis Peckham archiepiscopi Cantuariensis*, vol. 3, ed. C. T. Martin, Rolls Series 1886, 968.

[17] CP 25(1)/214/24, no. 18; CP 25(1)/214/26, no. 2.

[18] *Cal. Close Rolls, 1288-1296*, 160; CP 40/24, m. 78; *Close Rolls, 1268-72*, 297-9.

an administrator and adviser.[19] There is some evidence to indicate that Thomas may have conformed to this pattern, though all of it comes from a brief period immediately preceding his appointment as a royal justice. In 1271 he was acting as one of the auditors of Roger Bigod, earl of Norfolk, and in that same year put in an appearance at the Exchequer on the earl's behalf in connexion with the debts of the earl's predecessor.[20] The earl was married to Alina, the daughter of the former royalist justiciar, Philip Basset. There is also some evidence to suggest that Thomas Weyland may have been for a period in the early 1270s in the service of John FitzJohn, the husband of Philip Basset's other daughter, Margery.[21]

Thomas's other elder brother, William Weyland, had pursued a career perhaps best seen as a variant on this. He first went to Ireland in 1248 in the service of Henry III's half-brother, Aymer de Lusignan, and probably acted during the 1250s as seneschal of the earl of Norfolk's Irish liberty of Ross. He then entered the King's service in Ireland on appointment in 1257-8 as a justice of the eyres of counties Limerick and Tipperary. After the death of his elder brother John, William returned to England and was appointed in 1261 escheator of England south of the Trent, a post he held until the triumph of the Montfortian party at the battle of Lewes in 1264.[22] He subsequently returned to Ireland and by 1269 was acting as seneschal of another of the great Leinster liberties, that of Kildare. By 1271 he was once more back in England and was appointed a justice in eyre; he served in a number of eyres at the very end of Henry III's reign and was appointed to the Bench at the very beginning of the reign of Edward

[19] Examples in the Bench are Stephen Heym (1273-4), in the service of Richard, earl of Cornwall, during the 1250s and 1260s; Walter de Heliun (1276-1281), in the service of Robert Walerand from 1260 to 1273 and of Edmund, earl of Cornwall in 1274-5 (and after his period as a justice of the Bench in the service of the earl of Lancaster); Peter Mallore (1292-1308), probably in the service of Ellis de Rabayne and then of the earl of Lincoln; John of Mettingham (1290-1301), in the service of the earl of Lincoln. Examples in King's Bench are Roger Brabazon (1290-1316), in the service of the earl of Lancaster from 1275 to 1290; and Robert Malet (1290-5), in the service of the earl of Cornwall during the 1270s.

[20] SC6/932/12; E159/45, m. 8d (I owe this reference to the kindness of Dr. David Crook).

[21] *Close Rolls, 1268-72*, 297-9; BL Additional Ms. 28024, ff. 40^{r-v}; *Cal. Close Rolls, 1272-79*, 122.

[22] *Cal. Pat. Rolls, 1247-58*, 19; J. H. Bernard, 'Charters of the Cistercian abbey of Duiske in co. Kilkenny', *Proc. Roy. Irish. Acad.* xxv section C, 1920-2, 95-6; G. J. Hand, *English Law in Ireland, 1290-1324*, Cambridge 1967, 220-1; A. Wood, *List of Escheators for England and Wales*, List and Index Soc. lxxii, 1971, 1.

I.[23] It is possible that Thomas was for part of this time in the service of his brother William. It would certainly have given him the relevant experience of administration, particularly legal administration. But there is no real evidence that he was.

2

Thomas Weyland was first appointed as a royal justice at the very end of the reign of Henry III. In 1272 he sat as a justice for the latter part of the Essex eyre and was appointed a justice of the next eyre on the same circuit in Hertfordshire, though this did not, in the event, take place because of the death of Henry III in November, which brought a halt to all the eyre visitations.[24] In Michaelmas term 1274 he was appointed to serve as one of the justices of the Bench. Although two terms separate his appointment from the death of his elder brother William, he appears to have been appointed as a replacement for him. He then sat as a junior justice of the Bench for almost four years until the chief justice of the Bench, master Roger of Seaton, retired from office, probably through ill-health, at the end of Trinity term 1278.[25]

Thomas Weyland was his successor and held office as chief justice until the end of Trinity Term 1289. In the following Michaelmas term Ralph of Sandwich took Weyland's place, but only on a purely temporary basis; his permanent replacement, John of Mettingham, was not appointed until January 1290. Weyland's eleven years in office are not as impressive a period of service as the almost thirteen years enjoyed by his successor, Mettingham, but they represent almost a third of the entire reign and comfortably exceed the periods during which each of the other chief justices of the Bench of Edward's reign held office – one year in the case of Gilbert of Preston, the first chief justice of the reign, almost five years in the case of Weyland's immediate predecessor, master Roger of Seaton, and a little over seven years (including the period he remained in office at the beginning of Edward II's reign) in the case of Ralph de Hengham.[26]

Five justices was the most common complement of the Bench during the reign of Edward I, and for just under two thirds of the period during which Weyland sat as chief justice he had four junior

[23] P.R.O., Dublin RC7/1, 484; Crook, 137, 139.

[24] Crook, 140; *Cal. Pat. Rolls, 1266-72*, 711.

[25] *Select Cases . . . King's Bench*, vol. 1, cxxxv-cxxxvii; *Annales Monastici*, vol. 3, ed. H. R. Luard, Rolls Series 1866, 272; *Registrum Epistolarum . . . Johannis Peckham*, vol. 1, 57-8, 100-1.

[26] *Select Cases . . . King's Bench*, vol. 1, cxxxv-cxxxix.

colleagues there. For the remainder of the period Weyland had only three colleagues, the minimum complement of the court during Edward's reign.[27] These numbers, however, represent only the theoretical membership of the court – its membership as recorded in formal documents associated with the court; not the number of justices actually present and active there. John de Lovetot was nominally a justice of the Bench during the whole of Weyland's period as chief justice and was paid as such for the whole period. He was, however, abroad on official business for a number of the terms when the final concords record him as being present in the court at Westminster. When he handed in his plea rolls in December 1289, Lovetot claimed to have no plea rolls for fourteen of the terms during which he had nominally been a Bench justice (around one third of the total number of terms during which Weyland was chief justice of the court) because he had been abroad in those terms.[28] He was certainly abroad for some of them, but his own assize rolls indicate that for others of them he was in England and probably did sit in the Bench.[29]

The earliest surviving Year Book style reports of cases pleaded in the Bench come from the period at the very end of the reign of Henry III when Martin of Littlebury was chief justice of the court, and over a dozen such reports survive from the four year period when master Roger of Seaton was its chief justice (1274-8). It is, however, only from Thomas Weyland's period of office onwards that they begin to survive in any real quantity.[30] I have succeeded so far in locating and identifying reports of around eighty cases belonging to this period. Many are to be found in more than one manuscript; and a significant number of cases are reported in more than one version. So far none of them has been printed.[31]

[27] *Select Cases . . . King's Bench*, vol. 1, cxxxv-cxxxvii.

[28] *Select Cases . . . King's Bench*, vol. 1, clx.

[29] For evidence, for example, that he was at Westminster during the Easter, Trinity and Michaelmas terms of 1281 see JUST 1/1256, mm. 3d, 7, 7d, 12 and 13.

[30] For reports from Littlebury's period as chief justice see *Casus Placitorum*, ed. W. H. Dunham jr, Selden Soc. lxix, 1952, 79-81 and perhaps 77-78; Cambridge Univ. Lib. Ms. Dd. 7. 14, ff. 387a-b. For reports from Seaton's period as chief justice see *Casus Placitorum*, 49, 72-3, 96-7, 99-110, 121-6; Lincoln's Inn Ms. Misc. 87, ff. 68^{v}-69^{r} (and BL Ms. Harleian 1208, ff. 259^{v}-260^{v}); Cambridge Univ. Lib. Ms. Dd. 7. 14, ff. 401b, 403b-404a; Lincoln's Inn Ms. Hale 174, ff. 20^{v}, 83^{v}

[31] Manuscripts containing such reports include BL Mss. Additional 5925, 31826, 32088, 35116, 37657; Egerton 2811; Harleian 835, 1208; Lansdowne 467; Royal 10. A. V; Stowe 386; Cambridge Univ. Lib. Mss. Dd. 7. 14 and Hh. 3. 11; Lincoln's Inn Mss. Hale 174 and 188; Misc. 87 and 738. I am preparing an edition of all the pre-1290 Bench reports for the Selden Society.

The reports suggest some interesting conclusions about the way in which the Bench organised its business during Weyland's chief justiceship. Roger of Leicester sat as a justice of the Bench for the whole of the period, but not one of the reports even mentions him. It may just be that he never had anything to say that was considered worth reporting, but it is probable that there is a quite different explanation for this absence. From incidental mentions on the plea rolls it is known that in Trinity term 1276 and again in Trinity term 1287 he was sitting apart from his colleagues making adjournments in cases where litigants had been essoined; and that in Michaelmas term 1287 he and his colleague Ellis of Beckingham were sitting by themselves when they awarded judgment on a default.[32] The real reason for his absence is probably that he regularly sat apart from his colleagues, by himself or with a single companion, to deal with routine procedural matters which were of no interest to the reporters. John de Lovetot is mentioned in comparatively few reports. It is possible that this simply reflects the fact that Lovetot was often absent from the court, but again it is more probably to be explained as a consequence of the way in which the court managed its business. Certainly, four of the six reports in which Lovetot does appear feature him alone of all the justices. This may mean that when he was in the court he too sat by himself for much of the time, though hearing a more interesting class of business than his colleague Leicester.

For the reporters it was clearly two of the justices, William of Brompton and Thomas Weyland himself, who formed the main focus of attention. Weyland occurs in fifty-three of the reports; Brompton in thirty-four. The reports suggest that both justices may have heard some cases on their own. In fourteen reports Brompton alone is mentioned and in thirty-five only Weyland. When the two justices did sit with another justice it was most commonly with each other. They appear together but without any other colleagues in fourteen reports. Only in some four reports do as many as three of the justices appear together.

It cannot, of course, automatically be assumed that the failure of the reporter to note any remark by a justice means that he was not sitting in the court; but the general pattern of evidence from the reports taken with occasional references on the plea rolls themselves suggests that by the 1280s the justices of the Bench did not normally, if ever, sit together as a single court, and that much of the Bench's business was

[32] CP 40/17, m. 123; JUST 1/541B, m. 32d; CP 40/70, m. 58d.

heard separately by individual justices or small groups of justices. The reports also indicate that it was Weyland and Brompton who heard the most important and interesting cases and suggest that these two men were the leading justices in the court.

The reports also allow us to form some sort of impression of Thomas Weyland at work as a justice. In one case Alice, Andrew's widow, brought an action of dower claiming one third of a carucate of land against Joan, the widow of Andrew's brother, Alexander. Joan's serjeant claimed that Alexander had been the elder of the two brothers and so had been in possession of the land before Andrew; she had therefore been endowed before Alice, and the latter was not entitled to a dower share of land already allocated as dower to Joan. Alice's serjeant, however, claimed that Andrew had been the older of the two brothers, and had held the land first and so she had a good claim to dower in that land. Aware, perhaps, of the weakness of his client's case, Joan's serjeant then went for a victory on technical grounds. Joan had previously herself brough an action of dower against Alice in the king's court, and, when she had done so, Alice in her defence had not claimed that she was the widow of the older of the two brothers and thus dower was not due, and Joan had then recovered dower against her. Alice was, therefore, he claimed, estopped from making this claim now. Weyland made short work of this. If Alice's serjeant had pleaded badly on a previous occasion, he said, that was no reason now for depriving her of her right of action to recover her dower. Joan was made to traverse Alice's claim that her husband was the first seised and the dispute submitted to a jury.[33]

In another case we can see Weyland deciding an important point of statutory interpretation. When a plaintiff brought the action of *cessavit per biennium* created by chapter 21 of the Statute of Westminster II (1285) to recover a tenement held of him by a tenant who had not performed the services owed for the tenement for two years, did he have only to prove that the services had not been performed for two years or should he also be required to prove that the tenement concerned had not been open to distraint during that two year period? Weyland was quite clear that the latter was the case, and his reasoning was based, interestingly enough, not on the specific wording of the chapter concerned but on the intent of the makers of the statute, which had been to provide a remedy only where the common law was deficient, that is to say where the lord was unable to exercise his

[33] Cambridge Univ. Lib. Ms. Dd. 7. 14, f. 375a.

common law remedy for securing arrears of service, distraint.[34] Weyland's sureness and clarity on this point remind us also that he was the chief justice of the Bench at the time of the enactment of the statute; and that he may well himself have played some part in its drafting.

In a third case heard in 1287, Henry de Pierrepoint and his wife Annora avowed a distraint for six years' arrears of a rent of ten pounds said to be owed them by Richard Barry for a tenement he held of them at Bassingfield in Nottinghamshire. They were unable to show any seisin of the rent either by themselves or by any of the ancestors of Annora, but claimed that this was because Annora's ancestor, James of Holm, had died shortly after granting the land to Richard's father and before the first instalment of rent had fallen due. It also emerged, however, in the course of pleading, and partly through the questioning of the two justices Weyland and Brompton, that Richard and his father had held the land for twenty-six years without paying any rent for it, and that Annora was only a distant relation of James, though by now his nearest surviving heir. Weyland's judgment in the case is a classic example of a particular type of early common law judgment. Yes, he agreed, there was a hardship to the defendants if they were not now able to recover the rent by distraint, for their lack of seisin would also lose them any action of customs and services they might bring for the rent. But, he said, there would be a still greater hardship to the plaintiffs (and to other plaintiffs too) if the defendants were to be allowed to distrain for the rent without showing seisin of the services enjoyed by themselves or their ancestors as title to the services; and thus on the balance of convenience he found for the plaintiffs.[35]

The one thing that is missing from these reports, unfortunately, is any kind of personal touch. For his successors as chief justice of the Bench, John of Mettingham and Ralph de Hengham, the reporters give us anecdotes and moral stories, even the occasional proverb, which help to bring these men close to us as individuals. We know that his colleague Brompton on at least one occasion quoted an

[34] BL Additional Ms. 35116, f. 120^{r}. What seems to be a report of an earlier stage of pleading in the same case (in which several of the arguments employed in it are given an airing) is to be found in three manuscripts in closely related versions: BL Additional Ms. 5925, f. 94^{r}; BL Additional Ms. 31826, f. 221^{v}; BL Additional Ms. 35116, ff. 117^{r-v}.

[35] BL Additional Ms. 31826, ff. 58^{v}-59^{r}. Also reported in Lincoln's Inn Ms. Hale 188, ff. 24^{r-v}; BL. Harleian Ms. 835, f. 2^{r}. The plea roll enrolment of this case will be found on m. 97d of CP 40/69.

English proverb ('Won mon aveth mon, yenne aveth loverd to') but we have nothing of this sort for Weyland.[36] The nearest we come to a personal touch is in the report of a Bench case of 1289 where Weyland reminisces about how he had once been in a similar position to the plaintiff – the grantee of a wardship (in Weyland's case, one given or otherwise granted to him by the abbot of Bury St. Edmund's) against whom a widow had sought the body of an heir in an action of wardship, and how he had not been allowed to vouch the abbot because the voucher was contrary to law. The only other personal touch comes in a collection of reports where we have what may well be a caricature of Weyland's face in profile by a report of one of his speeches in a case, for it has what we are elsewhere told is Weyland's characteristic long beard.[37]

3

In his sketch of Weyland's life in the *Dictionary of National Biography* Tout claimed that, during his eleven years as chief justice of the Bench, Weyland '. . . had neglected no opportunity of furthering his own interest and building up a landed estate' and alleged that Weyland's conduct, which had always been 'questionable', had become 'exceptionally scandalous between 1286 and 1289, when the absence of Edward I and the chancellor Burnell on the continent removed the chief checks upon his action and that of his colleagues'.

It is certainly true that Thomas Weyland did make very substantial property acquisitions during the period he was chief justice of the Bench. These included at least seven manors or substantial property holdings in his home county of Suffolk, three manors or substantial holdings in Essex, and various other properties. From the purchase prices recorded in the associated final concords for some (though not all) of these acquisitions we know that he spent at least £1,150 on them, and perhaps half as much again: an average of some £150 a year. Clearly purchases on this scale could not have been funded from the £40 a year which Weyland received as his salary from the King for acting as the chief justice of the Bench.[38] But it is not necessary to

[36] Cambridge Univ. Lib. Ms. Dd. 7. 14, f. 401a.

[37] Cambridge Univ. Lib. Ms. Dd. 7. 14, ff. 239b-240a, 370b; *Bracton: On the Laws and Customs of England*, vol. 1, ed. G. E. Woodbine and S. E. Thorne, Cambridge, Mass. 1968, 83, note 2.

[38] C 62/55, m. 3, /56, mm. 6, 3, /57, mm. 9, 4, /59, m. 7, /60, mm. 4, 2, /61, mm. 8, 7, 1, /62, m. 3, /63, mm. 3, 2, 1, /64, m. 3, /65, mm. 4, 3.

assume that Weyland's acquisitions were wholly, or even largely, funded from the profits of judicial corruption, as Tout seems to imply. Thomas Weyland was in possession of property in England and Ireland worth at least £150 a year (and perhaps considerably more than that) *before* he became chief justice of the Bench. Of this about two-thirds had come to him by inheritance on the death of his elder brother William in 1274.[39] To this must be added the unknown, but apparently sizeable, income he derived from the two Essex manors (Brundon and Mashbury) held in dower by his second wife, Margery, of the endowment of her first husband, John of Moze, and profits of £20 a year from the lands at East Smithfield by the Tower of London which were owned by his stepson John of Moze, but whose income Weyland seems to have received up to the time of his downfall.[40] Such an income placed him, even in 1278, in the ranks of the upper gentry. More significantly, in the present context, it was also sufficiently large to have allowed him to finance many of his purchases out of current income and accumulated savings.

The only other evidence of Weyland's misconduct as a judge is the complaints made against him, as against almost all his colleagues in the judiciary, in 1289-90. In mid-October 1289 *auditores querelarum* were appointed to receive complaints of wrongs committed by the King's officials against his subjects during Edward I's absence in France. Three complaints seem to have been made to these *auditores* which alleged misconduct on the part of Weyland. Of these, the abbot of St. Évroult's complaint also named his fellow Bench justices as culprits but seems to be of an erroneous rather than a culpably and deliberately wrongful judgment. In any case it was not, apparently, successful.[41] William of Bardwell's complaint was directed mainly against Ralph de Hengham. Against Weyland it alleged only that he (and two other royal justices) had been in the court of King's Bench when a case brought by Bardwell had been heard there, and that all three of them had been there to give counsel and assistance to his opponent, the abbot of Bury St. Edmund's. Bardwell clearly thought such conduct improper; but, by contemporary standards, it would seem to have been at most on the borderline of acceptability.[42] In a

[39] The lands inherited from his brother were the Suffolk manors of Monewden and Brandeston, the Gloucestershire manor of Sodbury and the two Irish manors of Killoteran and Ballyconnery, both in county Waterford.

[40] CP 40/121, m. 209; *Cal. Inquisitions Miscellaneous*, vol. 1, no. 1505.

[41] *State Trials of the Reign of Edward the First, 1289-1293*, ed. T. F. Tout and H. Johnstone, Camden Soc. 3rd. series ix, 1906, 91-2.

[42] *State Trials*, 49-51.

different complaint of the same period which was directed principally against Weyland's colleague Brompton and alleged misconduct by him in the taking of the verdict of a jury in litigation in the Bench, Walter de Surdeval mentioned that John of Mettingham had been sitting on the bench with Brompton at the time of the alleged misconduct. In the course of the proceedings on this complaint, Mettingham is recorded as admitting that he had been in court, but as claiming that this was not in the role of justice but solely in that of a well-wisher (*benivolens*) to Surdeval's opponent, the prior of Sempringham. His reply seems to have been accepted by the *auditores querelarum* as a full and satisfactory answer, which entirely exculpated him.[43] The third complaint linked Weyland's name with those of Brompton and Hengham as bearing responsbility for the issuing of a writ of entry of novel form for the use of John Lovel in making a claim to an extensive holding at Stanford Rivers and Kelvedon Hatch in Essex as the remainderman under a settlement. The complainant, the tenant of these lands, John de Munteny, also complained that his exception against the writ had been wrongly disallowed and that the justices had wrongfully refused to seal the bill of exception to which he was entitled under the provisions of c. 31 of the Statute of Westminster II of 1285, which would record the exception he had put forward and the fact that it had been disallowed by the justices. Corruption was not alleged in this complaint; and what we seem to have here is a genuine conflict of opinion about whether or not the writ should have been made available to the plaintiff. Munteny seems to have had Chancery opinion on his side against the use of the writ, as also that of the post-1290 judiciary, but Hengham, Weyland and Brompton, the leading lights of the pre-1290 judiciary, seem to have thought otherwise. The refusal of a bill of exceptions was clearly wrong, but if Hengham had played some part in the authorisation of the issuing of the writ, it may well have seemed that there was little point in allowing such a bill.[44]

A further five complaints against Weyland were made directly to the King and his council in Parliament, as were many other of the complaints made against the justices at this time. That made by the bishop of Carlisle is easily dismissed. It is almost certain that the 'royal charter' which the bishop produced in a Bench case of 1287 concerning the right to present to the vacant church of Brough under Stainmore was only a letter of Richard I presenting a clerk to the

[43] JUST 1/541B, m. 36d.
[44] E 175/File 1, no. 7, m. 3; *Rot. Parl.*, vol. 1, 84–5.

vacant church and not a royal charter granting the advowson. The bishop was probably, therefore, not justified in claiming that Weyland and his colleagues had acted wrongly in not adjourning the case on the production of this document pending consultation with the king.[45] Margery and Violetta de Zoyn complained that Weyland had arranged for two final concords to be levied in the name of their now deceased brother John, while he was still a minor, one conveying the Essex manor of Chignall Zoyn to himself and other members of his family, the other conveying the Hertfordshire manor of Westmill to John's guardian, Thomas of Lewknor. These fines were certainly levied and the complaint sounds plausible.[46] The sisters, however, failed to recover either manor, despite bringing litigation for that purpose in the Bench in 1290 and 1294.[47] A third complaint by Thomas de Verdun alleged that Weyland had assisted his brother-in-law, William de Grey, in tricking him out of land worth £30 a year. Verdun had arranged to marry Grey's daughter and had agreed to grant this land to Grey, in order that Grey might then regrant it to the new couple. The grant to Grey had taken place as planned and the associated charter had been recorded on the Bench plea roll; Grey had promised to regrant the land to Verdun and his daughter but this agreement had not been put in writing or enrolled. The marriage had not taken place and he had lost his land. It is difficult to know what exactly to make of this story, since no defence to it is recorded. A calculated fraud is possible but seems unlikely. Some kind of dispute over marriage arrangements seems the most likely explanation. Verdun does not seem to have recovered his land.[48]

The remaining two complaints provide the most credible evidence for real wrongdoing on the part of Weyland. In one (which, formally speaking, is not a complaint at all) Robert of Ufford tried to make out a convincing case for being allowed an action of attaint to reverse the verdict of a jury in an action of trespass. What had been at stake in the action was the right to a ship which had been wrecked at Bawdsey in Suffolk. It was the general rule not to allow the use of attaint to reverse jury verdicts in actions of this kind, and in the event Ufford did not succeed in having the rule waived in this particular case. What Ufford alleged was that Weyland had taken the jury's verdict alone and without a colleague; had charged the jury incorrectly; and had

[45] *Rot. Parl.*, vol. 1, 23-4; CP 40/68, mm. 10d, 78.
[46] *Rot. Parl.*, vol. 1, 56-7.
[47] CP 40/86, m. 43; CP 40/104, m. 134; CP 40/146, m. 75d.
[48] SC 8/256, no. 12796; *Rot. Parl.* vol. 1, 47, no. 25 (summary only).

subsequently entered judgment in the case in the Bench without calling the parties to hear their judgment. He ascribed Weyland's misconduct to undue favour for Robert's opponent, the earl of Norfolk, and attributed this to the fact that Thomas was one of the earl's followers ('*mesneng*') at that time and his chief counsellor.[49] It is not difficult to find other evidence showing that Weyland continued to act as one of the earl's advisers after his appointment as a royal justice.[50] Indeed, the connexion must have been well-known and does not seem to have been the subject of any kind of official disapproval. Weyland was even appointed by royal letters patent to act as one of the two attorneys for the earl in England during his visit to Ireland in 1279.[51] Such a connexion can, moreover, be parallel both in John de Lovetot's service during the 1280s to Queen Eleanor and in Lambert of Threekingham's service while a justice of the Bench in the early fourteenth century to successive archbishops of York and at least one bishop of Durham.[52] What cannot be proved, however, is that the connexion did lead to misconduct in this particular instance: for that we only have Robert of Ufford's word. If things had turned out differently and it had been the earl who had been making the complaint he too could have given reasons why Weyland might have favoured his opponents. The chief justice is known to have been a tenant of Ufford's co-defendant, the prior of Butley, and on sufficiently good terms with him to have deposited his deeds for safe-keeping in his priory; and some degree of friendship between Weyland and Ufford himself seems to be indicated by the appearance of Ufford high in the list of witnesses to two unrelated deeds, both in Weyland's favour, of 1286 and 1287.[53]

The remaining complaint was one made by Hugh of Gosbeck. It

[49] *Select Cases in the Court of King's Bench*, vol. 2, ed. G. O. Sayles, Selden Soc. lvii, 1938, cxxxviii; and cf. *Rot. Parl.*, vol. 1, 53, no. 90.

[50] SC 6/997, no. 2; SC 6/997, no. 5.

[51] *Cal. Pat. Rolls, 1272-81*, 319.

[52] JUST 1/836, mm. 1, 2, 6; JUST 1/542, m. 12; J. C. Parsons, *The Court and Household of Eleanor of Castille in 1290*, Toronto 1977, 81; CP 40/23, m. 38. For Threekingham see *Register of Thomas Corbridge*, part 1, ed. W. Brown, Surtees Soc. cxxxviii, 1925, 223-4; part 2, ed. W. Brown and A. H. Thompson, Surtees Soc. cxli, 1928, 32, 73, 77, 121-3, 126, 128, 131; *Register of William Greenfield*, part 1, ed. W. Brown and A. H. Thompson, Surtees Soc. cxlv, 1931. 199; part 4, ed. W. Brown and A. H. Thompson, Surtees Soc. clii, 1938, 270, 342; part 5, ed. W. Brown and A. H. Thompson, Surtees Soc. cliii, 1940, 162, 166; *Registrum Palatinum Dunelmense*, vol. 2, ed. T. D. Hardy, Rolls Series 1874, 866-8, 945-6.

[53] *Cal. Inq. Misc.*, vol. 1, no. 1493; SC 8/151, no. 7536; E 40/3374; KB 27/107, m. 11.

concerned proceedings brought in the Bench in 1288 by William (son of Roger) of Braham by writ of cosinage with the object of recovering a rent of fifty (or fifty-six) shillings at Trimley and Kirton in Suffolk. The defendant in the case, William of Aldborough, had vouched Herbert Weyland (almost certainly a relation of Thomas) and his wife Margaret to warranty for the rent. They had warranted and in turn vouched the complainant to warranty. He had, he claimed, appeared in the Bench in Trinity term 1288, warranted and then traversed the demandant's claim that he was the next heir of the 'cousin' on whose seisin he had based his claim, and this issue had then gone to a jury. After the case had been adjourned, however, Weyland had, he alleged, seen to it that the relevant part of the plea roll entry had been erased and had then substituted for it a record that the complainant had departed in contempt of court and so judgment had been given against him. For this allegation there is confirmatory evidence. We do know that King and council reversed the judgment in the case on the grounds of manifest (though unspecified) error in the Hilary Parliament of 1290 and sent the case back to the Bench to be reheard. Indeed it was because of their responsibility for the recorded judgment in the case along with Thomas Weyland that his fellow Bench justices Brompton, Lovetot and Leicester and the chief clerk of the Bench, Robert of Littlebury, were heavily fined and made to pay damages to the complainant. The remaining Bench justice, Ellis of Beckingham, seems to have escaped punishment simply because in this one term alone he did not sit in the Bench, having been appointed as one of the justices of the Dorset eyre.[54] We can also see from the surviving entry of the case on Weyland's plea roll that the relevant part of the plea roll has been erased and then written over.[55] And there is a third and even more damning piece of evidence, which provides a motive for Weyland's wrongdoing. At the time of his downfall, Weyland was in possession of a rent-charge of approximately the same value in just these two Suffolk villages, an area of Suffolk in which he possessed no other property.[56] This suggests that the successful demandant, the only beneficiary of his wrongdoing, granted him some sort of interest in the rent in return for his assistance.

Although in this one case there is fairly conclusive evidence of

[54] CP 40/81, m. 102; JUST 1/541B, mm. 5, 10d, 12, 24d, 33; *Bartholomei de Cotton Historia Anglicana*, ed. H. R. Luard, Rolls Series 1859, 172-3.

[55] CP 40/73, m. 86d.

[56] E 372/139, m. 8d.

corruption on Weyland's part and it seems possible that he was guilty of misconduct in other cases too, the volume of accusations against him is surprisingly small, far fewer than the accusations against his colleague Brompton or against the chief justice of King's Bench, Ralph de Hengham, it is possible that his abjuration meant that many complainants who would have complained against him complained against his colleague Brompton instead. What is clear, however, is that the surviving evidence does not support the assertion that Weyland was guilty of corruption on any very considerable scale. It was certainly not judicial corruption that led to his downfall in 1289.

4

It was probably on 20 July 1289 that two of Thomas Weyland's servants in his Suffolk manor of Monewden committed a murder at a fair.[57] The victim is named in the official record of Weyland's trial as William Carwel of Ireland; but in the special commission appointed to inquire into the murder he is called Carewel le Forester.[58] He was, then, from Ireland and quite possibly of native Irish origin. It is tempting to identify him with the Cearbhaill Ó Foirchtern who in 1281 received a safe-conduct to visit his kinsman, the earl of Norfolk, in England, and to suggest that he was back in England on a return visit, but this cannot be proved.[59] The murder may have been unpremeditated, the result of the kind of drunken brawl that was common at markets and fairs. But perhaps, in view of Thomas Weyland's own Irish connexions, the killing was part of some wider Anglo-Irish feud to which Weyland and his servants had become parties. There is also another possibility: that there was a link between the murder and the bitter rifts which took place within the household of the earl of Norfolk in the later 1280s, pitting Robert of Benhall and Geoffrey Atwater of Ditchingham against other members of the earl's *familia* and the earl himself.[60] There is some evidence at least to suggest that Weyland took the side of Robert and Geoffrey in these disputes.[61] The victim may, then, have been Irish but have been killed

[57] JUST 3/87, m. 1.

[58] C 66/108, m. 9d.

[59] R. Frame, 'The Justiciar and the Murder of the MacMurroughs in 1282', *Irish Historical Studies* xvii, 1972, 223, 230.

[60] KB 27/114, mm. 35, 50d; KB 27/116, mm. 15d, 23; KB 27/118, mm. 23, 24d; KB 27/123, m. 9; KB 27/124, m. 26; KB 27/125, mm. 2d, 46d; KB 27/126, m. 58; JUST 1/1282, m. 32d; CP 40/116, m. 42.

[61] *Cal. Close Rolls, 1288-96*, 59.

because he was a supporter of the earl.

Thomas Weyland's involvement in the murder seems to have been solely that of an accessory after the fact, through having failed to have his servants arrested when they returned to Monewden, despite the fact that he knew of the murder. Just possibly, he actively sheltered them from arrest after their return. On 4 September 1289, only just over a month after the killing, special justices were appointed to inquire into it, with power to determine any indictments they received. By 19 September, they had tried and hanged Weyland's two servants at a special gaol delivery session. At that same session Thomas Weyland himself was indicted for having harboured the two murderers, and orders were given for his apprehension. He was duly arrested one evening in his home village of Witnesham by a clerk of the sheriff of Suffolk. Weyland asked to spend the night at home before being taken to Ipswich and was then able to make good his escape under cover of darkness. He eventually reached the Franciscan priory at Babwell, just outside Bury St. Edmund's, where he took the Franciscan habit and resumed clerical tonsure. Once his presence in the priory had become known, the men of the neighbourhood were set to guard it and soon Robert Malet was appointed by the King to take charge of arrangements for guarding him and then starving him out of the priory. Eventually, in mid-January 1290, Weyland surrendered and was taken under safe-conduct to London; once there, he seems to have been offered a choice between standing trial, perpetual imprisonment and abjuration of all of the King's lands.[62] His choice of this last option led to the gaol delivery session at the Tower in late February 1290 which I mentioned at the beginning of this paper.

The standard account of the 'State Trials' of 1289-93, that given by T. F. Tout and Hilda Johnstone in their introduction to the Camden series volume of *State Trials* published in 1906, links Weyland's downfall with the appointment by Edward I on 13 October 1289 of *auditores querelarum* to receive complaints of misconduct by the king's ministers during his three year absence in France: 'the immediate result of this inquiry was the gradual removal of the greatest offenders. Thomas de Weyland, Chief Justice of Common Pleas [was] the first to suffer . . .'.[63] This view is, however, clearly quite mistaken. The gaol delivery session at which Weyland was indicted

[62] JUST 3/87, m. 1; *Bracton*, vol. 1, 83, n. 2; *Annales Monastici*, vol. 3, 356; *Liber Memorandorum Ecclesie de Bernewelle*, ed. J. W. Clark, Cambridge 1907, 225.

[63] *State Trials*, xiii.

preceded by almost a month the appointment of the *auditores querelarum* and preceded by almost two months their first sessions. If there was a connexion between the appointment of the *auditores querelarum* and the indictment of Thomas Weyland then it was of the reverse kind: it was Weyland's indictment that led to the appointment of the *auditores* and not vice versa.

5

What happened to Thomas Weyland when he reached Dover in late February 1290? Geoffrey Hand, in an article published in 1970, was the first to draw attention to evidence that Thomas Weyland had subsequently reached Paris and was still there in 1292 when an emissary of Edward I canvassed the opinions of a number of Parisian legal experts on the Scottish succession question.[64] Until recently that was the last that was known of him. However, Dr. Henry Summerson has kindly drawn my attention to an entry on the Exchequer memoranda roll for 1297-8 which contains a reference to the death of Thomas Weyland; and further investigation has provided evidence that Thomas Weyland in fact died not long before 20 January 1298, and not in exile but back in England, at his wife's dower manor of Brundon.[65] No pardon to him seems to have been enrolled on the patent roll, but one was almost certainly granted, for it would have been very foolhardy for him to have returned to England without one.[66] John Weever tells us that a Thomas Weyland was one of the persons buried in the Suffolk priory of Woodbridge (perhaps in the priory church, now the parish church of the town); and since Thomas Weyland, the chief justice, is known to have been a benefactor to the priory, this may well be a reference to him.[67] Wherever he may lie and whatever his sins *requiescat in pace*.

[64] G. J. Hand, 'The Opinions of the Paris Lawyers upon the Scottish Succession Question', *Irish Jurist* v, 1970, 149.

[65] E 368/69, mm. 59, 85, 116, 120d.

[66] DL 25/1575.

[67] J. Weever, *Ancient Funerall Monuments*, London, 1631, 752-3.

4

The Administration of Criminal Justice in Late-Medieval England: Peace Sessions and Assizes

Edward Powell

The aim of this paper is to investigate the relationship between the justices of the peace and the assizes, the two principal agencies of criminal justice in England, during the formative period of their development in the second half of the fourteenth century. We know a great deal about the evolution of the JPs thanks to the exhaustive research work of Professor Putnam and her pupils, and virtually all the records of medieval peace sessions are now in print.[1] By comparison the history of medieval assizes has been neglected. Miss Gollancz's unpublished monograph on the circuit gaol delivery system was written fifty years ago, while the only general study of medieval assize work, concentrating on the decade between 1327 and 1336, appeared in 1950.[2] As a result of this imbalance, it is inevitable that a re-assessment of the relationship between JPs and assizes must be based on a critique of Putnam's work, and that is the form my argument will take.

Throughout her lengthy and detailed analysis of the emergence of the JPs in the fourteenth century, Putnam acknowledged no significant link between their activities and those of the assize justices. She regarded the latter, together with the justices in eyre, the court of King's Bench and commissions of trailbaston and oyer and terminer, as 'competitors' of the JPs in a struggle to acquire the lion's share of the ordinary jurisdiction of the Crown over felony and trespass.[3] According to Putnam's view, the JPs had seen off this competition by about 1390, and consolidated their judicial authority in the shires. She

[1] *Proceedings before the Justices of the Peace in the Fourteenth and Fifteenth Centuries: Edward III to Richard III*, ed. B. H. Putnam, Ames Foundation, London 1938. Editions of individual peace rolls are listed in D. J. Guth, *Late-Medieval England, 1377-1485*, Cambridge 1976, 8-16.

[2] M. Gollancz, 'The System of Gaol Delivery as Illustrated in the Extant Gaol Delivery Rolls of the Fifteenth Century', unpublished M.A. thesis, University of London, 1936; M. M. Taylor, 'The Justices of Assize', in *The English Government at Work, 1327-1336*, ed. J. F. Willard, W. A. Morris, W. H. Dunham, vol. 3, Cambridge, Mass. 1950, 219-47.

[3] Putnam, *Proceedings*, xxxvi-lvi.

saw as the prime mover behind the rise of the JPs the shire-knights who made up the Commons of Edward III's Parliaments, representatives of the class that was to fill the commissions of the peace. For half a century this group fought doggedly to obtain powers of determining for the old keepers of the peace, thereby transforming them into justices. Ultimately they succeeded, despite the persistent opposition of the central government and judiciary, which favoured a judicial system in the image of the old general eyre, with powerful centrally directed commissions staffed with central court judges and pleaders. It was not until the fifteenth century that the criminal jurisdiction of the JPs was challenged and finally overtaken by the circuit assize justices in their capacity as judges of gaol delivery. Only after 1400, Putnam argued, were assize justices regularly appointed JPs in each county of their circuit, thus acquiring the threefold commission of assize, gaol delivery and the peace which made them such a dominant feature of provincial government under the Tudors.[4]

This paper has three contentions: that the JPs and assize judges should in no sense be regarded as competitors, but rather as complementary to one another within a coherent judicial structure; that the practice of appointing assize judges to the peace commissions of their circuit occurred much earlier than Putnam realised, beginning in 1350; and that as a result of the omission of the assize judges from consideration, Putnam's analysis of the evolution of the peace commission between the 1340s and the 1390s is incomplete.

In order to prove these contentions it is necessary to follow Professor Putnam's footsteps by examining the frequent changes of the peace commission from the beginning of Edward III's reign, and then to relate those changes to the involvement of the assize justices in peace sessions' business. In the early years of Edward III's reign, between 1327 and 1344, there is no discernible link between the work of JPs and assize judges. The period was nevertheless of great importance in seeing the birth of the criminal jurisdiction of both sets of officials. The JPs first acquired the power to determine felonies in 1329, only to lose it almost at once, regaining it briefly in 1332 and between 1338 and 1344.[5] In 1328-29 the assize circuits were re-organized into six county groupings which closely resembled the permanent form of the sixteenth century and later, and a statute of

[4] Putnam, *Proceedings*, li-lvi.

[5] B. H. Putnam, 'The Transformation of the Keepers of the Peace into Justices of the Peace, 1327-80', *Transactions of the Royal Historical Society* 4th series xii, 1929, 24-41.

1330 authorized assize judges to deliver prisoners held in the gaols of their circuits.[6]

In 1344 the JPs were again reduced to mere keepers of the peace by the removal of their power to determine felonies and trespasses. New commissions of the peace were issued for all counties in July of that year and circuit justices were not included. The 1344 Parliament had enacted, however, that when it became necessary the keepers, 'with other wise and learned in the law shall be assigned to the King's commission to hear and determine felonies and trespasses done against the peace in the same counties'.[7] In practice, this meant that the keepers only acquired oyer and terminer powers through separate *ad hoc* commissions which included men of law.[8] Putnam correctly pointed out that the practice of 'afforcing' the keepers with lawyers foreshadows the quorum of the peace commission, the inner circle of justices, one of whom had to be present if cases were to be determined.[9] What she did not make clear was that the men of law named to 'afforce' the keepers of the peace regularly included the assize justices of the circuit in which the given county lay. William Cheltenham, for example, a junior assize justice on the north-western circuit in the 1340s, was frequently appointed in Worcestershire and Gloucestershire.[10] Similarly, William Bassett and William Shareshull, justices on the northern and south-western circuits respectively, acted with the keepers in the counties of their circuits.[11] The important point here is that even in its most primitive form the quorum of the peace commission already included circuit assize justices.

The Black Death of 1348-49 and the subsequent labour crisis precipitated a thorough overhaul of judicial administration, for which Putnam's monograph on the enforcement of the Statutes of Labourers remains the authoritative study.[12] The earliest systematic attempt to enforce the Ordinance of Labourers of 1349 was made with the issue of new peace commissions in February 1350, which were re-

[6] R. B. Pugh, *Imprisonment in Medieval England*, Cambridge 1968, 281-82.

[7] 18 Edward III, st. 2 c. 2.

[8] *Cal. Pat, Rolls, 1343-45*, 507, 510, 572-73; *1345-48*, 31, 105-7, 111, 175, 241, 301, 306, 318, 472.

[9] Putnam, 'Transformation', 42.

[10] *Cal. Pat. Rolls, 1343-45*, 507; *1345-48*, 106, 175-76, 241, 472; *1348-50*, 64.

[11] Bassett: *Cal. Pat. Rolls, 1343-45*, 507, 572; *1345-48*, 105. Shareshull: *Cal. Pat. Rolls, 1345-48*, 107, 301, 306.

[12] B. H. Putnam, *The Enforcement of the Statutes of Labourers during the First Decade after the Black Death*, Columbia, New York 1908.

issued with minor modifications after the Statute of Labourers in 1351.[13] The JPs were given the responsbility of putting the Ordinance into effect. They also regained the power to hear and determine felonies and trespasses, and for the first time such power was qualified by the inclusion of a quorum: one of two or three named justices was to be present if felonies were to be determined. A comparison of the 1350 and 1351 peace commissions with commissions of assize and gaol delivery reveals not only that assize justices were appointed to all the county benches of their circuits, but also that they invariably made up the quorum.[14] The JPs could not exercise their powers of determining cases of felony except in the presence of one of the assize judges.

Between 1352 and 1359 the government hived off the authority to enforce the labour laws to separate commissions for labourers, but otherwise the peace commission of 1350 survived with minor modifications until 1359, and assize justices continued to be appointed to the quorum of every commission. Broadly speaking, the relationship between the JPs and the justices of labourers was comparatively simple: commissions for labourers were granted to the same men as commissions of the peace, omitting the assize justices.[15]

In 1359 the brief experiment with justices of labourers was abandoned, and their duties restored to the JPs.[16] During the autumn of that year the government carried out the second major re-organization of criminal justice within a decade. It began on 22 October 1359 with a privy seal letter from the King ordering the re-allocation of assize circuits among the central court justices and serjeants.[17] On 30 October new assize commissions were issued following the King's instructions; on 4 November the commissions for labourers were recalled, and on 4 December new commissions of the peace were issued, the first full lists since 1351.[18] The JPs regained the power to enforce the Statutes of Labourers, but lost the duty to

[13] Putnam, *Statutes of Labourers*, 9-15.

[14] *Cal. Pat. Rolls, 1348-50*, 526-27; *1350-54*, 85-91. See also *Cal. Pat. Rolls, 1350-54*, 160, where the circuit justices received commissions to enquire into extortions committed under colour of the Statutes of Labourers. JUST 1 (Eyre Rolls, Assize Rolls, etc.) /1440-58; JUST 3 (Gaol Delivery Rolls) /136-141. Putnam, *Statutes of Labourers*, Appendix, 21-24.

[15] *Cal. Pat. Rolls, 1350-54*, 449-51, 508-9; *1354-58*, 59-62, 122-24.

[16] Putnam, 'Transformation', 45; *Proceedings*, xliv-v.

[17] *Select Cases in the Court of King's Bench*, vol. 7, ed. G. O. Sayles, Selden Soc. lxxxviii, 1971, lxiv-v.

[18] JUST 1/1458-64; *Cal. Close Rolls, 1354-60*, 655; *Foedera*, vol. 3 pt. 1, 463-64.

carry out military arrays within their shires, which had been part of the peace commission since 1338. Separate commissions of array had been issued on 3 October and 16 November, and henceforth the JPs were to be relieved permanently of their former responsibilities.[19] The determining powers of the JPs remained, together with the quorum for felonies, which as before was the exclusive preserve of the assize judges. The enrolment of the 1359 peace commissions on the patent rolls grouped counties according to assize circuits, and the assize justices were made accountable for the fines levied by JPs in each county of their circuit.[20] The overall effect of the changes in 1359 was to restore the *status quo* of 1350, but with the JPs now divested of their responsibilities for array.

Once more, however, the re-organization was to be short-lived. The famous statute of 1361, still seen as the legislative basis of the power of magistrates, formally conceded to the JPs the power to determine all felonies and trespasses at the King's suit.[21] The general issue of peace commissions which followed, in March 1361, is notable for our purposes in that it granted full determining powers without any form of quorum.[22] In consequence there were no circuit assize justices included in the commissions. Some central court justices and serjeants were appointed, but only in their home counties, such as John Cavendish in Suffolk. For three years, between 1361 and 1364, the JPs exercised totally unrestricted jurisdiction over felony and trespass precisely as the statute of 34 Edward III stipulated.[23] In this respect the period is unique in the fourteenth century: even during the years between 1338 and 1344 when JPs enjoyed determining powers without the involvement of assize justices, they were answerable to magnate supervisors. The government clearly regarded the three year experiment as a failure, because it was terminated in 1364 and JPs were deprived of all powers of determining. Instead their indictments were to be sent to the assize justices in their capacity as gaol delivery commissioners. As might be expected, the 1364 peace commissioners did not include assize judges except in their home counties.[24] In 1368 partly as a result of a parliamentary statute authorising JPs to hear and

[19] Putnam, *Proceedings*, xxviii.

[20] *Foedera*, vol. 3 pt. 1, 463-64.

[21] 34 Edward III c. 1.

[22] *Cal. Pat. Rolls, 1361-64*, 63-67; *Yorkshire Sessions of the Peace, 1361-64*, ed. B. H. Putnam, Yorkshire Arch. Soc. Record Series c, 1939, 1-3.

[23] See *Cal. Pat. Rolls, 1361-64*, 291-93.

[24] *Cal. Pat. Rolls, 1361-64*, 528-30; Putnam, 'Transformation', 46.

determine labour offences, the arrangement of 1350 and 1359 was restored.[25] The JPs regained their determining powers, and the assize justices were appointed to all counties in their circuits. The quorum for felonies was revived, and continued to be confined to the assize justices alone.[26]

The 1368 peace commission remained in force virtually unchanged until 1380. Full lists of commissions for all counties were issued in December 1375 and on Richard II's accession in 1377, and in both cases assize justices were appointed to all counties in their circuits and formed the quorum for felonies.[27] In the Parliament of 1380 a lengthy petition demanded that the powers of the JPs be substantially increased and the role of the quorum reduced.[28] The petition confirmed the important position that circuit justices enjoyed on the peace commission by requesting that JPs should have the power to determine notorious larcenies, murders, and homicides by malice aforethought without awaiting the presence of the assize judges. The resulting ordinance conceded this demand, and also conferred upon the JPs the power to hear and determine cases of extortion, livery and maintenance and armed conventicles. The changes were embodied in a fresh peace commission issued to all counties on 26 May 1380 and enrolled in the parliament rolls.[29] The quorum survived in attenuated form: it remained the exclusive preserve of the assize justices, but their presence was required only in cases of felony not included in the JPs' new general powers.[30] A new proviso clause required the presence of a justice of either bench or of assize for the determination of difficult cases of extortion.

The 1380 commission gave the JPs greater judicial authority than at any time since 1361-64, but once more the gains appear to have been short-lived. The decade of the 1380s is one of confusion and ambiguity in the history of the JPs. Putnam, relying on the work of her pupil Miss Sillem, argued that by the peace commission of 20 December 1382 the JPs again lost the power to determine felonies and common law trespasses, regaining it only in 1389.[31] However, Dr. J.

[25] 42 Edward III c. 6.

[26] *Cal. Pat. Rolls, 1367-70*, 191-95; Putnam, *Proceedings*, 203-5.

[27] *Cal. Pat. Rolls, 1374-77*, 136-39; *1377-80*, 44-48.

[28] *Rot. Parl.*, vol. 3, 83-85.

[29] *Rot. Parl.*, vol. 3, 84-5; R. Sillem, 'Commissions of the Peace, 1380-1485', *B.I.H.R.* x, 1932-33, 98-100; *Cal. Pat. Rolls, 1377-81*, 512-15.

[30] *Rot. Parl.*, vol. 3, 84-85: 'ad felonias predictas quarum determinacio superius declarata non existit . . . audiendas et terminandas'.

[31] Putnam, *Proceedings*, xxiv-v, xxviii-ix; Sillem, 'Commissions', 94-95.

B. Post has demonstrated quite convincingly that in practice the JPs continued to exercise their determining powers during the 1380s, and concluded that the omission of the oyer and terminer wording in the 1382 commission was accidental.[32] If this was the case, it is hard to understand why the omission was not rapidly corrected: in fact, as Post pointed out, it survived the general issue of peace commissions in July 1389. There was a second substantial modification in the 1382 commission which suggests that the omission was not a mistake: the quorum clause for determining was left out, exactly as one would expect if the power of determining felonies had been removed from the commission, and instead a quorum of five or six men of law, including the assize justices, was specified in the inquiry clause.[33] Why the presence of lawyers was deemed necessary merely for the taking of indictments is not clear, but the alteration of the size and purpose of the quorum implies a deliberate, albeit unsuccessful, attempt to modify the JPs' powers. These adjustments must be related to the general issue of powerful commissions to hear and determine treasons and felonies and to punish rebels, dated 21 December 1382 – the day after the issue of the peace commissions. Commissions of this kind had been issued twice before, in December 1381 and March 1382, and reflected the government's fear of renewed rebellion after the Peasants' Revolt.[34] The two sets of commissions of December 1382 complemented each other almost exactly, and in every county there was a substantial overlap of personnel on the two commissions which made it possible for them to hold combined sessions. The arrangements of 1382 resemble those of the 1350s, when two separate but overlapping groups of commissioners – the JPs and the justices of labourers – were entrusted with the administration of royal justice in the shires. The experiment of the 1380s was as short-lived as that of the 1350s, partly because it was too complicated, partly because of the form of the peace commission, which has confounded medieval clerks and modern scholars alike, was ill-drafted and ambiguous.

The general peace commission of November 1389 restored the JPs' powers to determine all offences, and instituted a new variation on the quorum. The commission specified two quorums: one for determining felonies, consisting of the assize justices alone; and a

[32] J. B. Post, 'The Peace Commissions of 1382', *E.H.R.* xci, 1976, 98-101.

[33] *Rolls of the Warwickshire and Coventry Sessions of the Peace, 1377-1397*, ed. E. G. Kimball, Dugdale Soc. xvi, 1939, 152-54; *Cal. Pat. Rolls, 1381-85*, 251-55.

[34] *Warwickshire Sessions*, 154-56; Post, 99-100; *Cal. Pat. Rolls, 1381-85*, 244-49.

second for all other offences in which the assize justices were joined by local men of law, usually the regular 'working' justices. In Oxfordshire, for example, the circuit justices Sir Robert Charlton and Sir John Hill comprised the felony quorum, and served with the lawyer John Rede and Nicholas Somerton, the *custos rotulorum* in 1390, on the quorum for trespass.[35]

Finally, in June 1394, a single, extended quorum was introduced, initially for felony, trespass and forestalling only, but soon for all offences over which the JPs had jurisdiction.[36] It differed from the old felony quorum in including not merely the assize justices, but also two or more local lawyers. This followed the statute enacted at the Parliament of 1394 which stipulated that two men of law of the county be appointed to all peace commissions, with power to deliver thieves and felons as often as was necessary to avoid undue delay in trying prisoners.[37] In the fifteenth century there were some minor changes and temporary modifications of the peace commission, but in its essentials the 1394 form of commission provided the basis for the jurisdiction of the JPs until the end of the sixteenth century.

What conclusions are to be drawn from the foregoing analysis of the involvement of assize justices in the work of the JPs through their inclusion in the quorum? First, it is striking how closely the determining powers of the JPs were regulated by the Crown, particularly as regards their felony jurisdiction. Only in the period between 1361 and 1364, and to a lesser degree between 1380 and 1382, did the JPs enjoy jurisdiction over felony without the constraint of a quorum. Secondly, the Crown was not faced with a stark choice between denying the JPs all judicial powers, as in 1364-68, and conceding them all, as in 1361-64. Between the two extremes lay a wide variety of options: separate commissions conferring determining power, as in 1344; a single quorum for felony, as in 1350, 1359 and 1368; two quorums, one for felony and one for trespass, as in 1389; and parallel commissions covering complementary areas of jurisdiction, as between 1352 and 1359 and between 1382 and 1389. The frequency and complexity of the changes in the peace commission in the second half of the fourteenth century suggest that their cause was not simply a struggle for control over local judicial administration between the King's judges and the county gentry,

[35] *Oxfordshire Sessions of the Peace in the Reign of Richard II*, ed. E. G. Kimball, Oxfordshire Record Soc. liii, 1983, 121-24; *Cal. Pat. Rolls, 1388-92*, 137-39.

[36] Putnam, *Proceedings*, xxv; *Cal. Pat. Rolls, 1391-96*, 435-41, 587.

[37] 17 Richard II c. 10.

with the latter emerging as ultimate victors. While Putnam is undoubtedly correct in emphasizing the determination of the Commons throughout Edward III's reign to secure and defend the JPs' criminal jurisdiction, the Crown's primary concern was to find the best method of dovetailing their powers with those of the assize circuit justices. There was no danger during the fourteenth century of the Crown losing permanent control over the administration of justice in the shires. By 1350 judicial visitations were far more regular and penetrating than they had been a hundred years earlier. The problems of the century arose from the massive expansion in the scope of royal jurisdiction, and the difficulties in reconciling the exercise of the King's lucrative judicial prerogatives with the demands of the local communities for efficient and impartial justice. The repeated adjustments made to the powers of the JPs, and the juggling with different types of commission in the 1350s and 1380s, taken in conjunction with the established routine of the assize and gaol delivery circuits, represent a cumulative series of short-term expedients to balance control against efficiency. The Crown's desire for an itinerant system of justice in the image of the old general eyre was tempered by the recognition that the assize justices should not be brought to a standstill by sheer weight of business, as the eyre had been, and that the law had to be enforced in the shire during the lengthy periods when the King's justices were closeted at Westminster. The solution ultimately hammered out in the 1394 peace commission proved workable in the long run because it established a generally acceptable balance between control and efficiency, between the interests of the Crown and those of the local communities.

Appendix:

Assize Circuit Judges Appointed to Peace Commissions, 1351-1394

Listed below are the names of assize judges appointed as JPs within their circuits by each general issue of county peace commissions between 1351 and 1394. The list has been compiled from the Calendars of Patent Rolls. Assize Rolls (PRO JUST 1/1440–1511) and Gaol Delivery Rolls (PRO JUST 3/136–85). The composition of the assize circuits was as follows:—

Home:	Essex, Herts., Kent, Midd., Surrey, Sussex.
East Anglian:	Beds., Bucks., Cambs., Hunts., Norf., Suff.
Southwestern:	Corn., Devon, Dors., Hants., Som., Wilts.
Northwestern:	Berks., Glos., Herefs., Oxon., Salop, Staffs., Worcs.
Midland:	Derbs., Leics., Lincs., Northants., Notts., Rutland, Warwicks.
Northern:	Cumb., Northumb., Westm., Yorks.

Berkshire and Oxfordshire formed part of the Southwestern circuit until 1359, when they were transferred to the East Anglian circuit. From 1368 they were permanently attached to the Northwestern circuit.

15 MARCH 1351:

Home:	Richard Willoughby, Henry Green & William Notton
East Anglian:	Richard Kelshall & Robert Thorpe
Southwestern:	William Shareshull, John Stowford & Richard Burton
Northwestern:	Roger Hillary, Richard de la Pole & William Cheltenham
Midland:	John Mowbray & William Skipwith
Northern:	William Bassett, Thomas Seaton, Thomas Fencotes & Roger Blakeston.

4 DECEMBER 1359:

Home:	William Thorpe & William Notton
East Anglian:	Robert Thorpe & John Knyvet
Southwestern:	Richard Burton & Henry Mutlow
Northwestern:	Henry Green & William Finchdean
Midland:	John Mowbray & Thomas Ingleby
Northern:	William Skipwith & William Witchingham

20 MARCH 1361:
Circuit judges not appointed to peace commissions.

8 MARCH 1364:
Circuit judges not appointed to peace commissions.

10 JULY 1368:

Home:	Robert Belknap & Thomas Ludlow
East Anglian:	Roger Kirton (alias Meres) & John Fencotes
Southwestern:	William Witchingham & Edmund Chelrey
Northwestern:	John Mowbray & William Wakebridge
Midland:	Thomas Ingleby & John Cavendish
Northern:	William Finchdean & Roger Fulthorpe

6 DECEMBER 1375:

Home:	Robert Belknap & Henry Hasty
East Anglian:	John Cavendish & John Holt
Southwestern:	Henry Percy & Walter Clopton
Northwestern:	Walter Perle & David Hanmer
Midland:	Thomas Ingleby & William Witchingham
Northern:	Roger Kirton & Roger Fulthorpe

2 JULY 1377:

Home:	Robert Belknap & Henry Hasty
East Anglian:	John Cavendish & John Holt
Southwestern:	Henry Percy & Walter Clopton
Northwestern:	David Hanmer & Roger Kirton
Midland:	William Skipwith & William Burgh
Northern:	Thomas Ingleby & Roger Fulthorpe

26 MAY 1380:

As 1377, except that Roger Kirton replaced Thomas Ingleby on the Northern circuit, and Robert Tresilian replaced Kirton on the Northwestern circuit.

20 DECEMBER 1382:

Home:	Robert Belknap & Walter Clopton
East Anglian:	John Holt & William Thurning
Southwestern:	Robert Tresilian & John Cary
Northwestern:	Robert Belknap & David Hanmer
Midland:	William Skipwith & William Burgh
Northern:	Roger Fulthorpe & Thomas Pinchbeck

15 JULY and 10 NOVEMBER 1389:

Home:	John Wadham & William Hankford
East Anglian:	John Cassy & William Gascoigne
Southwestern:	William Rykhill & William Brenchley
Northwestern:	Robert Charlton & John Hill
Midland:	William Thurning & Richard Sydenham
Northern:	John Markham & Hugh Huls

18 JUNE 1394:

As 1389.

5

The Henrician Assizes and the Enforcement of the Reformation

Amanda Bevan

The major problem facing any investigation into the assize system under Henry VIII is the loss of almost all the records. There is no single archival group of assize records for this period, such as the records of the clerks of assize which continue from the reign of Elizabeth I to that of Elizabeth II, or the various assize and gaol delivery rolls which start in the thirteenth century and peter out in the mid-fifteenth century.[1] All that survives for the first half of the sixteenth century is incidental material: sources which for the periods before and after the gap in the assize records exist as mere additions to the information available from the records of the assizes, but which for this period are the only things to survive. These peripheral sources are formal, occasional or personal: the various commissions issued to the assize judges; the records of individual cases called up into King's Bench; the letters written to, by or about the assize judges.[2]

Given this absence of a distinct corpus of assize records, it is not surprising that there has been a general lack of interest in the early sixteenth century assizes. For example, Cockburn's major study of the assizes between 1558 and 1714 gives a brief early history but makes little mention of the continuation of the assize system between the mid-fifteenth and the mid-sixteenth centuries. Similarly, the *Guide to the Contents of the Public Record Office* treats the records which survive on either side of the gap as emerging from different institutions of government, with no comment on any continuity or change which may have taken place in the intervening period. Elton even performs a vanishing trick with the assizes: mentioned in neither

[1] The ASSI group and the JUST group of records. See *Guide to the Contents of the Public Record Office*, vol. 1, London 1963, 123-31.

[2] Commissions and letters are calendared in *Letters and Papers, foreign and domestic, of the reign of Henry VIII . . .*, ed. J. S. Brewer, J. Gairdner and R. H. Brodie, London 1862-1932 (cited as *LP*). Records of cases called into King's Bench have been taken from P.R.O., King's Bench, Crown Side, Ancient Indictments, KB 9. For a fuller discussion of the sources, see A. S. Bevan, 'The Role of the Judiciary in Tudor Government, 1509-1547', unpublished Ph.D. thesis, University of Cambridge 1985.

the chapter on the ancient courts nor the chapter on local government, they disappear entirely from the *Tudor Constitution.*[3] In general, the unwritten assumptions have been that, during the period from which so little of their records survives, the assizes were not functioning, or were of little importance.

Sufficient evidence remains, however, to indicate that not only did the assize system itself continue to function at full force in the reign of Henry VIII, but also that important and previously unsuspected changes in the powers of the assize judges took place in that reign, in response to the political tensions of the 1530s – the divorce of Henry VIII and Katherine of Aragon, the break with Rome, the royal supremacy, and the inception of the official Reformation. The assize judges were entrusted with the final methods of enforcement of these changes throughout the realm: they were issued with new circuit commissions of oyer and terminer to use at the assizes for the trial of those who had traitorously opposed the political and religious transformations.

This 'discovery' is in itself a symptom of the problems of perception which affects views of the long-term history of the assize system. Historians of the medieval assizes have known for some time that any commission of oyer and terminer exercised at the assizes was likely to be a special commission sued by a party, and that general commissions of oyer and terminer were not usually linked to the assizes.[4] However, historians of the modern assizes (that is, of the assizes after the gap in the records) have tended to assume that the circuit or general commission of oyer and terminer was one of the ancient assize commissions, annexed to the justices commissioned to take the possessory assizes at about the same time as the commission of gaol delivery.[5] This belief has further obscured the changes which took place in the assize system in the 1530s. Elton, believing the assize judges to have a commission of oyer and terminer as a matter of

[3] J. S. Cockburn, *A History of English Assizes 1558-1714*, Cambridge 1972; *Guide to the Public Record Office*, 123-31; G. R. Elton, *The Tudor Constitution*, 2nd ed., Cambridge 1982.

[4] R. W. Kaeuper, 'Law and Order in Fourteenth Century England: the Evidence of Special Commissions of Oyer and Terminer', *Speculum* liv, 1979, 718-61; J. B. Avrutick, 'Commissions of Oyer and Terminer in fifteenth-century England', unpublished M.Phil. thesis, University of London 1967.

[5] W. Holdsworth, *A History of English Law*, vol. 1, London 1956, 274-78; Cockburn, 15-22, 59-61; J. H. Baker, 'Criminal Courts and Procedure at Common Law 1550-1800', in *Crime in England 1550-1800*, ed. J. S. Cockburn, London 1977, 27-8.

course, failed to recognize the emergence of the new circuit commission for what it was – not the issue of an odd commission here or there, but an addition to the powers of the assize judges which allowed the frequent and regular provision of local courts for the trial of treason.[6]

An investigation of the surviving assize records for the reign of Henry VIII indicates clearly that circuit commissions of oyer and terminer were not annexed to the assize commissions until the late 1530s, and were issued then in response to the problems of public order after the major rising known as the Pilgrimage of Grace.

Discussion of this new addition to the powers of the assize judges, already complicated by the general assumption that the circuit commission of oyer and terminer was one of the long-established assize commissions, is made still more difficult by the existence of various kinds of oyer and terminer commission. Many commissions had an oyer and terminer clause, to allow for the hearing and determining of offences or disputes. Classification of these various commissions is not always easy, and terms have not been used consistently. Holdsworth thought that such commissions might be 'either general, to enquire into all crimes committed within the area of the commission; or special, to enquire into a particular case, or a particular place, or into certain specified crimes'.[7] Avrutick further divided oyer and terminer commissions into three basic types: general, particular and combined.[8] Powell, writing of the commissions between 1262 and 1443, has stressed the flexibility of the form: 'oyer and terminer commissions formed a broad and heterogeneous group within the overall class of royal judicial commissions . . . One specialized variant of oyer and terminer, the commission of the peace, evolved during the fourteenth century . . . Such permanent adaptations apart, however, oyer and terminer commissions were extraordinary devices issued to deal with a particular case or group of cases'. Powell accepts the two broad categories of special commissions, initiated at the suit of the injured party, and general commissions, which were issued on the orders of the King and council to deal with a wide range of offences in a given county or group of counties.[9]

[6] G. R. Elton, *Policy and Police*, Cambridge 1972, 295-6.
[7] Holdsworth, 274.
[8] Avrutick, 17.
[9] 'List of Special Oyer and Terminer Proceedings 1262-1443, preserved in the Public Record Office in JUST 1', ed. E. Powell, unpublished list available in the Round Room of the Public Record Office, Chancery Lane, 1984.

A further difficulty in disentangling the history of the circuit commission of oyer and terminer has been that of confusion with the commission of the peace. Indictments taken before the one have been confused with indictments taken before the other. For example, Blatcher examined the crown side of the King's Bench plea roll for Michaelmas 1488, and concluded that of the cases which had originated before a lower court, thirty-two had come from commissions of oyer and terminer, and nine from sessions of the peace.[10] A re-examination in fact reverses these figures: nine cases from oyer and terminer, and thirty-four from the peace.[11] Such a misunderstanding may be based on the description of indictments before justices of the peace as being before 'justiciarii ad diversos felonias audiendum et terminandum necnon ad pacem'. This does suggest oyer and terminer, but in fact the description of commissioners of oyer and terminer in indictments is quite different: 'justiciarii . . . ad inquirendum . . . de quibuscunque prodicionibus, feloniis, murdris (etc.) . . . et ad easdem audienda et terminanda'. Variants of both phrases existed, but the basic differences remained in all varieties of phraseology.[12]

Confusion between the commissions of the peace and of oyer and terminer, and the belief that the latter was in regular use at the assizes from an early date, has in fact obscured the important part played by the commission of the peace, and the justices of the peace, at the assizes. Powell has now shown that from 1368 the full powers of the peace commission to determine felonies could in general only be exercised in the presence of the assize judges.[13] In the early sixteenth century, the peace commission was in frequent use at the assizes, where it appears to have been used in conjunction with the commission of gaol delivery, which had no explicit authority to take indictments. The assize judges sat with their fellow JPs at the assizes. Despite the loss of quarter sessions records, odd references survive as the result of specific cases being called into King's Bench. For example, a session of the peace was held at the Hereford assizes on 24 July 1531, when indictments were taken before Sir John Port and Thomas Willoughby (the assize judges), and James Baskervile, Nicholas Chippenham, John Buryton and Richard Warnecombe, JPs. Similarly, indictments were taken at a session of the peace held at

[10] M. Blatcher, *The Court of King's Bench 1450-1550*, London 1978, 47.
[11] KB 27/909, rex roll section.
[12] Avrutick, 55-6.
[13] E. Powell, above 49-57

the Northampton assizes on 19 July 1536 before Sir Anthony Fitzherbert (the assize judge), and Sir Thomas Gryffyn, Edward Mountague, Richard Knightley, Thomas Brudenell, John Hasilwood, Edward Warner, Robert Chauntrell, Thomas Cave, Edward Gryffyn and John Barners, JPs.[14] These examples could be multiplied, though in many cases the JPs are not all named but merely described as 'fellows'.[15]

These indictments called into King's Bench are evidence taken out of context. Surviving quarter sessions records from Norfolk show that the assizes included a session of the peace. In the quarter sessions roll for 24 Henry VIII are found, among others, two sessions of the peace, held at Norwich on 28 July 1532 and at Thetford on 19 March 1533, before the assize judges and other JPs for Norfolk. These were not the borough sessions, which were held at Norwich just before the assizes, on 22 July 1532 and 6 March 1533.[16] It seems reasonable to assume that the records of the assize sessions of the peace remained with the quarter sessions records of each county, and have since been lost for this period.

Even though it is clear that the assize judges were holding sessions of the peace at the assizes, this does not mean that the full authority of the commission of the peace could be exercised only at the assize sessions. This had been the case in the later fourteenth century, as Powell has shown: when the commissions of the peace were introduced, the power to hear and determine felonies could in general be used only in the presence of the assize judges who formed the quorum. By the early sixteenth century the quorum had increased in size, although it was still relatively small and was largely composed of the lawyers in the commission. However, the judges still had claims to effective supervision of their fellow JPs. These claims were expressed by Fitzherbert in the first purpose-written manual for JPs, published in 1538. Fitzherbert, in his careful gloss on the terms of the commission, made it clear that the unlearned JPs were to give way to those JPs learned on the law, and that the county JPs as a whole were to defer to the authority of those JPs who were judges of the King's Bench, Common Pleas or assize.[17] The judges of King's Bench and

[14] KB 9/530, m. 22; KB 9/535, m. 5.

[15] For example, KB 9/529, mm. 45, 56, 72; 530, m. 24; 531, mm. 2, 14; 532, m. 40; 533, m. 228; 534, m. 3; 535, mm. 53, 55; 537, m. 26; 977, mm. 16, 52, 53.

[16] Norwich and Norfolk Record Office, C/S3/24 Henry VIII, mm. 50o and 32o are the assize sessions of the peace; mm. 60 and 6b are the borough sessions.

[17] A. Fitzherbert, *The Newe Boke of the Justices of the Peas*, London 1538, fos. 5^v-6^v. See Bevan, 130-2.

Common Pleas were in fact frequent attenders of the quarter sessions in their own counties, and were able to advise on the law as a matter of course.[18]

The confusion that exists over the respective histories, on the one hand of the commission of the peace and, on the other of oyer and terminer, is typified by the response of the editors of *Letters and Papers* to the appearance of the new circuit commissions of oyer and terminer on the patent rolls. Commissions of oyer and terminer are described as commissions of the peace, and *vice versa*.[19] The editors failed to recognize the commissions of oyer and terminer as part of a regular new system, and described them differently almost every time they appeared on the patent rolls. Not all were in fact enrolled.[20] The gaps in the sequence and the various ways that the circuit commissions were calendared in *Letters and Papers* have led to further confusion. Thus Elton has stated that commissions of oyer and terminer were issued at the beginning of the reigns of Edward VI and Mary as nation-wide enquiries to redress grievances, following the example of the 1509 commission, which was issued for the political motive of disowning some of Henry VII's alleged extortionate officials.[21] In fact, the Edwardian and Marian commissions that he cites were simply the circuit commissions of oyer and terminer issued as a matter of course for the assizes.

The term 'circuit commission' is used here to differentiate the commissions of oyer and terminer issued as a matter of course to the assize judges from other general commissions of oyer and terminer issued before or after the introduction of the circuit commissions in the late 1530s. The circuit commissions are thus the same as the commissions of oyer and terminer described by Cockburn as the less important of the two major criminal commissions exercised at the assizes. Cockburn gives the gaol delivery commission pride of place in his edition of the Elizabethan and Jacobean Home circuit assize records. The continued use of the commission of the peace at the

18 Bevan, 132-4.

19 For example, commissions of oyer and terminer wrongly described as of the peace, *LP* xv, 282 (4-7), from Chancery, Patent Rolls, C 66/690, mm. 28d-29d. Commissions of the peace wrongly described as of oyer and terminer are *LP* xiii(1), 1309 (28) from C 66/678, m. 13d; *LP* xv, 733 (63), 831 (34, 47), 942 (12, 13, 39-41, 75) and *LP* xvi, 107 (4, 17, 29) from C 66/694, mm. 5d-10d.

20 For example, the Norfolk circuit commission of 4 February 1539 found at KB 9/541, m. 94.

21 G. R. Elton, 'Henry VII: A Restatement', in G. R. Elton, *Studies in Tudor and Stuart Politics and Government*, vol. 2, Cambridge 1974, 87.

assizes is ignored, although partially admitted in a footnote.[22]

The circuit commissions had several distinguishing characteristics. They were issued to cover the group of counties which made up an assize circuit. The commissioners were picked from the JPs of the counties on the circuit, although in the 1530s and 1540s not all counties had equal representation on the commission. The quorum was strictly limited to the assize judges plus a local judge if one happened to be available. Sir William Shelley of Sussex, a justice of Common Pleas, was on the quorum for the Home circuit commission: he was not at the time an assize judge, perhaps because of ill-health. This limited quorum had been in use before, in the early years of the commission of the peace.[23] It ensured that although the average size of the commission was in excess of thirty, it remained under the firm control of the assize judges.

The circuit commission of oyer and terminer had extremely wide terms of reference, allowing its members (in the presence of one of the quorum) to inquire into, hear and determine all offences committed in the counties and liberties within the circuit. However, the annexation of these commissions of oyer and terminer to the assizes in the late 1530s is explained by their possession of one vital attribute. The circuit commission of oyer and terminer specifically allowed for the trial of treason. It was to cope with the increase in the number of treason cases arising all over the realm that these commissions were first introduced. Treason could not be tried outside the court of King's Bench without a commission of oyer and terminer: the commission of the peace had no power to inquire for treason, and the commission of gaol delivery, not having the power to inquire for offences, could only clear the gaols of those indicted before others.[24] This had not proved a problem before the mid-1530s: the commissions of the peace and of gaol delivery worked in tandem at the assizes to inquire for and try felonies, and treasons were

[22] *Calendar of Assize Records: Home Circuit Indictments: Elizabeth I and James I: Introduction*, ed. J. S. Cockburn, London 1985, 6 fn 31A, 18-19.

[23] For example, *LP* xx(1), 622 (ii) from Chancery, Patent Rolls Supplementary, C 67/74, mm. 2-3.

[24] R. Brooke (died 1558), *La Graunde Abridgement*, vol. 3, London 1573, fo. 288^v: 'Justices de peace nont authoritie denquirer de treason'. E. Anderson (died 1605), *Les Reports*, London 1664, 111-13, cites the judicial ruling of 11 Eliz. that justices of gaol delivery could not proceed against persons imprisoned on suspicion of treason without a commission of oyer and terminer, in a report of 26 Eliz. arguing the opposite: the latter argument is based on an interpretation of the statute 1 Edward VI c.7.

sufficiently rare to be adequately dealt with by the issue of a special commission of oyer and terminer to a small group of local nobles, gentlemen and senior lawyers in the county involved.[25]

No commission fulfilling the requirements of a circuit commission was enrolled on the patent rolls in the reign of Henry VIII until 1538. The other assize commissions may be found in plenty: patents of assize, patents of association, commissions of gaol delivery and commissions of the peace were all enrolled in great numbers, even if not with exact regularity. However, the first circuit commissions were not enrolled until 30 Henry VIII, dated 4 July 1538.[26] On that day five commissions were issued, to the Home, Midland, Norfolk, Oxford and Western circuits: the Northern circuit did not receive a commission then or subsequently, as it was included in the commission of the council in the north.

Although these were the first circuit commissions to be entered on the patent roll, lack of enrolment does not necessarily mean that other commissions were not issued. In order to check that circuit commissions were not in regular use at the assizes before 1538, a full examination was made of the various records called up into King's Bench in the reign of Henry VIII, and filed in the term files now known as the Ancient Indictments. Several commissions of oyer and terminer issued before 1538 were discovered that had not been enrolled, but they were for single counties and were issued for the trial of specific (though unnamed) traitors. The only exceptions were two sets of general commissions issued over several counties in 1509 and 1518. The 1509 commissions are well known: those of 1518 do not appear to have been noticed before. Both were in operation over the summer months, the 1509 sessions being held from July to October, the 1518 sessions at the assizes themselves. However, although the 1518 commissions included treason in their remit, they do not appear to have been used for the trial of traitors. Instead, they were used for felony, and also against extortionate officials.[27] It may be to the point that after the 1518 sessions the assize judges were required to give to the council 'a true report of the misdemeanors in theire severall circuits that is to say whoe be reteyners of oppressers or mainteyners of wrongfull causes or otherwise misbehaved persons in theire said severall circuites'.[28]

[25] For examples, see Bevan, 229-34.
[26] *LP* xii(1), 1519 (12-16) from C 66/678, m. 36d.
[27] KB 9/971, mm. 22-128 (1518 sessions); 453, mm. 1-470 (1509 sessions).
[28] BL Lansdowne Ms. 639, fo. 54^{v}.

The commissions of 1509 and 1518 were not issued solely or mainly for the trial of traitors (although Empson and Dudley suffered under the former); on one occasion, however, circuit commissions were issued to the assize judges and others for exercise at the assizes to try traitors. This was in February 1495, when Henry VII issued such commissions for the Lent assize circuits as a response to the Perkin Warbeck conspiracy.[29] In 1495, 1509 and 1518 the commissions were used for a brief time only and were not reissued for the next assize circuit. They were issued for reasons of political necessity in 1495 and 1509; the cause of the 1518 issue is unknown, but it may have been part of Wolsey's campaign to tighten law enforcement. On each of these three occasions, therefore, circuit commissions of oyer and terminer had been issued in response to a particular political situation or decision, not as part of a regular series of commissions issued to the assize judges for each circuit. It is possible that the issue of circuit commissions in the late 1530s may have been intended to be similarly short-lived: in fact, the commissions were discovered to be necessary for the protection of new policies, and what had been emergency provisions for the local trial of treason became a part of the normal powers of the assize judges.

The early 1530s saw the promulgation of a series of increasingly radical policies: the divorce of Henry VIII and Catherine of Aragon; the new marriage with Anne Boleyn; the break with the papacy that had been required to accomplish these marital rearrangements; and the declaration that the King was the supreme head on earth of the church of England. By the end of 1534 the political changes establishing the royal supremacy were effectively complete. Nevertheless, it was not until late 1534 that these new developments were provided with a legal sanction to enforce their acceptance throughout the realm. The 1534 Treason Act (26 Henry VIII c.13) declared it treason for anyone, by written or spoken word or by planned or executed deed, to deprive the King or Queen of any of their titles, or to declare the King a heretic, schismatic, infidel or usurper. Anyone who committed such an offence after 1 February 1535, and was lawfully convicted thereof according to the laws and customs of the realm, was to be adjudged a traitor and to suffer the usual penalties.

However, the 1534 Treason Act, the cornerstone of the legal

[29] KB 9/934; *Cal. Pat. Rolls, 1494-1509*, 30.

protection of the Henrician Reformation, made no provision for the actual trial of treasons. By July 1538 a system of twice-yearly courts held in every shire of the realm for the trial of treason cases was in place. Was 1538 the first year of this new system, or was it simply the first year for which an enrolled commission survives on the patent rolls? It must be remembered that Chancery in the 1530s was extremely inefficient at enrolling commissions of all kinds: 1538 is the year in which enrolment practice began to improve. In fact, examination of the assize reports written by some of the assize judges, and particularly of the records returned into King's Bench, has shown that no system of commissions covering the country was set up either at the time the Treason Act was passed, or for more than two years after. In 1535 and 1536 commissions of oyer and terminer were still issued solely on the old *ad hoc* basis for the trial of people caught up by the old or new treason acts. Treason trials took place, but the Crown felt able to cope with treasonable murmurings without the development of any new methods of control. Not until after the Pilgrimage of Grace, in late 1536 and early 1537, was it thought necessary to institute a regular system of control throughout the realm.

In the first two years after the passing of the Treason Act the Crown was content to use the old method of issuing commissions as and when cases of treason arose throughout the realm. Some examples will illustrate this. The first person tried for offences against the new statute was George Baburney, a tailor of Newport Pagnell. In February 1535, three weeks after it became treason to do so, he informed a group of fellow drinkers that the king was 'an heretyk a thieff an harlotte and a traytour to god and his lawes, and before midsomer day next comyng he trustyd and wold play at foteball with his hed'. Baburney also declared that the King had no title to the Crown, for the King of Scots was the rightful King: he wished that 'the swerd of vengeans myght light upon our seid soveraigne lord and of all his councell'.[30] These treasonable words were reported by the bailiff of Newport Pagnell on the next day, to the assize judges at the Buckinghamshire Lent assizes. However, no action could be taken then and there, as the assize judges had no authority to act. Not until March was a commission of oyer and terminer, directed to six local men, sent down to the county. Even then, the trial did not take place until 8 April: the two senior local

[30] KB 9/531, m. 8.

lawyers named to the quorum were also assize judges on other circuits, and the sessions had to await their return home. Baburney was condemned to the usual traitor's death: he was the first person to suffer under the new law.[31]

The next example, apart from the London trials of the Carthusians, Bishop Fisher and Sir Thomas More, is an oyer and terminer commission which was actually exercised at the summer assizes of 1535 at York, for the trial of several clerics who had spoken against the royal supremacy. This commission had not been issued at the same time as the assize commissions: it was sent north after the assize judges, in such haste that the judges were able to give the local members of the commission only two days notice of the existence of the commission and of the session; as a result, some did not sit.[32] Only one offender, a monk of Jervaulx, was executed for treasonable words at this York session, but two more were respited because the judges were unsure of the proper interpretation of the new statute. Jenney, one of the assize judges, informed Cromwell that 'there ys more endicted of treason but for that the wordes war to us dowghtfull whether they made high treason or nott we wuld not therfore procede to tharreyngment of them untyll your maistership and other of the kinges councell were made pryvye to the same for your further advice therin to be had'.[33] One of these cases, a priest who called the King a lollard, was well within the scope of the Treason Act, but another was actually a loophole in the new law. The parson of Winestead had preached in support of the Pope without attacking the King.[34] In 1536 this was made an offence, with the same penalties as those incurred for praemunire (28 Henry VIII c.10).

A third example of the difficulties encountered by the recipients of these *ad hoc* commissions comes from September 1535, when a commission of oyer and terminer was sent to the council in the marches of Wales for the trial of the prior of Worcester and one of his monks, accused of treasonable words. On receipt of this commission the council discussed it at length. Although Sir Thomas Englefield (a judge of Common Pleas, justice of Chester and the leading lawyer seconded to the regional council) was included in the

[31] *LP* xi, 215 (misdated to 1536), from State Papers, Henry VIII, General Series, SP 1/105, fo. 233; KB 9/531, mm. 5-11.

[32] KB 9/533, m. 54.

[33] *LP* xi, 37 (1) from SP 1/95, fo. 38.

[34] KB 9/533, mm. 44-5.

quorum, neither he nor the rest of the councillors knew what to do with the commission. Englefield, busy about the Welsh marches, had not attended the London trials of More, Fisher and the others earlier in the year, and had thus missed discussions of judicial interpretation with his fellow judges. The council in the marches finally wrote to Cromwell that 'forasmoche as suche matters be in thiese parties rare and no fourme of indictemente knowen, hit is thought to us by your favour that before this matter be here attempted, that indictementes be drawen uppon the booke of the instruccions by the kinges graces lerned counsaile. That don, then the opinions of all the judges be knowen agaynst whom the matter shall weye to be treyson, and against whom the matter will bere to be mesprycion'.[35]

This traditional system of issuing commissions, as and when the occasion arose, to a small group of local gentlemen under the direction of a serjeant-at-law or a judge who was either resident in the county or was the assize judge, might have continued unaltered had it not been for the Pilgrimage of Grace.[36] This major rising, which convulsed first Lincolnshire and then the northern counties, lasted between October 1536 and early 1537. There were rumours supporting the rebels throughout the rest of the country, and the rebel army had hopes that the King's forces sent up to halt them would come over to their side. In fact, the rebels dispersed of their own accord, having received the promise of a pardon, which was subsequently withdrawn.

The early months of 1537 were spent in mopping up after the rebellion in the counties worst affected. Three commissions of oyer and terminer were sent out, one to Lincolnshire, one to Lancashire and one for the northern counties under the rule of the council in the north. Each was issued to loyal noblemen and lawyers, and to local gentlemen of rather more suspect loyalty: each was kept busy trying and executing those rebels who had been declared outside the pardon.[37] However, in the other parts of the realm which had not been directly affected by the Pilgrimage of Grace, the judges riding the Lent assize circuits of 1537 were not equipped with commissions

[35] *LP* ix, 510 from SP 1/97, fo. 94. See Elton, *Policy and Police*, 124–7, for a fuller discussion of the affair: to the sources used there should be added State Papers, Henry VIII, Theological Tracts, SP 5/4, fos. 154–8.

[36] See M. H. and R. Dodds, *The Pilgrimage of Grace 1536-1537 and the Exeter Conspiracy 1538*, Cambridge 1915.

[37] Bevan, 248–52.

of oyer and terminer. Without them they had no power to try any treason that might have cropped up in sympathy with the rebellion. This caused frustration among those local gentry who were trying to keep their shires quiet. Sir William Godolphin, a JP of Cornwall, wrote to Cromwell in the late spring of 1537 of his futile attempts to bring to trial one Carpyssacke , who had tried to revive the Pilgrimage in the south-west. Godolphin complained that 'I have ben at every gaylle delivere and assyssys to geve evydens ayenste the traytour Carpyssacke . . . [and] have ben answeryd furste by Sir John Chomownd at the gaylle delyvere that he had none attoryte to enquer for hy trayson. So was the answer off justes of assysse, wher for y moste hertely desyr yowr good lordschyppe to have thys in rembrans to speoke to the justes off the assysse Mr Wyllyby and that hys jugmente be to be hangyd at Helston towne ys ende and ther to remayne yn chaynnys'.[38]

In Lent 1537, therefore, the judges of the Western circuit did not have a circuit commission of oyer and terminer which would allow them to try any treason on the circuit. By the summer of 1537, however, on at least three of the assize circuits such commissions are known to have been employed – a full year before any enrolment on the patent rolls. The Norfolk circuit received a commission which was certainly used at the Norwich assizes for the trial of the residue of the Walsingham plotters, whose conspiracy to start a rising in Norfolk has been described as the most serious plot south of the Trent in these years.[39] The judges of the Midland circuit also received and exercised a similar commission, while the Oxford circuit commission was used for treason trials at the Worcester and Stafford assizes.[40] Carpyssacke appears to have gone untried in 1537, as the summer Cornish assizes were abandoned for fear of plague.[41]

The annexation of commissions of oyer and terminer to the assize commissions can therefore be shown to have begun in the summer of 1537, as a response to fears of another major collapse of public order in the face of controversial royal policy. As we have seen, the issue of such commissions at at time of danger to the Crown was not unprecedented: Henry VII had issued similar commissions in February 1495. Then it was in response to a defined crisis – the Perkin Warbeck conspiracy – and the commission did not become

[38] *LP* xii(1), 1127 from BL Cotton Appendix L, fo. 75.
[39] KB 9/538, mm. 3-18; Elton, *Policy and Police*, 144-51.
[40] KB 9/542, m. 12; *LP* xii(2), 515 from SP 1/124, fos. 34-5.
[41] *LP* xii(2), 690 from SP 1/124, fo. 224.

standard issue. In the late 1530s, however, a short-term solution was not possible: the threat of crisis had become endemic.

The circuit commissions of oyer and terminer, issued twice a year with the other assize commissions from the summer of 1537, had a double virtue in the eyes of the Crown. First, they set up a regular system of courts over the whole realm for the local trial of treason and the subsequent display of the consequences of treasonable activity. Secondly, the bulk of the commissioners, who sat on the bench but could not act without the assize judges, were chosen from eminent members of the commissions of the peace over the circuit. These men, the leaders of their county societies, were thus required to make a public display of their support for the King's new policies, while being kept under the firm control of the assize judges. The presence of the JPs on the commission at the assizes was an enforced demonstration of their support of crown policy: their absence from the quorum meant that they were not entirely to be trusted.

Such gentlemen had to take care to behave with diligence: the assize judges were reporting on the state of the shires to Cromwell, and any disinclination to give public support to the new policies would have been noted. Gentlemen could even be browbeaten into a public display of loyalty: it was not merely their support that was wanted, but the effect that it would have on the county. A notable example comes from the Gloucester assizes of Lent 1538, where two men were to be tried for treason – a certain John Payne and the Marquis of Exeter's bear-keeper. This trial was reported to Cromwell by the president of the council in the marches who sat with the assize judges and other commissioners. 'Att the triall of the ij traytours that your lordeshipp sent we caused Sir John Bridges, Sir John Huddleston, and others of the best of the benche to be on that enqueste, Sir John Bridges somewhat grudging to that, sayeng that hit hath not beane seen that he or suche other shulde be taken from the benche to goo uppon suche tryall, wherunto he was aunswered that he was not to good to serve the king, and the olde wountes shulde be broken and so fynally he was contented'.[42] Neither Huddleston nor Bridges was included in the next commission. Those of the JPs who were named to be on the circuit commissions of oyer and terminer were thus doubly trapped, flattered by this mark of approval, and forced by it to a demonstration of perhaps insincere support for the new policies which would serve to impress

[42] *LP* xiii(1), 519 from SP 1/130, fos. 63–4.

the assembled local populace at the assizes with the need for public acceptance of the changes.

Throughout the rest of Henry VIII's reign, commissions of oyer and terminer for the circuits continued to be issued to the assize judges and to selected JPs of the counties on the circuits.[43] To some extent the issue of these commissions may have become a matter of course even by the 1540s. Although by these commissions each county had a twice-yearly court for the trial of treasons, the older form of commission, directed to a few men in a single county, continued to be issued. Thus James Malett was tried before an Essex comission of oyer and terminer in November 1542 for saying 'woo worth them that began the devorce betwene the kyng and quene Kateryn for syns we had never good world'.[44] Perhaps such commissions were issued to deal immediately with treasons which occurred between the assizes, or for cases of particular sensitivity, such as the trials of the abbots of Colchester, Reading and Glastonbury.

In addition, a new form of oyer and terminer commission emerged following the passing in 1542 of an act which allowed for the trial outside the shire of people who had been examined by three members of the council, and who were by them vehemently suspected of treason (33 Henry VIII c.23). This new form of commission was directed solely to the judges of King's Bench and Common Pleas; it specifically named both the suspect and the councillors who had conducted the examination. Thus in November 1543, William Cobden, a priest of Chichester, was examined before Paulet, Baker and Dacres of the council, and was tried the next day in Westminster Hall for preaching that 'Henry ys not by the grace of God kyng of England Fraunce ore Irelond'. Cobden was sent back to Chichester for execution.[45]

Nevertheless, the circuit commissions of oyer and terminer continued to be used at the assizes for cases of treason. For example, at the Essex assizes in the summer of 1541, Roger Covert was indicted for treasonably declaring that 'nether kyng nor emperoar maye make lawes to putt any man to deth but only for dedely syne'.[46] However, the commission was also being used to try offences other than treason: at the Derby assizes of July 1543, four

[43] For example, *LP* xvii, 443 (24-6); *LP* xx(1), 622 (ii, iv), 623 (iv).
[44] KB 9/533, mm. 1-8.
[45] KB 9/533, mm. 9-10.
[46] KB 9/550, m. 13.

cases of forcible entry and one of assault were tried before the oyer and terminer commissioners.[47] Similar examples may be found: rather surprisingly they all seem to come from Midland circuit. This may be the result of the assize clerk's preference for noting down one commission rather than another: on other circuits similar cases were being dealt with by the commission of the peace. Such possible diversity became an accepted part of the assize system, though one which has caused confusion since.

The circuit commissions of oyer and terminer, as introduced in the late 1530s, duplicated the oyer and terminer powers of the peace commissions for the trial of felonies and lesser offences, while possessing a superior jurisdiction to both gaol delivery and peace commissions. It may be that the addition of this new commission, in the tight control of a quorum composed of the assize judges alone, implied a derogation of the commission of the peace: after the introduction of the new commission it appears to have become more usual for serious crimes to be directed from the quarter sessions to the assizes and the quorum of the peace, no longer restricted by the need for legal expertise, could swell to provide honorific status for more and more members of the commission of the peace. The relationship between these various commissions at the assizes in the mid-Tudor period appears to have been complex, and almost impossible to explicate fully. An entry on commissions and commissioners in Brooke's *Abridgement* does something to indicate the extent of the jurisdictional overlapping of the 1550s. 'The justices of gaol delivery are also in the commission of the peace and by that they indict and then deliver the gaol . . . the justices of oyer and terminer cannot by this authority arraign any prisoners but those who are indicted before them, but the contrary if they have commission of gaol delivery as well, which note, for these two can be executed at one and the same time'.[48] It appears likely that from 1537 these three commissions were used both consecutively and concurrently at the assizes. The history of the powers of the sixteenth-century assize judges is by no means as straightforward as it has seemed.

[47] KB 9/556, mm. 58-62, 69-70.

[48] Brooke, *La Graunde Abridgement*, vol. 1, London 1573, fo. 149^{v}.

6

Strategies of Rhetoric in St. German's Doctor and Student

R. J. Schoeck

Commonplaces, precisely because they are shaped and utilized to formulate the obvious, often have a way of not spelling out in detail what contemporaries could take for granted. In his splendid introduction to the Selden Society edition of *Doctor and Student* J. L. Barton wrote that, 'it is only when the Doctor has completed his examinations and asks the Student to tell him something of the grounds of the law of England that it becomes clear that if these be commonplace definitions, they are certainly not being put to commonplace use'.[1] It is thus necessary to re-establish the context of 1528 for a fresh reading of the *Doctor and Student*, as well as to investigate further the question of sources. Unless we make this effort, it would be difficult to comprehend, to cite one problem of interpretation, why Thomas More took St. German to be so dangerous an adversary in his *Apology* and *The Debellation of Salem and Bizance*, which he wrote in response to St. German's *A Treatise Concerning the Division Between the Spiritualty and Temporalty* (1532) and *A Dialogue Betwixt two Englishmen, whereof One was Called Salem, and the Other Byzance* (1533). More's controversy with St. German has been definitively treated by J. B. Trapp in his edition of the *Apology*, and I shall not deal further with it here.[2] I shall be concerned rather with the rhetorical strategies employed by St. German to argue his case for the independence of common law from canon law and its jurisdiction.

I have recently published a fresh examination of evidence concerning the biography of Christopher St. German, in which there are some disturbing *lacunae*. But we do know that on his maternal side there were connections which provided links with the legal families of the Yelvertons, Pastons, Coningsbys, and Blennerhassetts, as well as the Greys and Calthorps of Norfolk and

[1] St. German's *Doctor and Student*, ed. T. F. T. Plucknett and J. L. Barton, Selden Soc. xci, 1974, xxiv.

[2] *The Apology*, ed. J. B. Trapp, vol. 9 in The Complete Works of St. Thomas More, New Haven 1979.

surrounding counties.[3] How much this background contributed to his success in the law we cannot yet say, but it is clear that he rose to prominence in the profession. Outside the Middle Temple, where he began his studies around or just before 1480, he was one of the counsellors who sat in the Court of Requests and he himself referred to his practice in the Star Chamber. In certain documents of the period, St. German is styled as 'Doctor', but nothing is known of any studies outside England or whether in fact he received a doctorate in civil or canon law.[4] We may conclude that St. German came of a good family rather well placed and well connected, and that he had influential friends, leading to his being regarded as an important common lawyer in the early years of the sixteenth century. Some time around 1520, at the age of about sixty, he apparently retired from active legal practice and enjoyed his private library, which seems to have been a remarkable one – it 'exceeded any one or two that belonged to a person or persons of his profession' according to the tradition reported by Anthony à Wood – and his contemporary reputation was one of great learning and exemplary piety and charity. He came out of retirement and, it would seem, studied theology and canon law in the mid-1520s; and by 1528 he produced his remarkable *Dialogus de fundamentis legum Anglie et de conscientia* – first published in Latin, of which the 1528 is the only extant edition, though a 1523 edition of similar title was reported by Ames.[5] Nearly seventy, St. German became an

[3] See R. J. Schoeck, 'The Family of Christopher St. German', *Notes and Queries* xxxi, 1984, 165-9; and on the legal aspects of his family connections, R. J. Schoeck, '"That Most Erudite of Tudor Lawyers", Christopher St. German,' *Journal of the Rocky Mountain Medieval and Renaissance Association* iv, 1983, 107-24, especially 108-9.

[4] 'Doctour' or 'Dr.' in a manuscript list in the hand of Sir Julius Caesar as having sat as 'Counselor to the King': printed in *Select Cases in the Court of Requests A.D. 1497-1569*, ed. I. S. Leadam, Selden Soc. xii, 1898, cix. See also *The Ancient State Authoritie and Proceedings of the Court of Requests*, ed. L. M. Hill, Cambridge 1975, 30 note 1.

[5] See *Doctor and Student*, lxix, which gives the entry in J. Ames' *Typographical Antiquities*, ed. W. Herbert, T. F. Dibdin, London 1816, vol. 3, 86. Although no copies of this reported edition are known today, Ames' reputation as a careful bibliographer, together with the detailed description, especially of the colophon, give considerable credence to the likelihood of a 1523 edition. A 1523 publication date would be of some significance: that would be the year after the continental publication of Marsilius of Padua's *Defensor Pacis* in 1522. The question of St. German's possible knowledge and use of Marsilius is an important question, but one which lies outside the province of this paper: see *Doctor and Student*, xxi, and Schoeck, 'That Most Erudite of Tudor Lawyers', 119-21.

increasingly radical writer and thinker, and after 1532 was engaged in the controversy with More; it was he (in the words of J. W. Allen), who 'expressed most clearly the nature and implications of the change that the Tudor government was bringing about, and in fact seems to have been a bellwether of much of that change'.[6] Key passages in *Doctor and Student* show how St. German was able not only to express that change but to contribute to it.

There is little arcane about St. German's principal sources, for with one exception they are conventional ancient and medieval authorities: the ancient sources are the Bible, Aristotle, Augustine, and Justinian; and the medieval, Isidore, Gratian, Aquinas, and the surprising St. Bridget of Sweden (on whom, according to John Bale, St. German wrote a treatise that has not survived).[7] But in addition to these there are citations of or attributions to Petrus de Aliaco, Panormitanus, and other canonist writers; as well as Gerson, and d'Ailly – in fact, for much of the *Doctor and Student*, citations are drawn overwhelmingly from three scholastic theologians: Aquinas, Gerson, and d'Ailly. It is quite remarkable that a writer on the English common law should draw so heavily from theology and the canon law, and so little from the native common law tradition (there are points where he might have made greater use of Fortescue, for example, than he does).[8] To these observations must be added the point that St. German was not writing a technical treatise for a purely professional audience – a point to which I shall return – and that there are clearly borrowings or adaptations which are not acknowledged. In sum, while St. German's knowledge of Aristotle and Augustine appears to be quite conventional, and may not all be first-hand, his handling of medieval sources – Aquinas and Gerson especially, but certain canon law texts as well – indicates first-hand

[6] J. W. Allen, *A History of Political Thought in the Sixteenth Century*, 2nd ed., London 1941, 165. Barton has commented on St. German's place in the royal propaganda campaign, *Doctor and Student*, xii ff.; for further detail see D. S. Berkowitz, *Humanist Scholarship and Public Order*, Washington, D.C. 1984, 19 ff.

[7] The attribution of a work on St. Bridget of Sweden we owe to Bale, but nothing more is known of it. St. Bridget (c. 1303-1373) was canonized in 1391, and along with penitential practices and charitable works she devoted herself to urging reforms within the Church. On the strength of Bale's attribution it would seem probable that St. German had a special devotion to St. Brigit.

[8] St. German does cite Fortescue's *De Laudibus Legum Anglie* (*Doctor and Student*, 282), and Barton argues that St. German seems to have taken the term 'maxim' from Fortescue's *De Laudibus* (*ibid*, lii). But St. German does not appear to have made use of Fortescue on the natural law.

knowledge, particularly of scholastic treatments of law.[9] One further point: despite Barton's statement that 'St. German may not have been so good a canonist as he is sometimes represented',[10] nearly all of his introduction seems rather to argue that he was, and more than a dozen texts of the canon law tradition are cited there and in the notes to the text. Yet let me pay tribute: Barton writes in his preface that 'to place St. German's work in the context of his age is a task which requires more learning than [he is] master of': for a definitive study of St. German's thought that is true enough, but what Barton has done in the edition of *Doctor and Student* is of great use to others.[11]

In a work originally entitled 'a dialogue concerning the foundations of the English law and of conscience', it is clear that we must follow in the footsteps of the Student of the common law when he asks the Doctor for assistance:

> But in some cases one can be aided by that sort of equity in the king's chancery by the writ sub poena bycause it can not be wel declaryd where a man shal be holpen by conscyence and where not/ but it be fyrste knowen what conscyence is/ therfore bycause it perteyneth to the moste properely/ to treate of the nature and qualytie of conscyence/ therfore I praye the that thou wylte make me some bryef declaracyon of the nature and qyalytie of conscyence . . .

And the Doctor replies:

> I wyll with good wyll do as thou sayste & to the intent that thou mayst the better understande that I shall saye of conscyence/ I shall fyrste shewe the what sinderesis is/ & then what reason is/ and then what conscyence is. And howe these thre dyffer amonge them selfe I shall somwhat touche.[12]

In all of this approach there is no medieval *accessus ad auctores*, though he seems to be echoing the tenor as well as following the thought of

[9] *Doctor and Student*, 'Canon Law, Conscience, and the Chancellor', xxxix ff.

[10] *Doctor and Student*, lxvi; and see xxviii.

[11] It would be helpful if we had first-hand knowledge of St. German's books, but none has been identified. Nonetheless, a close reading of St. German's definitions and a comparison of them with his sources is needed – J. Hunter has made a start in his dissertation on *Doctor and Student*, unpublished Ph.D. thesis, University of Colorado 1984. Further, much more study is needed of the text of *Doctor and Student*, for Plucknett and Barton have carried their collation only through the 1532 edition of the Second Dialogue. As Professor Michael MacDonald's paper on the text of *Doctor and Student* (given at the IANLS Congress, Amsterdam, 1973) demonstrated, corrections and modifications in the text continued almost continuously.

[12] *Doctor and Student*, 79 ('But . . . subpoena' trans. from Latin version).

Aquinas and Gerson.

First, *synderesis – vis motiva seu potentia naturalis anime rationalis* – 'Sinderesis is a naturall power [the Latin includes the sense of 'motive force'] of the [rational] soul, set [always] in the highest part therof, moving and stirring it to good and abhorring evil'.[13] A little further he adds that 'this sinderesis is the begynnynge of all thynges that may be lernyd by speculacyon or studye'. St. German is clearly laying an intellectualist foundation for the moral order, and we note that he has called sinderesis 'a spark of reason' [*scintilla rationis*], going on to quote from the pseudo-Dionysius, *De Divinis Nominibus*, cap. 7, which had been used first by Aquinas and then by Gerson. But Gerson had employed *scintilla rationis* to describe – and the quotation from the pseudo-Dionysius to explain – *intelligentia simplex*, which for Gerson was a cognitive not an affective faculty, dealing with intellectual truth, not moral action. Instead, Gerson makes the evaluation of moral quality a function belonging to affection, and not cognition. The difference between St. German's concept of the faculties, which are crucial in his exposition of sinderesis and the functioning of conscience, and that found in Gerson's analysis, is striking. In the summation of J. Hunter:

> St. German is quite definite that basic moral principles are things known by virtue of a cognitive power; moral quality is accessible to the same rational faculty by which pure speculative axioms are known, and is self-evident in the same way. The affective faculties have a place in moral action . . . But the natural inclination to pursue good and abhor evil – at least so far as its content is concerned – is a product of knowledge, not will.[14]

St. German continues his building of a structure of intellectualist psychology of the faculties in chapter 14, now following Aquinas more directly, and stressing reason as the power of the human soul which guides and motivates man's moral actions. It is not only cognitive but also motive (*non solum cognitiva sed etiam motiva*).

We may move with St. German to the use of this psychological foundation both for human law and the law of reason and for the spiritual function and supernatural foundation of the divine law. St. German incorporates Thomistic natural law into his primary division of law: everything which may be known by reason alone. In his secondary law of reason St. German includes precepts derived

[13] *Doctor and Student*, 80-81.
[14] Hunter, thesis.

from the application of principles of the law of reason primary to strictly human customs or law. For St. German conscience is not that subjective sense of right and wrong – in the sense of Selden's comparison of the breadth of the Chancellor's conscience to the length of his foot – but rather something to be determined by revelation and reason. Thus conscience, Barton observes, 'which is the art of translating this general rule into specific rules of conduct to be followed in particular situations, is a form of applied knowledge.' Conscience, we are told more than once, must always be founded upon some law.[15]

From this theory of the structure of synderesis, reason and conscience, and of their role in the system of common law, St. German is able to move – through the dialogue between Doctor and Student, through the cases which the Student of the law adduces, and by virtue of his theory of the faculties and of the kinds of law – to a position from which he can simply but effectively disregard certain canon law claims to authority and jurisdiction. At times this argument is conveyed by such devices as (in commenting on cases of inheritance which have been cited):

> And therefore since the survivor has the right according to the law of the land (which has to judge upon temporal things) [*habet de temporalibus judicare*], so he has the right before any other tribunal whatsoever.

In the English version of 1531 is added:

> in this case the Iugis of the spyrytuell courte must Iuge the wyl to be voyde as the law of the realme is that it is. And yet there is no suche law of forfeyture of goodes by outlagarye in the spyrytuell lawe.[16]

The implication here is clear: that the judgment of the ecclesiastical judges is based entirely upon the law of the realm, and is to follow that law.

St. German achieves the first of his intentions in this work: to supply a collection of cases which took the English law, rather than the civil or canon law, as the law whose effect in conscience was to be considered. At the very least the effect is a displacement of the canon law. The claims of the Church and its canonists to have the power to intervene in cases – especially those of conscience – is being

15 *Doctor and Student*, xxvi.
16 *Doctor and Student*, 45.

vigorously challenged.[17] One may wonder whether St. German had been one of that select group of common lawyers and theologians who argued the points of the Standish-Kidderminster dispute at Blackfriars on 10 March 1515. Certainly, the King's assertions of his sovereignty and jurisdiction foreshadow the more philosophical and theoretical position of St. German a decade later. The words of the King – 'Wherefore know you well that we will maintain the right of our Crown and of our temporal jurisdiction, as well in this point as in all others, in as ample a wise as any of our progenitors have done before us'[18] – could not be seen as contradicting this first line of development of *Doctor and Student*; and that line led to a questioning of the jurisdiction of the canon law and a justification of Chancery jurisdiction.[19] At the very least the Standish-Kidderminster dispute was a collision of the spiritual and temporal laws, and there were echoes of this dispute in the Fifth Lateran Council at the same time.

In the *Division Between the Spiritualty and Temporalty* St. German had alleged or assumed a division, which would inevitably be a lessening of the spiritualty. In *Doctor and Student* St. German was doing nothing less than challenging the traditional system of canon law, with its authority, procedures and jurisdictions. More's main line of defence of the canon law was the consent of the general council, and he argued: 'against this general approbation he layeth his own reason. And what is his own irrefragable reason that he layeth against all this?' And the answer has been provided by St. German in those chapters on sinderesis, reason and conscience: that sinderesis does not err or sin, that:

> While reason is concerned with principles which, as soon as their terms are apprehended and known, cannot fail to be known, and cannot be disputed, it may then be called sinderesis, irrespective of whether they are principles of speculation or of action, and irrespective of whether they pertain to the higher or lower part of reason. And reason taken in this sense is always virgin, that is to say, it persist ever inviolate . . .[20]

[17] St. German lived through both the Hunne Affair and the Standish-Kidderminster dispute, in both of which the conflict of common law with the canon law was at issue. One might well put it that St. German was writing to supply a collection of cases of conscience which took the English law, rather than the civil or canon law, as that law whose effect on conscience was to be considered: see *Doctor and Student*, xx.

[18] Quotation in R. J. Schoeck, 'Common Law and Canon Law in Their Relation to Thomas More', in *Action and Contemplation: Proceedings of the Symposium Held at St. John's University, 1970*, ed. R. S. Sylvester, New Haven 1972, 36.

[19] See *Doctor and Student*, xlviii.

[20] *Doctor and Student*, 87 (trans. from Latin version).

The rhetorical strategies of St. German have yet to be examined in detail. At the very beginning, in the Prologue to the First Dialogue, the author writes that it is human law that governs what is justly held and what is not:

> So when St. Augustine says that the sin is not remitted unless the thing taken is restored, English law tells us which taking is just and which unjust; and so the law is the best guide whether restitution is due or not.[21]

Lex anglie, that is to say, *est optima interpres:* at the outset the main thrust is anticipated – that the canon law will be bypassed and that the common law will be established as *optima interpres*, not only as to whether restitution is due or not (as in this case) but in may other areas as well. And for authority he goes back to St. Augustine, as the Reformers do. Thus St. German does not deny the force of authority; he simply goes back to a patristic source, not recognizing or not using canonical authorities. This is much the point, it would seem, in the frequent citation of *Summa Angelica*. St. German may have made mistakes in his citations, or even his readings, of points in canon law.[22] But let us note, he cites the authority of the *Summa Angelica* – a manual written by a canonist, but intended primarily for the use of confessors – and declares only that 'many be of oppynyon': he neither gives it as generally received opinion nor does he endow it with the weight of his own support. In effect, the *Summa Angelica* is brought into the discussion but left with no more authority than that it is the repository of opinion. There is a fair amount of canon law citation or allusion: Gratian, Panormitanus, Petrus de Aliaco, and others; but those citations are not made in a conventional fashion, and many are not identified or tied to a text. The Selden Society edition does not index all those named in the text, and there are many others; we cannot yet speak as though we had all the evidence of St. German's use and knowledge of the canon law. St. German, in my reading, wants to by-pass the canon law, not credit it with authority.

Although St. German's treatise is called a 'dialogue', it is strikingly different from the dialogues of contemporary Renaissance humanists whose work he is most likely to have known: from More's *Utopia* and the *Colloquies* of Erasmus to the *Boke of the Governour* and the Platonic dialogues of Sir Thomas Elyot. That

21 *Doctor and Student*, 5 (trans. from Latin version).
22 See note 10 above.

difference must have been deliberate. Hunter has singled out William of Ockham's *Dialogus* as an example from the late medieval scholastic tradition which provides many of *Doctor and Student*'s characteristics. The introduction of character is perfunctory and non-Ciceronian; there is little attention to the mechanics of oral conversation (a point on which More was later to chastise St. German); and there is little interest in the usual humanistic setting or occasion. Hunter argues that St. German's dialogue is more closely allied to the scholastic than to the humanistic, and, he goes on,

> The chapters, in fact, are set up explicitly in the form of disputations, with the Discipulus posing propositions for debate and raising objections, and the Magister answering the objections and resolving the question.[23]

But as well as the *quaestio disputata* there are the quasi-dialogic or dialectic forms of the common law itself: the moots and bolts, the close readings of specific statutes in the Readings at the Inns – all of these need to be considered more closely in a final formal analysis of *Doctor and Student*.

We do not have to be reminded here of the impressive influence of *Doctor and Student* through the age of Blackstone, and that it was both 'a basic handbook for law students' and a fundamental and original treatise on equity. Holdsworth, and more recently Plucknett, have commented on St. German's place in the development of equity in the English common law, and I shall not attempt to add to their comments.[24] Still more recently, Knafla has observed that Ellesmere's 'understanding of equity was derived from Saint-German and Plowden'.[25]

But still more, *Doctor and Student* was also a significant treatise on political thought, one which makes impressive uses of deliberative rhetoric. While we do not yet know its full role in the later history of English political thought, it seems certain that its influence was wide and strong outside the Inns of Court, an influence perhaps spread and strengthened by the very influence of the common lawyers who

[23] Hunter, thesis, chapter 7.

[24] See W. S. Holdsworth, *Some Makers of English Law*, Cambridge 1966, 95 ff., and *Sources and Literature of English Law*, Oxford 1925, 185 ff.; S.F.C. Milsom, *Historical Foundations of the Common Law*, London 1969, 80 ff. For a modern study of Chancery, see W. J. Jones, *The Elizabethan Court of Chancery*, Oxford 1967, and T. F. T. Plucknett, *A Concise History of the Common Law*, 5th ed., London 1956, 673 ff.

[25] L. A. Knafla, *Law and Politics in Jacobean England: The Tracts of Lord Chancellor Ellesmere*, Cambridge 1977, 161 ff.

were doubtless its earliest readers. Certainly More's responses to St. German in the *Apology* and *Debellation* had, ironically enough, the effect of encapsulating many quotations from St. German (often of considerable length) in his own long piece of polemical writing. In this and in many other ways, St. German's thought percolated into the world of Tudor thought and letters.

The theory of Parliamentary power owes much to St. German, beginning with the notions implicit in *Doctor and Student*, developed especially in *A Treatise Concerning the Division Between the Spiritualty and Temporalty* and carried to an extreme in the final treatises that argued for a Parliamentary responsibility in the determination of doctrine. Later in his seventies we find St. German sitting with bishops to determine theological matters: in its way, this is surely as potent a symbol of the shift from clergy to laity as More's becoming Lord Chancellor and his being asked by the Bishop of London to write in defence of the Church.

While there is still much that we do not know about St. German's life and career, and while full studies of his works remain to be done, we are surely in a position to go farther than J. W. Allen's statement that St. German was the one who 'expressed most clearly the nature and implications of the change that the Tudor government was bringing about'.

7

Usury in the Elizabethan Exchequer

Norman L. Jones

Violent crime has always been in fashion. The crowds that went to Tyburn and the historians of crime share an enthusiasm for it which they do not have for the less spectacular, if more frequent, infractions of economic regulations. Perhaps that is the reason that, with the exception of M. G. Davies's book on the enforcement of English apprenticeship, so little attention has been paid to laws designed to control English economic life in the sixteenth century.[1] Economic offences, however, have a great deal to teach us about an economy in the throes of becoming capitalist, about the assumptions of the men who made and administered the laws, and about the Exchequer, which played a major role in enforcing the economic regulations.

The laws concerning usury provide an excellent *entrée* to the problems of nascent capitalism and to the courts which sought to check its more egregious effects. Recognized by scholars of economic and intellectual history as a touchstone of modernization, the usury statutes have been studied, their evolution ascribed to the advance of modern ideas about capital and to the influence of the doctrines of John Calvin, but no one has taken the time to explore what the statutes meant in practice.[2] The purpose of this paper is, therefore, to introduce the reader to the problem of usury as it was legally conceived, and to explore briefly the operations of the court of Exchequer against usurers in the period 1545-1624. Along the

[1] M. G. Davies, *The Enforcement of English Apprenticeship 1563-1642, A Study in Applied Mercantilism*, Cambridge, Mass. 1956.

[2] D. M. Palliser, *The Age of Elizabeth*, London 1983, 294-5, is a good representative of the economic argument. The best exponent of the usury laws as an index of modernization and secularization is R. H. Tawney, *Religion and the Rise of Capitalism*, Harmondsworth 1980, 183-4. First published in 1926, it had been preceded by Tawney's edition of *The Discourse on Usury* by Sir Thomas Wilson, London 1925, in which he wrote the best introduction to the practice of usury in England. Benjamin Nelson, a latter-day disciple of Weber, goes further out on a limb to link the liberalization of the usury law with Calvinism. See his *The Idea of Usury. From Tribal Brotherhood to Universal Otherhood*, Princeton 1949, 83-6.

way we shall ask a series of questions. What was the structure of enforcement provided by the statutes? Against whom was the law enforced? What happened to someone accused of usury?

The place to begin is conveniently obvious: with the terms of the three statutes that cover the period 1545-1624. They spell out the courts, the forms of enforcement and the punishments used to deal with usurers. 37 Henry VIII c. 9 comes first in chronology and first in importance, since it was the father of most later statutes on usury in the common law world. Henry VIII's law, replacing 11 Henry VII c. 8, was unique in that it dealt with usury in purely secular terms, and that it allowed the most generous legal rate of interest England would see for several hundred years. Establishing ten per cent per annum as the maximum, it ordered that any person who lent money, gave credit on goods, or mortgaged property at over that rate should:

> forfeyt and lose for every such offence the treble value of the wares and merchaundizes and other thinge or thinges so bargayned solde eschaunged or shifted, and the treble value of the yssues and profytts of the saide Mannors Lands Tenements and Hereditaments so had taken or receyved by reason of any such bargayne sale or morgage, and also shall have and suffer ymprisonment of his body, and make fyne and ransome at the Kings will and pleasure; the moytie of which forfeyture of the said treble value shalbe to the Kinge, and the other moytie to him or them that will sue for the same, in any of the Kings Courts by accion of debte bill playnte or informacion . . .[3]

In practice, it meant that convicted offenders would forfeit three times the principal of loans or mortgages carrying an interest rate of more than ten per cent. Although the statute provides that they might be imprisoned, there is no record of anyone suffering in that way. A person who knew of an infraction could bring a suit in the courts of King's Bench, Common Pleas or Exchequer and if he was successful the court would award him half of the fine, the other half going to the Crown. Although any of the courts of record could be used, the Exchequer, dealing with the royal revenues, seems to have been the most popular venue for usury cases. Moreover, though writs of debt, bills and plaints could be used to begin an action, the most popular technique was to lay an information.

When 35 Henry VIII c. 9 was repealed by 5 & 6 Edward VI c. 20 in 1552, the liberal ten per cent ceiling was abolished, and lending at

[3] 37 Henry VIII c. 9. 5.

interest once again became illegal. At the same time however, the punishment for usury became much less harsh. Still triable in the courts of record, the penalty was reduced to forfeiture of the principal and interest, half going to the informer and half to the Crown as before.

The Edwardian statute, under which there were many cases in the 1560s, was replaced by 13 Elizabeth I c. 8 in 1571, and at the same time the provisions of 37 Henry VIII c. 9 were revived, though with certain important modifications. Carefully drafted to punish as many usurers as possible, the new statute defined the offence more precisely and widened the number of courts with jurisdiction. First, it declared that contracts made for more than ten per cent were void, as well as punishable with treble forfeiture. Second, it created a new class of usury offenders, the brokers, who were to be punished 'as in praemunire'. Third, though loans of over ten per cent carried treble forfeiture, loans at under ten per cent were also made illegal and were punished by forfeiture of the interest. Fourth, justices of oyer and terminer, justices of the peace, mayors, sheriffs and city bailiffs were empowered to hear and determine complaints against usurers. Other important points in the statute included a reservation of the rights of the ecclesiastical courts to punish usurers, and a proviso that ordered the judges to interpret the statute 'most strongly' against usurers.[4]

As far as the judges in the courts of record were concerned, usury was defined rather exactly. 11 Henry VII c. 8 had borrowed its definition from the canon law, and it continued in effect throughout the next century. Usury occurred when anyone lent 'money to and for a tyme, taking for the same loan any thing more besides or above the money lente by wey of contracte of covenaunte at the tyme of the same lone . . .' Time and again the judges, no matter which statute was in force, agreed that the elements of bargain, loan and corruption had to be present for a transaction to be usurious. If the bargain was not sealed by a corrupt contract there could be no usury, leading a commentator in 1594 to opine:

> I observe . . . how no usurie is condemned but that which is imposed upon the borrower by way of contract or covenant . . . if there were no contract for gaine there was no breach of the Lawe, so that the borrower was not barred by this, but that he

[4] 13 Eliz. I c. 8. 2, 3, 4, 5, 8, 6.

might gratifie the lender at his owne election.[5]

In court it was fairly easy to establish that a bargain had been made and a contract agreed upon, but it was difficult to prove the corrupt nature of that covenant. That it was necessary to do so was explained by the justices of Common Pleas who held that 'the corrupt agreement . . . makes it usury; and it is the intent makes it to be so, or not so'.[6] Since intent was hard to establish, the justices relied on a calculation of risk in establishing whether a bargain was *bona fide*. If the lender ran a risk that he might lose the principal and/or interest the loan was not oppressive, corrupt and usurious.[7]

In practice, the barons of the Exchequer received a majority of the informations which purported to show that someone had intentionally made a usurious bargain, and nearly all of the informations they received came from informers. Suing on behalf of themselves and of the Crown they followed the form of the *qui tam* action that was generally used for the control of 'oppressions'. The philosophy behind the *qui tam* action, which awarded the informer half the fine, was both sensible and economical: the oppressed victim was given a financial incentive to prosecute his oppressor. By definition in usury cases the borrower was a victim, in need of the law's aid to resist the power of the evil lender. The framers of the usury legislation assumed of usury, as of oppressions in general, that it was 'for the most part wrought by the superior in countenance, abilitie, or office, to the inferior in the same: for the oppressor . . . is alwayes offering hard measure to them who are to deale with him, untill they be able and willing to resist him'.[8] And so the right to sue the oppressor was created.

Although the oppressed were armed against their oppressors by the law, in reality they seldom began actions for usury; instead, professional informers used the *qui tam* action to augment their incomes. If the suit against a man charged with an oppression reached a successful conclusion or a composition the informer shared in the fine; if it did not the informer could use the threat of a suit to force someone to pay protection money. Either way the

[5] *The Death of Usury Or the Disgrace of Usurers. With Explanation of the Statutes now in Force Concerning Usury*, Cambridge 1594, 20. The definition was enunciated by the justices and barons in several cases. For example: *Tanfield* v. *Finche*, *ER* 78, 293 (Cro. Eliz. 27); *Sir Wollaston Dixie's Case*, *ER* 74, 89 (1 Leonard, 96).

[6] *Button* v. *Downham*, *ER* 78, 882 (Cro. Eliz. 643).

[7] See, for example, *Bedingfield* v. *Ashley*, *ER* 78, 973 (Cro. Eliz. 741).

[8] Ferdinand Pulton, *De Pace Regis et Regni*, London 1609, 91.

statutes against oppressions, which included anti-social activities such as destroying the fry of fish, hoarding fuel or food to drive up the price, exporting certain food stuffs, importing wool cards, and a number of other things, created a minor legal industry.

Not surprisingly, informers were intensely disliked in Tudor society. Their extortions and their willingness to cause others trouble for their own profit made them unlovable creatures. However, the courts could hardly have functioned without them, since they took the place of the police force the Crown did not have. A vast majority of recorded usury cases were brought by informers, and because popular demands for their control forced parliamentary action in the 1560s and 70s, some evidence has remained of how they operated.

The course followed by an informer to bring pressure to bear on someone who had committed an offence was much the same both before and after the various reforms through the century. He began by suing out a process or writ, which he bought from a clerk of the court, without beginning an official court action. If that failed to bring the accused to his senses, inducing him to pay off the informer, the next step was to file an information, which cost the informer over ten shillings. This information, if it was to withstand scrutiny in court, had to contain certain particulars: the name of the offender, the name of his 'victim', the place where the offence occurred, the approximate date of the offence, the amount lent and a claim that usurious interest had been charged, offending against the statute. The reference to the statute had to be carefully spelled out, as did the place of the offence and the other particulars, but the information need not specify the rate of interest, though after 1571 many of the informations did. Since the defendant's guilt depended only on the fact of usury, and since the fine depended on the amount lent, it was immaterial to the court whether the borrower paid ten and a half per cent or a hundred and fifty per cent. Often, thankfully, the informer did specify the terms of the loan, since it was those terms that proved the corrupt nature of the bargain.

The clerks of the remembrancer's office wrote up a bill incorporating all of this and took it to one or more of the barons of the Exchequer, before whom the informer swore to the veracity of the allegations. If the barons accepted the bill, they ordered that process begin by the issuing of a writ of *venire facias*, directing the sheriff of the county in which the offence occurred to bring in the accused. This done, the clerks took the bill and rewrote it on a long strip of parchment (called a rotulet), adding the fact that so-and-so (the informer) had come before Baron such-and-such on a certain date and sworn to the truth of the following allegations. After the facts of the case they noted that the informer had petitioned the court to be awarded his half of the fine, specifying the amount. Then they recorded the issuance. Any further developments in the case, such as the appearance of the accused, the issue of a writ to empanel a jury, and the verdict or composition, were later added to the rotulet.

Once the information had been neatly written out in Latin and a writ of *venire facias* despatched to the sheriff, something should have happened, but often it did not, as far as the court was concerned. David Lidington has found that of the 13,649 actions begun in the Exchequer between Michaelmas 1559 and Trinity 1570, less than one per cent were pursued to a verdict; an overwhelming eighty-four per cent went no further than the filing of the information and the issue of a writ.[9]

However, the fact that the court has no record of further proceedings does not mean that the matter was dropped. For the informer, the information was often nothing more than a way of pressuring the accused into 'compounding' with him. Rather than go to all the expense of a trial (every step in a prosecution cost the informer money), he was generally quite willing to accept a lesser amount. The accused was relieved to get off with less expense than he would have had even if acquitted, since lawyers were expensive. Only the Crown was hurt, losing whatever fine might have accrued to it on conviction, if the informer failed to tell the court of their agreement. He was supposed to do so, but some of them were surprisingly forgetful. Of course it is highly possible that informers got what they wanted without filing an information at all; the mere threat of the action being enough to persuade people to pay protection money.

The Crown, however, had no objection in principle to allowing offenders to compound for their crimes. Trials were expensive, and convictions were hard to get from juries, so the courts were quite willing to accept compositions, as long as the informer shared with the Crown. This was so much the case that the Exchequer was

[9] I wish to thank David Lidington for allowing me to see the draft of his Cambridge Ph.D. dissertation and the manuscript of his paper 'Mesne Process in Penal Actions at the Elizabethan Exchequer', now in *Journal of Legal History* vi, 1985. The best introduction to Elizabethan informers available in print is in Davies, 40-62. See also G. R. Elton, 'Informing for Profit: A Sidelight on Tudor Methods of Law Enforcement', *Cambridge Historical Journal* xi, 1954, 149-167.

under orders to settle for fines whenever possible.[10] Moreover, Tudor courts often acted as arbitrators encouraging out of court settlements, and composition was a form of out of court settlement in penal actions.[11]

For most of the period under review informing on usury was a fitful activity. Only from July 1571 until April 1575 was there an attempt to encourage prosecutions, though whether it was intentional on the part of the Privy Council is doubtful. During those years two courtiers, Mackwilliam and Colshill, held a monopoly on the searching out and trying of offenders against the usury law, as well as most other oppressions. Intended to last seven years, the grant gave them the right, with the knowledge and approval of at least two of the chief legal officers, to compound for offences against the statutes, a service for which they had the statutory half of the fine, plus ten per cent. Moreover, they also had the right to request the treasurer or barons of the Exchequer to get patents of pardon from the Lord Chancellor, releasing the accused from the payment of the Crown's share of the fine. Lastly, the grant declared that no justice could fine or compound with an offender unless Mackwilliam and Colshill were privy to the case. These powers were granted because 'it is reported that there is great remissness in the execution of the statutes aforesaid, partly caused by the corrupt dealings of those called promoters or informers'.[12]

Their patent was revoked in 1575, but while they had it they made good use of it.[13] Prosecutions, already rising in the 1560s, stayed high during their tenure. In the Exchequer the record for informations was set in 1566 with 166, dropping sharply to 25 in 1571, the year the new usury statute was passed. As Mackwilliam and Colshill got into their stride the informations started to rise again, from 49 in 1572, to 148, to 116, to 161 in the year their patent was repealed. After that the number plummeted. Just before the Privy Council took away the patent, the Exchequer investigated the activities of some of the informers, so giving us a chance of seeing how the system worked.

What did the informers have to say for themselves? Thomas Veale, putatively a London haberdasher, admitted having sworn out

[10] E 159/341, 'Brevia directa baronibus', Easter term, 2 Eliz.

[11] See J. A. Sharpe, *Crime in Early Modern England 1550-1750*, London 1984, 45-46 for a general discussion of arbitration and out of court settlement.

[12] *Cal. Pat. Rolls, 1570-71*, 279.

[13] *Acts of the Privy Council, 1571-75*, 371.

71 processes for usury in the Exchequer, acting for three deputies of Mackwilliam and Colshill. He denied compounding out of court and prolonging suits, but that was to be expected. Certainly the evidence bears out Veale's activities, since there are dozens of informations with his name on them.[14] The team of Nicholas Wright and William Rochester had sworn out about 25 processes for usury, getting writs of *venire facias* for a few, but mostly subpoenas. Wright admitted compounding with some of the accused. For instance, Robert Ringwood had paid him 50 shillings, and had paid Mackwilliam and Colshill 40 shillings. Wright said that he had always given the court notice, and that he never deliberately prolonged suits. What he did not say was whether he inadvertently left suits pending. One of his brother informers told the court that he never 'delaied nor suffered to be contynued and not prosecuted with effect to thende to dryve the parties by longe sute to compounde and agree with hym', but he admitted delaying suits. 'He was not abell', he said, 'to followe soe manie sutes at once for want of money'. Perhaps he should have borrowed some operating capital.[15]

Another haberdasher, William Riseham, was pursuing usurers all over England. All but one of the processes he sued out were from the Exchequer, and they were against people from London, Hull, Hertfordshire, Devon and Dorset. How he could achieve such range is illustrated by a composition detailed by Thomas Bunnynge of Denton, Norfolk. Bunnynge hounded a man named Foxe with two informations for usury in the Exchequer, 'divers' processes out of Common Pleas, and an attachment, before finally making a deal. Foxe, who if convicted would have owed Bunnynge £504, gave him his bond to pay £40 in cash and work off the rest. He was to 'geve so manie trewe notices of usury as shuld amount [to] . . . lx li. for this deponents parte'. For default 'or lack of so manie trewe notes' he was to pay a penalty.[16] The evidence is very shadowy, but some of the leading informers must have built up intelligence networks through this and other methods.

The compositions themselves varied in value, and often the Queen was the loser, even when the court was informed. Many cases ended like the one against Mr. Drewery. The informer made composition 'before Justice Sothcott and that the quenes Majestie

[14] E 133/2/242.
[15] E 133/2/284.
[16] E 133/2/284.

hath for a fyne v li. and this deponent is to have xx li. when the said Drewery or any for hym doth recover the money lent'. It was kind of the court to forgive £15 of the Queen's fine, and to await the repayment of the loan so patiently, especially since Drewery's conviction would have nullified the contract![17] This kind of generous composition is not at all unusual in Tudor courts, and it could cost the Crown a great deal of money. Take for instance the bargain struck by Stephen Slanye, a London skinner. He was condemned to pay a penalty of £7,800, split between the Queen and Robert Midleton, the informer; Slanye had been caught imposing a usurious mortgage on Sir Warham St. Leger. At the request of Mackwilliam and Colshill Slanye was pardoned from paying the £3,900 he owed the Queen. One wonders how much Slanye had to pay Mackwilliam and Colshill for the favour.[18] Presumably Midleton, if he collected the fine, retired a rich man.

Of course, not all cases were begun simply for profit. There were those in which an aggrieved party wanted the process to go to the bitter end, dragging the accused through as much mud as possible. Like many Tudor lawsuits, the charge of usury was often levelled as an offensive or defensive measure in connection with suits commenced in other courts, and sometimes a plaintiff might lodge charges in more than one court, maximizing both the vexation and the legal leverage. The case of *Fenton* v. *Blomer* in the Chancery is an example. Fenton had begun an action for usury against Blomer in the Exchequer, where defendants were not required to give evidence under oath. Then he put a bill into Chancery, making the same charge, hoping that the Chancery would force him to admit under oath details that were not forthcoming in the Exchequer.[19]

There were even, strange to say, instances in which the injured party sought justice against an oppressor by suing him for usury. It is impossible to calculate how many cases like this there were since the records are too sparse, and because many who wanted someone prosecuted did not inform in their own names but sought out an informer, gave him the details, and let him proceed. Whether the informer and the accuser shared the costs and profits is not known, though at times they undoubtedly did.

The rage of John Marmyon brought on a dispute that can stand for these revenge suits. Marmyon had been caught in the toils of one

[17] E 133/2/284.

[18] *Cal. Pat. Rolls, 1574-5*, 517.

[19] W. J. Jones, *The Elizabethan Court of Chancery*, Oxford 1967, 209 note 3.

lender and in order to save his lands he had been forced to accept a very expensive loan from a second, Thomas Skinner. Then when Skinner whether by accident or design failed to pay the money owed on his first debt, Marmyon was arrested and imprisoned in the Fleet. After this indignity came the last straw: Skinner asked for £7 interest that was owing; and the broker demanded a higher fee for arranging the loan with Skinner. When Hayes, the broker, confronted the prisoner with these requests, Marmyon exploded. 'Ys yt not suffycyent for me to paye xxxvii li. for the lone and interest of cclii li. xvii s. x d. but that I must consyder yew also?', he shouted. 'Yt was a greate shame that suche unresonable usury was permytted', and he swore that he would speak 'hys full mynde and consyence in yt, yf ever he myghte come yn place'. Shortly afterwards it occurred to him that he need not 'come in place' to get his revenge: all he needed was an informer. To that end he called Nicholas Lewis, a servant of the Warden of the Fleet, and told him the details of the loan. Marmyon, said Lewis, was 'very well pleased that thys deponent sholde have exhibytyed this matter by informacion to the Excheker and adiuryst hym so to do'. Later, after he had been released from prison, Marmyon, sitting at breakfast at the sign of the Golden Calf in Thames Street, was heard to say that if an information was begun against Skinner, he would testify against him, even though he had given Skinner his bond to 'save him harmless' from such a suit.[20]

Of course a charge of usury could help one escape one's debts, and occasionally the borrower himself is found to have brought in the information. Hugh Newman of Dynton, Wiltshire, laid an information in Trinity term 1569 against a Poole merchant who had lent him money. Sometimes neighbours would do the job for you, as witness the mutual backscratching of Richard Richardson and John Dissell. Richardson accused John Taylor of making a usurious loan to John Dissell; *quid pro quo*, Dissell then laid an information for usury against William Saunder, alleging a usurious loan to Richardson.[21]

David Lidington has discovered yet another use for informers in usury cases. A man who had lent money might procure an informer to put in an information for usury against him. Then the lender would compound with the informer for a small fee, thereby

[20] E 133/1/32.

[21] Newman: E 159/358, rot. 47. Richardson and Dissell: E 159/356, rots. 74; 74d. My thanks to David Lidington for these cases.

escaping the threat of anyone else, including the borrower, bringing an action against him for the loan. Following this strategy, James Langrake, a well-known informer, brought an action for usury against his son, George, another well-known informer.[22]

Once an action had been commenced, and if the accused did not compound for the offence before being tried, the exchequer machinery ground slowly on. Term after term the accused was cited to appear, though he seldom did, or did so a year or two late. If he did appear, and the barons thought it worthwhile to continue, the sheriff was ordered to impanel a jury. Often this was not done. If one was impanelled the informer frequently did not come forward to present the evidence in the case; and if he did, juries seem to have been reluctant to convict.

If the action led to a trial the defendant had several pleas that might allow him to escape. The most obvious was 'not guilty', and juries were often willing to believe it. Another plea which did not involve the defendant in difficult technical manoeuvres was to admit that a corrupt bargain had been made, but to claim that he had not accepted the interest. Since the law on usury grew out of canon law, whether or not a contract was usurious depended upon the intentions of the parties, so a change of heart was considered by the courts to expiate the lender. The contract, *qua* contract, remained void because it was corrupt, but the lender was not punished with triple forfeiture.

Brown and Fulsbye's Case in the Common Pleas illustrates this. Brown had borrowed £80 from Fulsbye, and had bound himself to pay £90 in one year's time. When his day of payment came, Brown offered Fulsbye the £90, but Fulsbye, after counting it out, gave Brown back the £10 interest. The court ruled that this was not usury within the statute 'to make a treble forfeiture; but yet in that case the obligation itself is void'.[23] The King's Bench had made a similar ruling four years before, in 1577, though it had not dealt with the question of whether the contract for the principal was valid if the usury was not taken. It simply held that if anyone contracts for twenty per cent interest and takes none of it, he is not punishable by the statute; but if he takes so much as as shilling then the whole contract is affirmed, and he will suffer accordingly.[24]

[22] My thanks to David Lidington for sharing his knowledge of informers and their mysterious ways. See note 9 above.

[23] *ER* 74, 717-8 (4 Leonard, 43).

[24] *ER* 78, 286 (Cro. Eliz. 20), *Mallory* v. *Bird* sub *Pollard* v. *Scholly*.

If the defendant could not make an 'honest' defence, however, he had to fall back on the legal skills of his counsel, who might find a technical way to escape the charge. The most popular was to challenge the form of the information, since if it did not meet an exact legal standard the case woud be thrown out. The fact that this standard was so exact left many opportunities for defendants.

Sir Wollaston Dixie, who had been Lord Mayor of London in 1585, succeeded in getting his conviction overturned on such technicalities. He had pleaded not guilty in the Exchequer to an information filed by a professional informer, Simon Addams, in 1587. In instructing the jury the barons had said that 'the information being exhibited for the loan of money, that the evidence was not proceeding or leading to the issue'. This was because the information said that Dixie had made a corrupt loan, when in fact he had made a corrupt bargain for cloth. Despite the barons, the jury convicted Dixie and awarded Addams and the Queen the forfeiture. Dixie, sensing that the barons had handed him a ready-made loophole, moved in arrest of judgment that the evidence did not maintain the information. In the statute, his counsel claimed, 'there are three things . . . and three words, i.e. bargain, loan, and chevisaunce, and these three are several things'. Therefore, since the information said loan but gave evidence of a corrupt bargain in cloth, Dixie's conviction ought to be dismissed.

The barons debated this claim at length, demonstrating in the process how complex a problem informations could be, and what opportunities they opened for the defendant in a usury case. Baron Manwood, laying down the important rule that in usury cases there must be a corrupt bargain for lending in excess of the statutory rate, expatiated on informations:

> There was a case in this Court in the time of this Queen, that the defendant had taken more than ten pounds in the hundred pounds, but in the information no corruption in the bargain was alledged; and therefore judgment was given against the informer: but in the case at bar corruption is set forth *in facto*, and therefore as to that the information is good enough: as unto the forbearing and giving days of payment the same is alledged in the information, but not according to the statute, for the statute is in the disjunctive, but the information is in the copulative . . .

On that Dixie looked as if he was going to lose, but Manwood went on to explain that, since the plea was not guilty, all points of the statute had to be taken into account. Following that principle, the baron found some other problems with the information. The place where the corrupt bargain had occurred was not explicitly stated:

'ergo no visne for it to be tried, ergo no trial can be, ergo, no issue for it'. Further, he noted that the offence had to have occurred within the year, and this information, because it did not show whose money it was, was not good.

On those grounds, rather than the ones he alleged in plea, Dixie was found not guilty. Addams and Attorney General Popham filed a writ of error in the Exchequer, arguing that it was not necessary to show the place where the corrupt bargain was made, for the offence punishable under the statute was the receipt of excessive usury, not the contract. Since the contract is but the inducement to the receipt, they said, only the place of receipt needed to be shown to prove usury. The appeal was adjourned.[25]

How the information was to specify the place of the offence was a recurring problem. Most informations in the Exchequer claim that it occurred in two places, a certain county and in Westminster. The reasons for this dual claim are not readily apparent, and they do not seem to have been clear to the courts either, giving a defendant with good counsel a way out. Manwood, by now chief baron, held in 1590 that an information on a usurious mortgage was invalid because it alleged that the lender had taken the 'issues, rents and profits' of Welsh land while in Middlesex. Manwood said that although the defendant could have taken the rents in Middlesex, he could not have taken the issues and profits anywhere but where the land was. Citing a case in which an information for converting wood to charcoal had been dismissed because it should have been laid where the wood was cut, not where it was coked, the Barons ruled that the information should have been laid in Glamorganshire.[26] The information was dismissed.

In another example of these technical pleadings a man named Ken from Somerset had been convicted in the Exchequer 'upon an information exhibited by a subject against him upon a statute of usury, before Baron Birche, alone, out of Court, and also out of Term'. He had come before Birche freely, without the sheriff of Somerset returning the writ of *venire facias* awarded against him, even though the offence was supposed, in the information, to have occurred in Middlesex. The offense alleged was that he had taken £80 interest on a loan of £500. After his conviction Ken brought a writ of error into the Exchequer, claiming a number of faults in the information and errors of fact. First, he said that he had not accepted

[25] *ER* 74, 89-90 (1 Leonard, 96), *Sir Wollaston Dixie's Case.*

[26] *ER* 74, 657 (3 Leonard, 238), *Owen Morgan's Case.*

the £80 or any parcel thereof for gain, 'for the forbearing *and* giving day of payment' of the £500. He had only received £40. The jury found, however, that he had taken the £40 for 'lending *and* giving day' for £150, part of the £500. Thus, though still guilty, the amount of his forfeiture was reduced from £1500 to £450. Nonetheless, Ken hoped to get the entire conviction overturned, and he pressed his argument that there were three errors in the information: it was not alleged precisely who lent the £500; the information had said that the amount forborne was £300, while the jury found that only £150 was forborne; and in the statute the words 'forbearing, [or] giving day of payment and forebearance, are disjunctively separate'. In the information the words were copulative, as the jury had found, and so the information was not in accord with the statute. It was a good, complex argument, and it left the barons puzzled. They called in the two chief justices for advice, and the last we hear of the case it is still under consideration.[27]

Assuming that people, having exhausted their attempts to escape punishment, were convicted – and despite the odds some were – what happened to them? Were they fined and imprisoned as the statute allowed? There is no evidence that anyone was ever imprisoned as the result of a usury conviction, unless it was on an action for debt stemming from non-payment of the penalty awarded to the informer. Those the jurors found culpable were assigned the full fine, as stipulated in the statute that currently governed, but it is likely that the convict did not pay the full amount. Even after conviction composition remained a possibility, as the case of Richard Rogers demonstrates. Rogers, a London goldsmith, was convicted of usury and fined £1200 in 1574. The Queen gave a quarter of her £600 share to four of her littermen, but they discovered to their consternation that after the conviction Rogers had compounded with Mackwilliam and Colshill for £450, making their quarter worth only £112/10/- instead of the £150 they had expected. They carried their complaint to the earl of Leicester and he intervened on their behalf, so that they eventually got their money, but Rogers only paid an additional £37/10/-. Thus his total fine to the Queen was only £487/10/- instead of the £600 awarded by the court.[28]

We have seen that Mackwilliam and Colshill were empowered to arrange partial pardons, and there are cases of full pardons. In 1556 Richmond Herald at Arms was pardoned, in consideration for his

[27] *ER* 73, 823-4 (3 Dyer, 367b), *Ken's Case.*
[28] SP 46/7, fos. 57; 106. E 123/5, fo. 238.

service, of all usuries charged against him in any court.[29] In 1591 George Casbolt was discharged of £150 forfeited for taking usury above ten per cent.[30] And in James's reign there are several examples, including one in which the pardon was made for usury offences even though there was no information against the man receiving it.[31]

If a person knew that he had made loans which put him in danger of punishment or harassment for usury he could protect himself by buying into the general pardon enacted whenever Parliament met. With a little luck in the timing of Parliament's meetings, a man might escape by getting his name on the pardon roll. This way out continued to be available until 1601, when usury was excepted from the act, after which the exception became a standard feature of Acts of Pardon. Why it was made impossible for usurers to buy a pardon is not certain. It might have been because usury convictions were too valuable as a source of crown income. However, in the Acts of Pardon usury always appears in the middle of a list of spiritual offences: adultery, incest, fornication, simony, usury, and disturbing of common prayer, which leads one to suspect that the exception arose out of pressure from the bishops or others who still connected usury with sin.[32]

After it became impossible to obtain a pardon through the Act of Pardon the Crown began to sell pardons on an individual basis. It thus remained possible for someone with enough influence and money to protect himself from prosecution by purchasing, as Thomas Hill did, a pardon for offences committed against the statute of usury, for which there were no informations against him.[33] Despite the possible paths of escape however, most people, whether through lack of foresight, ignorance or bad luck did not escape unscathed once an information against them had been filed. Either they compounded or they bore the costs of an expensive trial in the hope of escaping; most seem to have compounded in order to control the damage.

Ironically, the system did seem to have some dissuasive effect on the populace. You had to be careful because you never knew when someone might turn you in, and once an action was begun it was costly no matter what the outcome. After the Parliament of 1571 tightened up the statute against usury it became possible to punish

[29] *Cal. Pat. Rolls, 1555-57*, 16.
[30] *Calendar of State Papers Domestic* (henceforth *CSP Dom*), *1591-94*, 238.
[31] *CSP Dom., 1619-23*, 182.
[32] 43 Eliz. I c. 19; 3 Jac. I c. 27; 7 Jac. I c. 24; 21 Jac. I c. 35.
[33] *CSP Dom., 1619-23*, 182. Other examples at: 231, 236.

brokers who arranged loans at more than ten per cent, as well as those who made the loans. This, however, seems to have been an option little exercised, since the informer made no profit from it. When the barons took evidence in usury cases they often enquired about the broker's fee, but they did not do anything about it. The only case of a broker being punished under the statute comes from the Middlesex quarter sessions. In 1576 Rowland was convicted of having brokered a loan of £500 at twenty per cent interest.[34]

The question of the statutes' effectiveness remains. If very few people were actually convicted, did the usury laws do what Parliament seems to have intended them to do? The answer is a highly qualified 'yes'. The reason we can give an affirmative answer is that the contracts commonly used between persons involved in loans clearly show the influence of the statutes. People worked very hard to find forms which would protect them from the operation of the law, while giving them security in their loans. For instance, the popularity of the annuity was in part due to its legality as a way of lending money without seeming to charge interest. So long as the principal was never repaid in a lump sum the annuity was a sale of money, not rental of money, and was legal.[35] There are many more forms of contract made popular by the usury statutes, and in them we find the real proof of the public's fear.

In another sense we can speculate that the 1571 statute, setting what amounted to a ten per cent ceiling (prosecutions for loans under ten per cent are almost unknown) was effective because it seems to have lowered interest rates from an average of thirty per cent before 1571 to about twenty per cent afterward. Ten per cent became the floor, and the ceiling for honest lenders.[36] The reasons for the statutes' effectiveness rests with the informal system of enforcement run by the informers, who used the power of the courts to back their demands. Few were convicted of usury, but many paid the informers and the Crown as if they had been convicted, and many more went in fear.

34 *Middlesex County Records*, vol. 1, ed. J. C. Jeaffreson, London 1886.

35 See *Dr. Goad's Case* as reported in *Tanfield* v. *Finche*, *ER* 78, 293 (Cro. Eliz. 27–28).

36 This observation is based on a survey of the available evidence on pre and post 1571 loans, especially on the informations filed in the Exchequer.

8

Knowledge of the English Criminal Law in Poland at the Turn of the Eighteenth and Nineteenth Centuries

W. M. Bartel

One of the results of English interest in establishing trade relations with the Baltic area, and especially with Poland, was the setting up of intellectual contacts between the two kingdoms at the end of the middle ages. Both countries, though situated at the opposite edges of Europe, belonged to the sphere of Latin Christian culture. Both, too, proceeded along a parallel path at a certain period of their history, possessing Parliaments (in Polish: *Sejm*) at a time when the absolutist European states deprived their subjects of decisive influence over the management of public affairs. Both, thanks in part to their active universities, became important centres of intellectual activity.[1]

During the seventeenth and eighteenth centuries mutual Anglo-Polish relations underwent a significant change. Unfavourable political circumstances in east-central Europe, as well as a manifold domestic crisis, explain why the old Republic, especially in the first half of the eighteenth century, faced the necessity of undertaking radical reforms in order to avert the loss of independence, threatened by the surrounding hostile powers whose military might was gradually increasing.[2] No wonder then that England, engrossed at the time in its own serious problems, no longer saw in Poland its equal partner. The representatives of the Polish reform movement, however, looked at that time to the West in search of inspiration in their endeavours to prepare a programme for the renovation of the state. Montesquieu attracted the attention of the Poles to England,

[1] R. Dyboski, 'Anglo-Polish Cultural Relations', *The Contemporary Review* clv, 1939, 585-89. See also *Polish Law Throughout the Ages*, ed. W. J. Wagner, Stanford, California 1970, 222, 232-7; 246-7, 249-50.

[2] Polish observers were concerned with the shortcomings of their parliament and executive; also with the rational formulation of civil rights, at that time jealously guarded as the exclusive possession and privilege of the nobility. See A. Gieysztor *et al.*, *History of Poland*, Warsaw 1979, 180-287; G. N. Clark, *The Seventeenth Century*, Oxford 1960, Index 'Poland'. The drawbacks and pitfalls of the unlimited freedom of the Polish nobility had been keenly perceived by Montesquieu, *De l'Esprit des lois*, Paris 1749, bk. xi ch v.

which was beginning to build a parliamentary-cabinet system, imitated later on the Continent and elsewhere. Personal contacts encouraged growing Polish interests in the English model. The last King of Poland, Stanislaw August Poniatowski, was a great admirer of the English form of government and before his accession to the throne in 1764, while travelling in Europe, spent a considerable time in Britain carefully observing political and social life.[3]

Initially, the issue of codification or reform of the Polish civil and criminal law was not given noticeable attention, either within the reform party or within the sphere of interests of Stanislaw August Poniatowski, although the first step in this direction was made in the 1730s. It was then that the first written collection of Polish laws came to be published under the title *Volumina Legum*.[4] The idea of codification gained currency in Poland in the 1770s and the reformers began to search for models and food for thought and reflection in western Europe. In doing this, they could not fail, as will be shown below, to encounter England. Britain, in contrast with continental countries, did not manifest any interest in a systematic ordering of the laws operating within it. Still, I believe, many eighteenth-century lay Englishmen, remaining outside the legal profession or the Houses of Parliament, were interested in learning about the entirety of the legal order operating in their country, and this fact may account for public interest in Blackstone's *Commentaries on the Laws of England*. The usefulness of the products of human thought is measured by the yardstick of practical application, and as we know 'Blackstone' maintained its practical value late into the nineteenth century, despite sharp criticism from writers like Jeremy Bentham, the inventor of the modern concept of codification.[5]

[3] J. Niéc, *Mlodość ostatniego elekta St. A. Poniatowski, 1732-1764* ('The Youth of the Last Elect, Stanislaw August Poniatowski, 1732-1764'), Krakow 1935, 91 ff. He was elected King of Poland in 1764 and abdicated the throne in 1795.

[4] *Polski Slownik Biograficzny* ('Polish Biographical Dictionary'), henceforth *PBD*, vol. 13, 471-77; *Encyklopedia Powszechna PWN* ('Universal Encyclopedia PWN'), vol. 4, 760; St. Kutrzeba, *Historia źródel dawnego prawa polskiego* ('History of the Sources of Old Polish Law'), vol. 1, Lwow 1925, 241-49; Z. Kaczmarczyk and B. Lesnodorski, *Historia państwa i prawa Polski* ('Polish Constitutional and Legal History'), vol. 2 ed. J. Bardach, Warszawa 1966, 472.

[5] W. Holdsworth, *A History of English Law*, vol. 12, London 1938, 702 ff, and *Sources and Literature of English Law*, Oxford 1952, 156-59; C. K. Allen, *Law in the Making*, Oxford 1961, 115; J. H. Baker, *An Introduction to English Legal History*, London 1974, 76, 118; S. F. C. Milsom, *The Nature of Blackstone's Achievement*, London 1981. See also J. Goldberg, 'James Kent, the American Blackstone, the Early Years', in *Law-Making and Law-Makers* ed. A. Harding, London 1980, 157-58.

The *Commentaries* became well known on the Continent chiefly due to the French, who were then going through a period of fascination by everything English.[6] The most distinguished representative of French legal science, the champion of the cause of the humanitarian reform of European criminal law, Jacques-Pierre Brissot de Warville (1754-1793), the editor of the ten-volume *Bibliothèque Philosophique du Legislateur, du Politique, du Jurisconsulte* of 1782-85, presented his readers with works, dissertations and essays by eminent authors written in French, English, Italian, German and Spanish. But the merit for the pioneering work of bringing Blackstone's *Commentaries* – initially only the fourth book – into circulation in France belonged to the ex-Jesuit scholar, Fr. Gabriel François Coyer (1707-1782).[7] Coyer published his free translation in the two-volume *Commentaire sur le code criminel d'Angleterre* in Paris in 1776, faithfully preserving the order of the original, but changing the current numbers of the chapters in the second volume.[8] Coyer adhered to the humanitarian principles propagated by the contemporary representatives of the school of the law of nature, stating explicitly in his 'Translator's Preface'; 'I do not dare claim that the laws which I undertook to translate correspond in all respects . . . to the just image of legislation. Let the reader himself solve the dilemma'. In this respect he was right in thinking that the English criminal law presented in the fourth volume of the *Commentaries* was marked by a high degree of severity;[9] without closing his eyes to the negative aspects of the subject of his investigation however, Coyer believed that the insular system 'was one of the better models and patterns of a true criminal legislation'.

The entire work of Blackstone became known in France, as well as in Poland where knowledge of English was a rare phenomenon, through de Gomicourt, who published his translation in Brussels between 1774 and 1776.[10] The translation was imprecise, and what is

[6] Voltaire's interest in England in the 1720s and 1730s is well known. On the later period see J. Grieder, *Anglomania in France, 1740-1789: Fact, Fiction and Political Discourse*, Geneva 1985.

[7] See L. Adams, *Coyer and the Enlightenment*, Studies on Voltaire and the Eighteenth Century ed. T. Besterman cxxiii, Banbury 1974.

[8] Book 4 of the *Commentaries* contains thirty-three chapters; Coyer placed chs. i-xvii in vol. 1 of his translation; vol. 2 contains the remainder numbered separately i-xvi.

[9] Holdsworth, *Sources*, 158. Blackstone, though too apt to defend indiscriminately all the rules of English law, was by no means blind to its defects.

[10] A. P. Damiens de Gomicourt, *Commentaires sur les lois anglaises*, 2 vols, Brussels 1774-76.

worse, written in poor French ('ni exacte ni française' it has been said), but it still gave some idea of the original. It may well be that this text became known to a man among the close collaborators of King Stanislaw August Poniatowski of Poland, namely Fr. Teodor Ostrowski (1750-1802), a priest whose order, the Piarists, greatly contributed to the development of Polish culture. One may assume that Blackstone's intention to present the entirety of the English legal order became a source of inspiration for Ostrowski, who set out, like Blackstone in England, to write a practical and non-technical handbook of Polish Law. He realised his intention fairly speedily by publishing in Warsaw, in 1787, *Prawo cywilne narodu polskiego* ('The Civil Law of the Polish Nation').[11]

As he was preparing the part of this book devoted to criminal law and its procedure, Ostrowski stressed a number of positive as well as negative features of the institutions and rules discussed there. He compared them with the systems of criminal legislation in other countries, which he became familiar with via French writings, and he also made use of *Commentaire sur le code criminel d'Angleterre* by Fr. Coyer, whose works had been known earlier in Poland.[12] Ostrowski thus undertook the task of making Blackstone's views accessible to the Polish reader.[13] He explained why he was concerned precisely with this part of Sir William's work in his 'Polish Translator's Introduction'. In his opinion, Polish criminal law contained so many gaps that only the most serious offences had been given a legislative formulation. Penal sanctions, deprived of precise definition, created a situation which was dangerous for the legal system because the judges, deprived of adequate directives and guidelines, passed arbitrary sentences. But for Ostrowski the most serious drawback of Polish criminal law was the lack of universally applied rules of criminal procedure. In such a situation it was essential to look for foreign models with which to amend these flaws in the Polish legal system. Ostrowski believed that models were not

[11] See Z. Zdrójkowski, *Teodor Ostrowski, 1750-1802*, Warszawa 1956; *PBD*, vol. 23, 578-79. 'The Civil Law' enjoyed great popularity and Ostrowski lived long enough to see its second edition.

[12] Coyer wrote *Histoire de Jean Sobieski, roi de Pologne*, 2 vols., Varsovie 1761, and his *Oeuvres* were published in Paris and Warsaw in 1764. See note 7 above.

[13] T. Ostrowski, *Prawo kriminalne angielskie przez Wilhelma Blakstona zebrane a przez X.T. Ostrowskiego S.P. wytlumaczone i uwagami do prawa polskiego pomnozone* ('English Criminal Law collected by Wilhelm – sic! – Blackstone and translated by Fr. T. Ostrowski, enhanced with remarks pertaining to Polish law'), 2 vols, Warszawa 1786. Cited as Ostrowski.

to be sought in Roman Law because it did not correspond to the Polish form of government and the legal outlook of Polish people; they ought to be sought in a legal system which had grown on a soil of political structure, customs and intellectual make-up resembling what was found in Poland.[14] Ostrowski saw a model of this nature in the criminal legislation of the English nation because: 'The character of this nation, its domestic policies, the manner of public debates, and, most important, the almost universal consensus regarding national and civil liberties, present too clear and obvious an image for our Republic'.[15] Well informed about the reforms of criminal law introduced in his lifetime throughout the world, he also pointed out the changes taking place in the sphere of criminal law in the 'Confederated American States': 'whose . . . system of criminal laws, more appropriate to the republican form of government, should be deemed a better model than any other by a republic having such a reform in mind'.[16]

Basing himself on these models Ostrowski claimed that there were favourable conditions for the introduction of a reform of criminal law in his country, reminding his readers that the punishment for magic and witchcraft had recently been abolished in Poland, and mentioning that *inter alia* the Poles were the first in continental Europe to give up torture as a means of obtaining evidence in criminal procedure.[17] He went on to express his hope that the introduction of an outline of English criminal law to his fellow countrymen would be more useful than the proposal of a new, ready-made draft of a criminal code, no matter how perfect it might be. He also argued that as the Polish Parliament, the *Sejm*, had adapted to its needs models provided by the British Parliament, then there was no reason why Poland should not adopt English models also in the sphere of criminal law, in order to introduce necessary amendments and corrections.[18] What Ostrowski was giving to his readers, then, was not a manual for carrying out reforms, but material for critical reflection and analysis.

'English Criminal Law, written by William Blackstone, collected

[14] An opinion shared also by the Polish nobility, which feared the introduction of absolutist ideas, above all those derived from Roman Law.

[15] Ostrowski, vol.1, 5. While hardly free from exaggeration, this opinion can still be considered valid in principle.

[16] Ostrowski, vol.1, 10.

[17] *Volumina Legum*, vol.8, ed. J. Ohryzko, Petersburg 1860, 282-83.

[18] Ostrowski, vol.1, 12.

and translated by Fr. T. Ostrowski . . .' corresponds in its structure to *Commentaire sur le code criminel d'Angleterre* by Fr. Coyer; the chapter titles added by Ostrowski faithfully render the content of the English original. But the Polish translation of Coyer's text is free in character. In striving for maximum concentration of his Polish text he explicitly dropped the background explanations about English history, because these did not belong to the legal subject matter proper. He did, however, announce the publication in the near future of a history of England where the reader of 'Criminal Law' would be able to find answers to questions about influence on the process of formation of criminal legislation. As an orthodox Catholic, Ostrowski was also often offended by the critical remarks about Papists included by Blackstone in Book IV of the *Commentaries*; our translator loyally informs readers with 'sensitive conscience' that they should approach these remarks critically, as it is only natural: 'that what in their country may be judged . . . as proper, in another is regarded . . . as indecorous'.[19]

Ostrowski's valuable original contribution lies in the 'Remarks', generally stated briefly, placed after each translated chapter of Blackstone-Coyer.[20] They ought to be read in close connection with the text of a given chapter, because Ostrowski included in them only selected questions directly related to the Polish criminal law system. Apart from this, he attempted a broader reflection on the problem of humanizing criminal law, on the basis not only of discussions carried on in the European literature of the age of Enlightenment, but also of models from classical antiquity. A detailed presentation of all this material would go beyond the purpose and limits of the present paper, so I shall divide his arguments into several thematic groups and illustrate them with selected examples.

In the first group I would like to include problems that today fall within the scope of the science of criminology. Analysing the sources of crime, Ostrowski pointed out first of all social inequalities

[19] Ostrowski, vol.1, 18.

[20] Only the last chapter in Vol.2, 'Poczatki, wrost i ulepszenie stopniowe praw angiels' ('Of the Rise, Progress and Gradual Improvement of the Laws of England' in Blackstone) does not have any 'Remarks' related to it. Ostrowski wrote: 'after each chapter I have appended my "Remarks", where concentrating in more detail on the laws of my country, I have shown many times the similarities existing between our legislation and that of England. I have provided some ideas of improving our country's criminal laws. Finally I have demonstrated how these two laws agree with or diverge from politics and natural law', vol.1, 13. See Zdrójkowski, 180-198.

and contrasts existing in his day, including the destructive effects of economic deprivation. He advised the undertaking of measures designed to raise the level of morality and education among the lowest layers of the population.[21] Ostrowski stressed the educational and pedagogical function of work. For example, when considering the penalty of banishment, he suggested that those convicted should not be expelled from the territory of a given country, as this may only contribute to the spreading of evil, 'carried' by the criminal into neighbouring countries. He used the example of countries with colonies (including Britain), where criminals were deported and settled in the overseas deserts to be used as convict labour forces. To the authorities of countries without overseas territories, Ostrowski suggested that they could send outlaws into deep forests and swampy areas and have them do useful work there.[22]

In the next group of problems Ostrowski considered the question of legal reform. He stated that one should not absorb foreign models uncritically without first answering the question of whether these models will be appropriate to the social context in which they will function. He also believed that interruption in the continuity of development of legal institutions turns out to be detrimental to the state in the long run.[23] Another important quality of good law is clarity and brevity. The legislator ought to make the content of operating laws generally accessible to the widest circles of the population. In connection with this Ostrowski quotes a passage from an instruction by Catherine II, the Empress of Russia, which prescribed that: 'The book of laws . . . should have as small a format as possible, so that everybody may be able to buy it . . . at a low price'.[24] One means of publicizing the regulations of the criminal law could be the method, based on English and French models, by which leaflets were thrown out at times of public execution, containing a brief description of the punished crime, as well as the motives for the court's verdict accompanied by the relevant passages from the appropriate criminal laws.[25]

[21] Ostrowski, vol. 1, 37-41. At 39, he recommends 'enlightening this part of the Nation, which we as a rule hold to be guilty only because of its ignorance and simplicity'.

[22] Ostrowski, vol. 2, 224-27.

[23] Ostrowski, vol. 1, 159-60.

[24] Ostrowski, vol. 1, 55-56.

[25] Ostrowski, vol. 2, 232-33: 'In this way the judges, taking heed of the judgement of the public, will be more wary . . . villains and criminals will not be afraid . . . of the judges but of the verdict of the law, and finally the common people, secure under the custody of law, will have in the persons of the judges not tyrants but fathers full of justice'.

The third group of problems dealt with by Ostrowski comprises reflections on crime and punishment and on criminal procedure. According to Ostrowski the basic inadequacy of Polish criminal law is the lack of regulations that would define responsibility for a crime precisely with regard to the age and the intention of the criminal.[26] The Polish legislators should follow Blackstone in differentiating degrees of responsibility and weight of punishment, depending on whether the perpetrator of crime was a ringleader, accomplice, helper or just well-wisher.[27] The purpose of punishment should be to deter the potential criminal from committing the crime, and the degree of severity of punishment should be carefully weighed. The English legislator is right, according to Ostrowski, in stating the principle that when a given act is penalized by capital punishment, imprisonment or corporal punishment, the judge has no right to 'exchange one for the other'.[28] He believed, however, that in the case of a verdict of capital punishment one should, following the English example, 'prefer the need for the punishment's moderation, according to attenuating or aggravating circumstances'.[29] In his analysis of the regulations which made it possible to disrupt the proper functioning of the system of justice, Ostrowski came to the conclusion that both in England and in Poland legislation aimed in the same degree at 'securing to the citizens that which is their due in court according to the law'.[30] Still he admitted that England was ahead of Poland in the precision of elaborate legal rules designed to eliminate manipulation of trials, prescribing rewards for helping police in prompt discovery of crime committed, punishing bribe-taking judges, and providing rules for the proper administration of prisons and prison organization.

Ostrowski praised the fact that in England regulations facilitating prompt capture of criminals have existed without interruption; at the same time deploring that similar laws existing in Poland since the middle ages had fallen into oblivion, and that their application was considered in his day an unnecessary factor complicating life.[31] Formalism, Ostrowski claimed, must not be given undue significance in a criminal trial. In Poland, as well as in England and other European countries, the failure to meet prescribed time deadlines for the completion of the trial can, in effect, render 'the entire courtroom drudgery' useless. This flaw can be prevented by

[26] Ostrowski, vol. 1, 53-54.
[27] Ostrowski, vol. 1, 61-62.
[28] Ostrowski, vol. 2, 220.
[29] Ostrowski, vol. 1, 313.
[30] Ostrowski, vol. 1, 179.
[31] Ostrowski, vol. 2, 56-57.

means of a decree prolonging the course of procedure, probably a rather expensive solution for the parties involved in the trial, but still desirable because, 'To cancel the sentence because of an unfulfilled minor procedural point, is to offend the court itself and the wronged party in the trial, and at the same time it is to open a wide gate through which many crimes may escape unpunished'.[32]

The aspect of English law in which Ostrowski saw models particularly deserving of faithful imitation was the organization of the judiciary. In the Polish system, the court called *grodzki* judged the nobility in the first instance for the commission of such serious crimes as arson, highway robbery, invasion of somebody's home and rape. In contrast with other courts designed to hear cases involving the nobility, the *grodzki* court was presided over by only one judge, whose professional competence could often be seriously questioned, a state of affairs which created serious dangers for the proper administration of criminal justice.[33] For this reason Ostrowski proposed a reform of the organization of this court. Moreover, he wished, following the English model, where the court of King's Bench reviewed the verdicts passed in criminal courts of lower rank, to endow an institution with the right to oversee the activities of the *grodzki* court, or even to introduce the principle by which all verdicts of capital punishment passed in these courts should obtain approval from the King and his council.[34]

Ostrowski also discussed the jury system operating in England. He thought it to be a significant factor in the process of arriving at the material truth in the course of a trial, and did not share the opinion that it allegedly drew out unduly the course of procedure. Moreover he believed that because a jury is composed of persons possessing legal status and social rank equal to that of the defendant, they constitute an essential guarantee of 'the security of every citizen'. But despite the numerous positive aspects of this institution which he presented, Ostrowski did not support the idea of introducing it in Poland and only confined himself to drawing the reader's attention to the subject.[35] Ostrowski's interest was also

[32] Ostrowski, vol. 2, 230-31.

[33] S. Kutrzeba, *Historia Ustroju Polski w Zarysie-Korona* ('An Outline of Polish Constitutional History – the Crown'), 8th ed. Warszawa 1949, 226.

[34] Ostrowski, vol. 2, 105.

[35] Ostrowski, vol. 2, 36: 'This way of conducting a trial is so inseparable from national freedom that each Englishman considers it one of the greatest liberties'. Polish writing and legal practice returned to the subject of the jury system many times in the nineteenth century.

greatly aroused by the office of the coroner, who guaranteed the life and health of the criminal in gaol till the announcement of his sentence, and might also: 'protect prisoners against malicious misbehaviour of the managers of public prisons, who by the daily spectacle of human misery had grown hard hearts'. For, as Ostrowski remarked as a conclusion to his reflections, 'In this context it is fitting to mention our prisons and their gaolers'.[36]

After a very general survey of a number of questions presented by Ostrowski in his 'Remarks' to 'English Criminal Law', one feels tempted to ask whether the 'Remarks' were directly applied to Polish criminal law of the late eighteenth century. The answer is in the negative. As mentioned above, it was the author's intention to present to the circle of theoreticians and practitioners, as well as to the general 'enlightened public', the problems of criminal legislation as it existed in England; a country in which Poles were becoming interested in the search for material with which to reform a state threatened by the loss of independence. It is, however, obvious that the bulk of information contained in the pages of Fr. Ostrowski's work enriched the discussions that were going on in Poland on the project of codifying the law, attempted repeatedly since the 1770s. This led to the formation, by a decree of the *Sejm*, of a special committee whose task was to draw up the Code of Stanislaw August. In preparing 'a civil code together with civil procedure, and a criminal code with criminal procedure', the committee was only not to base itself on the existing Polish and Lithuanian laws, but also to draw on 'laws from other . . . foreign legal systems'.[37] The committee, with Fr. Teodor Ostrowski as one of its members, began its work in 1792, but did not manage to progress very far.[38] The next year the second partition of Poland took place, and two years later Poland vanished for a long time from the political map of Europe.[39]

This very fact brought about, naturally enough, the atrophy of systematic reflection about the state that had been so vivid among Polish public opinion in the preceding decade and had been

[36] Ostrowski, vol. 2, 34-35. See below for early nineteenth-century concern about the penal system.

[37] *Volumina Legum*, vol. 9, 220; *Kodeks Stanislawa Augusta – Zbiór Dokumentów* ('The Code of Stanislaw August – a Collection of Documents'), ed. S. Borowski, Warszawa 1938, 20.

[38] The committee invited Fr. Teodor Ostrowski to meet on 12 October 1791, *Kodeks* ed. Borowski, 35.

[39] Gieysztor, 332-34.

expressed in an outpouring of books and commentaries. The absolutist governments of the partitioning powers, Austria, Prussia and Russia, undertook a brutal liquidation of the existing legal order on Polish soil on a wave of Germanisation or Russification; and because of censorship Polish intellectual contacts with the West were completely cut off.[40] A slight improvement took place during the period of the Napoleonic wars, when in 1807 the Duchy of Warsaw, the Grand Empire's satellite state, was established on a part of the former Polish territory. It was then that the School of Law and Administration came into existence in Warsaw, while in Crakow the University was still operating, as before.[41] The study of law was dominated by French and German influence, as Napoleon's isolationist policy was a severe obstacle to contacts with England, including those in the sphere of intellectual research. The situation was somewhat changed after the Congress of Vienna of 1815 which erected on the ruins of the Duchy of Warsaw the Kingdom of Poland, known also as the Congress Kingdom, which maintained personal union with Russia, and a miniature Free City of Crakow, under the 'protection' of Austria, Prussia and Russia. Both of these dependent state creations enjoyed liberal constitutions in the first period of their existence, until 1830,[42] and steps were taken to codify the law. These efforts were particularly energetic in the Kingdom of Poland, where the codification of the criminal law had been successfully completed by 1818, and the civil law by 1825.[43]

During their debates over the drafts of the criminal code, and subsequently, theoreticians and practitioners had drawn English law into the sphere of their research. And again, as in the eighteenth century, Poles still largely ignorant of the English language were helped by legal literature in French. It is through this mediation that they came to know in translation many of the works of Jeremy Bentham (1748-1832), author of the famous sentence: 'Whatever is not in the code of laws, ought not to be law'; among them were: *Traités de legislation civile et pénale* (Paris 1802) and *Théorie des Peines*

[40] Gieysztor, 338-40; A. Brücker, *Dzieje Kultury Polskie* ('A History of Polish Culture'), vol. 4, Krakow 1946, chs. 1, 4, 11.

[41] *Historia Państwa i Prawa Polski* ('Polish Constitutional and Legal History'), vol. 3, ed. J. Bardach and M. Senkowska-Gluck, Warszawa 1981, 66-167.

[42] Gieysztor, ch. 15; Bardach and Gluck, vol. 3, ch. vi.

[43] Bardach and Gluck, vol. 3, 230-32. In the Free City of Crakow, changes in existing civil and criminal laws were not made, despite the formation of a codification committee, *ibid.*, 822-23.

et des Récompenses (London 1811).[44] Nobody however became interested in these translations in Poland, and nobody performed a task similar to that of Ostrowski with Book IV of Blackstone's *Commentaries* translated by Coyer.

Another figure who attracted much attention besides Bentham, was the philanthropist John Howard (1726?-1790).[45] His works: *The State of the Prisons in England and Wales* (1777) and *An Account of the Principal Lazarettos* (1789) were translated into French by 1800,[46] and his views became known in Poland through notes and commentaries found in French legal literature. In Polish literature concerning criminal law from the period of the debate mentioned above one can name two authors who, acquainted with the work of Blackstone, also familiarized their readers with the ideas and concepts of Bentham and Howard: Julian Ursyn Niemcewicz (1757-1841) and Józef Pawlikowski (c.1768-1829).[47] The former wrote 'Of Public Prisons: that is Houses of Penance', the latter 'Of Criminal Law'.[48] Both were men of merit in their patriotic struggle for the independence of Poland, both held republican-democratic views, both adhered to the humanitarian trend in the theory and practice of criminal law represented by Cesare Beccaria (1738-1794) and Gaetano Filangieri (1752-1788). They did not devote much attention to the English criminal law in general, confining themselves to stressing its high quality, though making some critical remarks on questions of detail.[49]

[44] See J. Zagar, *Bentham et la France*, Paris 1957.

[45] D. L. Howard, *John Howard*, London 1958; and M. Southwood, *John Howard*, London 1958; are both outline biographies. Blackstone encouraged Howard to carry out a reform of prisons in England according to the models of Rasp and Spin-Houses in Holland. Howard also visited prisons in Poland, perhaps during his trip to Russia in 1781: see J. Pawlikowski, below note 48, 124-5; T. Czacki, *O Litewskich i Polskich Prawach* ('On Lithuanian and Polish Laws') vol. 1, Krakow 1861, 219 note 1.

[46] *Etat des prisons, des hôpitaux et des maisons de force*, trans. J. P. Bérenger, 2 vols., Paris 1788; *Histoire des principaux Lazarets de l'Europe*, 2 vols., Paris 1799-1804 (published by the Ministère de l'Intérieur).

[47] Niemcewicz: *PBD*, vol. 22, 771-80; Pawlikowski, *PBD*, vol. 25, 446-52.

[48] J. U. Niemcewicz, *O wiezieniach publicznych czyli domach pokufy*, Warszawa 1818; J. Pawlikowski, *O prawach kryminalnych*, Warszawa 1818.

[49] Niemcewicz, 11-12, praised particularly 'trial by jury and the reasonable procedure . . . established for the protection of the defendant'. Pawlikowski, 36, accepted and praised the institution of the English jury, but criticized the principle of unanimous decisions. Niemcewicz, 11-12, concluded with regret that 'even in this enlightened country there are penalties as unjust as in other European countries'.

Their chief interest lay in the system of prisons, whose reform had been discussed in Poland for more than a hundred years.[50] Therefore they concentrated on the problem of the function of punishment and its administration. They proclaimed the idea of the resocializing, as we like to call it nowadays, function of imprisonment. Reflecting upon the inefficiency of penalties administered in the past, Pawlikowski states that this was the result of lack of proportion between the severity of the penalty and the nature of the crime committed; he also expressed the conviction that a rationally adjusted penal sanction is able to improve and resocialize every convicted prisoner. Those who claim that 'a man, imprisoned once for a crime, can never be improved', are wrong. He adds that 'The immortal Howard has rubbed off the rust of prejudice . . . by his efforts, and has shown the world that a man may fall into murder and crime, but that he does not shed all of his soul's nobility for ever, and that he willingly returns to it when society does not frustrate his efforts'. These views and proposals for concrete solutions had been given flesh by 'the famous sect of Quakers' which offered its charitable service to a government prison in Philadelphia 'in order to fulfill the wishes, and realize the precepts of Howard'.[51] Niemcewicz wrote similarly: 'Howard, this active and indefatigable friend of man . . . had strongly awakened . . . the sentiments of justice and humanity through which the law-giver saw the need to make the grand work of improvement', in the criminal code of the State of Pennsylvania.[52] Niemcewicz, staying as an emigrant in America at that time, had got directly in touch with the prisons of that area, reformed under the influence of Howard's concepts and the Quakers' practical application. The Philadelphian model, as he says, had found its imitators in almost every state of the Union, so in his work he confined himself to a description, in very great detail, of a prison in New York. At the end of his reflections Niemcewicz

[50] The first modern 'house of correction', based on Dutch models, was established in Warsaw in 1733: *Biblioteka Warszawska*, vol. 1, Warszawa 1890, 214-21; but serious reforms in the Polish prison system were undertaken only during the reign of Stanislaw August Poniatowski: J. Rafacz, *Wiezienie marszalkowskie* ('The Marshal's Prison'), Lwow 1932, 9ff. See also M. Senkowska, *Kara Wiezienia w Królestwie Polskim w pierwszej polowie XIX wieku* ('The Penalty of Imprisonment in the Kingdom of Poland in the first half of the Nineteenth Century'), Warszawa 1961; and for comparative material P. Spierenberg, *The Spectacle of Suffering*, Cambridge 1984.

[51] Pawlikowski, 114, 118, 119.

[52] Niemcewicz, 9-10, 12-13.

stated that the organization of prisons in the Kingdom of Poland should be shaped according to the American models.[53]

This project converged, in its general outline, with the views held by the Prince François La Rochefoucauld Liancourt (1747-1827), an *émigré* from revolutionary France who praised the work of Howard in a brochure *Des prisons de Philadelphie*.[54] But despite Niemcewicz's efforts – he approached the authorities concerned with an appropriate memorandum – his humanitarian plan was never realized.[55]

A few sentences should be devoted to an attempt aimed at adapting the views of Jeremy Bentham in the reorganization of the prison system in the Kingdom of Poland. The King of Poland and Tzar Alexander I of Russia, when visiting the prisons of Warsaw in 1818, were critical about their condition and ordered the application of necessary reforms. The legal framework for this enterprise was to be provided by a special government committee headed by Franciszek Ksawery Potocki (1775-1837), the judge of the Court of the Highest Instance.[56] Under his supervision the 'Project of a General and Particular Improvement of the Administration and Condition of Public Prisons in the Kingdom of Poland' was created. Apart from this, he himself prepared 'Remarks on the Project'.[57] Undoubtedly, the influence of the plans of Bentham and other humanitarians had made itself felt in the arrangement of these two works. On the other hand, however, Potocki desired to compromise them with the severe system of penalties existing in the Polish Code from 1818. All in all, this author borrowed from Bentham and other reformers, including Niemcewicz, the need for a very precise definition of formal aspects of the prison regime, while accepting at the same time the application of penalties such as periodical starvation or sleeping on bare planks. He also believed that the introduction of obligatory informing among prisoners would contribute to their moral improvement! It is difficult to conclude that Potocki sincerely desired the realization of the

[53] Niemcewicz, 13-14, 27-53. He stayed with intervals in America 1797-1807 (followng his imprisonment in Russia 1794-96), of which one year was spent in Philadelphia. In 1806 he obtained American citizenship.

[54] *Des prisons de Philadelphie. Par un Européen*, Philadelphia 1796. See Senkowska, 23.

[55] Senkowska, 26.

[56] Potocki: *PBD*, vol. 28, 88-91.

[57] *Projekt ogólnego i szczególnego ulepszenia administracji i stanu wiezień publicznych w Królestwie Polskim*; and *Uwagi do Projektu*.

humanitarian assumptions contained in the thought of Bentham.[58]

I am well aware of the fact that the sketch outlined here of knowledge of the English criminal law literature in Poland is far from being complete, and is not free from defects. I think, however, that I have managed to point out the need for undertaking more extensive studies on the subject of the influence of English legal culture on Polish legal culture in the period discussed here, and also later on. This problem contains threads which might well become starting points for a wider comparative study.

[58] The measure of his far-reaching conservatism, so characteristic of Potocki, was his firmly negative attitude towards the introduction of trial by jury in Poland.

9

The Appointment of Sheriffs and the Administration of Justice in Nineteenth-Century Ireland★

John McEldowney

> There is nothing I know which is more surprising to an Englishman than the mode of nominating the Sheriffs in Ireland. I know that this is a most convenient patronage to the Government, but I know also that I cannot hint in the House of Commons at such a source of patronage, and I confess I have great doubts as to the legitimacy of it.
>
> Sir Robert Peel to Lord Whitworth, 8 April 1816[1]

1

The office of sheriff held a prominent position in the administration of law and justice in nineteenth-century Ireland.[2] As Sir Robert Peel confided to Attorney-General Saurin in April 1816: 'When English members hear that the Sheriff appoints the Grand Jury, that the Grand Jury tax the county, that the Sheriff has considerable influence at elections, and that the Sheriff is appointed openly on the recommendation of the member supporting the Government they are startled not a little'.[3] Peel ought to have added that the sheriff also selected the jurors to be summoned which gave him an important influence in the very heart of the criminal and civil justice system.[4]

The Irish experience was in contrast to the position in England where as Maitland observed, 'a very noticeable feature in English history is the decline and fall of the sheriff, a decline and fall which

★I am very grateful for help and advice from Mr. D. E. C. Yale, Christ's College, Cambridge, and Professor P. O'Higgins, Trinity College, Dublin. I am also grateful to the Nuffield Foundation for financial assistance in undertaking this research. Also to the Law School at the University of Warwick for sabbatical leave. Errors are my responsibility alone.

1 C. S. Parker, *Sir Robert Peel*, London 1891, 222: Peel to Attorney-General Saurin, 8 April 1816.

2 J. M. McLennan, *Memoir of Thomas Drummond*, Edinburgh 1867, 305.

3 Parker, 222.

4 McLennan, 305.

goes on continuously for centuries'.[5] Nevertheless, it is necessary to examine how the sheriff was appointed in England, because in theory English statute law applied in Ireland from the end of the fifteenth century, under Poynings' Act, and also how English statute law was adopted in Ireland, because there is no adequate historical study of the office of sheriff in Ireland.[6] It is intended to explain how the Irish sheriff was appointed and, despite attempts to enforce statutes to the contrary, how the office of sheriff developed as a source of patronage depending on the government of the day.

2

Blackstone wrote that the office of sheriff was of great antiquity and of Anglo-Saxon origin.[7] In Norman times the sheriff was the principal officer of the shire and his duties combined administrative and judicial business. Various attempts were made to ensure that the Crown had control; the sheriff's tenure was limited to one year and the Exchequer attempted to exercise strict annual accounting.[8]

Uncertainty and confusion surrounded the law on the appointment of sheriffs. Some were hereditary. Blackstone mentioned the examples of Westmoreland and the City of London.[9] In general, as sheriffs were more effectively subjected to central government in the thirteenth century, demands arose for local election, especially after 1258. This principle was enshrined in a statute in 1300, 28 Edward I c. 8, but practice continued to vary widely. The appointment of sheriffs was in the Exchequer, and no one was likely to be appointed who did not enjoy the King's confidence.[10]

[5] F. W. Maitland, *The Constitutional History of England*, Cambridge 1919, 233.

[6] The main practitioners' guide is G. Y. Dixon and W. L. Gilliland, *The Law relating to Sheriffs in Ireland*, Dublin 1888.

[7] W. Blackstone *Commentaries on the Laws of England*, vol. 1, 12th ed., London 1896, 339.

[8] The early history may be found in W. A. Morris, *The Medieval English Sheriff to 1300*, Manchester 1927.

[9] Blackstone, 339. Five counties had hereditary sheriffs in 1300: Cornwall, Rutland, Westmoreland, Worcestershire and Lancashire; of these Westmoreland survived until 13 and 14 Vict. c. 30. The elected sheriffs of London and Middlesex formed a special case from the early twelfth century.

[10] Election of sheriffs, according to Blackstone, was as follows: the people chose twelve persons, and three were nominated, 'ex quibus rex unum confirmabat'. On thirteenth-century practice see H. Cam, *The Hundred and the Hundred Rolls*, London 1930, 59-67; D. A. Carpenter, 'The Decline of the Curial Sheriff in England', *E.H.R.* xci, 1976.

Between 1300 and 1340 a series of statutes was enacted which attempted to regulate the appointment of sheriffs, partly out of a desire to clarify an area of confusion, but more obviously as a by-product of political conflict. The baronial Ordinances forced on Edward II in 1311 shifted the method of appointment to the chancellor and the council assisted by the treasurer and barons of the Exchequer, and required appointment to be expressed in a commission under the great seal. These arrangements were given more permanence in the Statute of Lincoln of 1316, 9 Edward II stat. 2, and survived Edward's recovery of personal power in 1322.[11]

In 1340, during another political crisis,[12] the interpretation of 9 Edward II stat 2 was further complicated by the introduction of 14 Edward III c. 7. In practice sheriffs had continued in office beyond a year, although in theory the Statute of Lincoln had insisted on an annual appointment of sheriffs. 14 Edward III c. 7. enacted that after a year elapsed another sheriff could be appointed and the procedure laid down was '. . . by the chancellor, treasurer, and chief baron of the Exchequer taking to them the chief justice of the one Bench and of the other, if they be present'. But no mention was made under 14 Edward III c. 7. of all the judges and it is unclear if 14 Edward III c. 7 was intended to repeal 9 Edward II. The early fourteenth-century statutes were never more than provisional guides in the middle ages, always interpreted flexibly and occasionally liable to be disregarded altogether out of political expediency. But this did not prevent later observers seeing them as definitive statements and basing their own arguments upon them.

Nineteenth-century commentators in general were concerned, or prepared, to read back into the early statutes the evolved practice of allowing greater judicial influence over the appointment of sheriffs. The Irish Chief Baron Henry Joy[13] writing in 1837 thus explained that 'The safe course was to give the nomination [of the sheriffs] to

[11] On these statutes and their political context see: J. Conway Davies, 'The Statute of Lincoln, 1316, and the Appointment of Sheriffs', *Law Quarterly Review* xxxiii, 1917, 78-86; W. A. Morris, 'The Sheriff', in *The English Government at Work, 1327-1336*, vol. 2, ed. W. A. Morris and J. R. Strayer, Cambridge, Mass. 1947; R. C. Palmer, *The County Courts of Medieval England, 1150-1350*, Princeton 1982, 28-35.

[12] See N. M. Fryde, 'Edward III's Removal of his Ministers and Judges, 1340-1', *B.I.H.R.* xlviii, 1975; W. R. Jones, 'Rex et Ministri: English Local Government and the Crisis of 1341,' *Journal of British Studies* xiii, 1973.

[13] Henry Joy, youngest son of Henry Joy of Belfast, owner of the Belfast Newsletter. Tory, voted against the Union 1798. Solicitor-General 1822, Attorney-General 1827, Chief Baron of the Irish Exchequer Court 1831-1838.

the Twelve Judges, which complied with the Requisition of both Statutes; as if all the Justices are present according to 9 Edward II; the Chief Baron and Chief Justices must be present according to 14 Edward III . . .'.[14]

Joy's interpretation is supported by Blackstone's explanation that after the Statute of Cambridge of 1388 (12 Richard II c. 2.) the custom was:

> . . . that all the judges, together with the other great officers and privy counsellors meet in the Exchequer on the morrow of all Souls yearly (which day is now altered to the morrow of St. Martin by the late act for abbreviating Michaelmas term) and then and there the judges propose three persons to be reported (if approved of) to the King who afterwards appoints one of them to be sheriff . . .[15]

The development of the judges meeting to appoint the sheriffs was gradual. The vagueness and uncertainty surrounding the effect of 9 Edward II allowed custom to develop and become the settled law. Nevertheless this is hardly a satisfactory explanation for a shift from the appointment of the sheriff by the chancellor, treasurer and justices to the judges alone, which by the eighteenth and nineteenth centuries is taken to be settled law.

Blackstone had difficulty in providing a satisfactory explanation. He suggested that there was probably a subsequent statute to 9 Edward II and 14 Edward III but admitted it was '. . . not now to be found among our printed laws'.[16] Blackstone's reasons for supposing that there was an unrecorded statute are controversial. The practice allowing the justices alone to recommend the appointment of sheriffs had materially differed from the directions of all the previous statutes. Fortescue mentioned the practice of the judges appointing sheriffs,[17] and Blackstone believed that Fortescue would hardly have accepted the legality of the practice were it not for a statute. According to Blackstone Sir Edward Coke mentioned a statute transcribed from the Council Book of 3 March, 34 Hen. VI.

The Irish Chief Baron, Henry Joy, gave three reasons why he

[14] Hatherton Papers, Stafford Record Office, D260/M/01/2188: 'Correspondence relating to the appointment of sheriffs in Ireland', cited as Correspondence. The same material is in House of Lords Sessional Papers 1838, xviii, 883. See also: 'letters respecting the mode of appointing sheriffs in Ireland', Parliamentary Papers 1817, viii, 465.

[15] Correspondence, 1837.

[16] Blackstone, 339.

[17] *Fortescue: De laudibus legum Anglie*, ed. S. B. Chrimes, Cambridge 1942, 52-55.

disagreed with Blackstone's belief that such a statute existed. First, he could not find a statute in the Statute Book nor on the parliament roll. If such a statute had been passed it would have been subsequent to the 23 Henry VI which in large measure confirmed 14 Edward III, and '. . . it is not to be supposed that in the short interval between that [23 Henry VI] and the 34 Henry VI all trace of that Statute should be lost . . .'[18] Secondly, Henry Joy observed that Coke only mentioned 9 Edward II and 14 Edward III as the law. Thirdly, Joy referred to the opinion of Lord Chief Justice Hobard and Sir George Cooke who mention 9 Edward II as the law.

Henry Joy's opinion was that 'a reasonable construction' was given to the statute. He concluded that the law was:

> not to consider the appointment of Sheriff absolutely and definitely vested in the Judges, exclusive of the approbation of the King, by whose patent they were to be appointed; but that the Judges should have the Initiation and the King the Completion of the appointment . . .

Joy's interpretation is confirmed by modern historians, not least Chrimes.[19] It was widely held that the King had a discretion to select but the judges were to submit a number of names, normally three, out of which the selection was to be made.

Undoubtedly this was a practice which depended on 'a reasonable' interpretation of the statutes but there were frequent complaints that the whole procedure of selection via nomination was ignored. Blackstone asserted that there was authority for the King selecting the sheriff, without recourse to the judges' nomination and mentioned a case in the fifth year of Elizabeth, but Henry Joy also disagreed with Blackstone's interpretation of the law on this point. The case mentioned by Blackstone, Joy argued, was a memorandum arising from the plague when the judges could not meet to nominate sheriffs. Joy concluded:

> I do not find it any where holden that where there has been a nomination by the judges pursuant to the Statute the King can by His Prerogative whole pass by the Person so nominated; still less that He could do so without assigning any sufficient Reason for doing it.[20]

Such controvery and difference of opinion over the meaning and application of the statutes persisted; the inherited system of appointment for sheriffs was open to abuse and a source of patronage.

18 Correspondence: H. Joy to T. Drummond, 14 June 1837.
19 In *Fortescue: De laudibus*, 169–72.
20 Correspondence: H. Joy to T. Drummond, 14 June 1837.

This helps to explain the continuing interest of nineteenth-century commentators and politicians in the interpretation of the medieval statutes.

3

Ireland has been claimed to be the first adventure of the Common Law,[21] and the appearance of the sheriff in Ireland was an indication of the adoption of English law, though that process was never completed in the middle ages. 'Almost four centuries later this lordship of Ireland became a kingdom attached to the English crown, but even by that time the Common Law had not spread throughout the whole island . . .', as Dr. Donaldson explains.[22]

Two limitations on the operation of the Common Law in Ireland added to the confused state of whether English law applied. The first limitation was uncertainty surrounding the exact territory covered by the Anglo-Norman influence. The second limitation was access to the courts by the native Irish. A further consideration is the incomplete survival of records to guide us in knowing how the law was applied. In part because of this, comparatively little is known of the medieval Irish system for the appointment of sheriffs.[23] During the thirteenth century sheriffs could be appointed by the Irish justiciar or treasurer, or by direct mandate from England. From 1293 sheriffs and bailiffs who answered at the Irish Exchequer were to be appointed and removed by the treasurer and barons in Ireland (though exceptions were still made in practice). In 1341 it was required that the treasurer had to have the advice and assent of the justiciary, chancellor and others of the council. In 1355 the English government tried another approach: local election in each county on an annual basis, though it is uncertain for how long the practice persisted.[24] Through all this can be seen the same problems as in England, notably rivalries between royal officials and powerful local interests, on which was

[21] The term is borrowed from A. G. Donaldson, *Some Comparative Aspects of Irish Law*, Cambridge 1957, 3.

[22] Donaldson, 5-6.

[23] For outline accounts see: A. J. Otway-Ruthven, *A History of Medieval Ireland*, London 1968, 173-79; A. J. Otway-Ruthven, 'Anglo-Irish Shire Government', *Irish Historical Studies* v, 1946-7, 1-28; G. J. Hand, *English Law in Ireland 1290-1324*, Cambridge 1967, 135-6; H. G. Richardson, 'English Institutions in Medieval Ireland', *Irish Historical Studies* i, 1938-9, 382-92.

[24] Otway-Ruthven, *History*, 176-77. R. Frame, *English Lordship in Ireland 1318-1361*, Oxford 1982, analyses the political background to these changes.

superimposed in Ireland endemic tension between the institutions of Dublin and those of Westminster. Whatever the vagueness and uncertainties surrounding the applicability of the law, Poynings' law, 10 Henry VII c. 4, attempted to settle the question for the future.[25] The Irish Parliament accepted that English statute law in existence at the end of the fifteenth century applied to Ireland. The question arises, what was the Irish experience in the appointment of sheriffs?[26] One of the first Irish statutes of importance was 10 Henry VII c. 5. D. B. Quinn noted 'An act of 1494 (10 Henry VII c. 5.) put appointments into the hands of the treasurer and, in fact, the office tended to fall permanently into the hands of local families who used its considerable powers for their own aggrandisement'.[27] In theory Poynings' Act made the English statutes, 9 Edward II and 14 Edward III, applicable to Ireland. This introduced to Ireland the same confusion over the method of appointment as had been experienced in England. In addition the English law had difficulties of adaptation in Ireland.

Throughout the sixteenth and seventeenth centuries one of the abuses most frequently complained of was the appointment of sheriffs by the Crown without reference to the judges. But there were many others, and *The Calendar of State Papers, Ireland*,[28] gives details of those commonly alleged about the system of appointment. A brief mention may be made of the more prominent abuses. In 1586 Lord Burghley, Lord High Treasurer of England, received a complaint from Chancellor Archbishop Loftus:

> Also, where both by custom and statutes established in that behalf the choice of sheriffs in the several counties belongest to the nomination of me, the Chancellor, the Treasurer, the two Chief Justices and Chief Baron of the Exchequer; in this thing his Lordship, both against the law and to the great offence and oppression of Her Majesty's people, overruleth us all, appointing such sheriffs in several counties as have not been chosen by us, even of his own servants and followers, and expressly

[25] Donaldson, 5-6; Irish Statutes, vol. 1, 1768, 44. See D. B. Quinn, 'The Early Interpretation of Poynings' Law, 1494-1534', *Irish Historical Studies* ii, 1940-41, 241-54; R. Dudley Edwards and T. W. Moody, 'The History of Poynings' Law, Part I 1494-1615', *ibid.*, 415-24.

[26] In this paper we are concerned only with the appointment of sheriffs in all the counties of Ireland. In cities, for example in Dublin, sheriffs were elected by the corporation. This was so in Cork, Limerick, Waterford, Kilkenny, and the town of Drogheda.

[27] D. B. Quinn, 'Anglo-Irish Local Government 1485-1534', *Irish Historical Studies* i, 1938-9, 357.

[28] *Calendar of State Papers relating to Ireland*, cited as *C.S.P.I.*

> against law, continuing divers of them in that office for two or three years together.[29]

Complaints were regularly received that some counties had no sheriff appointed. In 1604 in County Tyrone no sheriff was appointed and the efficiency of the law was thereby reduced.[30] A common complaint was that sheriffs who were appointed had no land in the county where they held their position. This was clearly in breach of statute and it was suggested in 1607 that in the Counties of Tyrone and Armagh 'retainers' were appointed sheriff who had no land in the county.[31] Corruption was alleged in the appointment of sheriffs and also that the sheriffs themselves were of poor ability and little integrity.

Allegations were often made that sheriffs were guilty of misconduct in carrying out their duties. Election notices were frequently controversial. In 1613 the sheriff in County Cavan persuaded some freeholders not to vote on the day of the election and then returned two candidates who had no residence in the county. A similar abuse occurred in County Armagh in the same year. Such was the extent of the abuses that commissioners were sent to Ireland to inquire into the grievances, and after investigation a total of fourteen instances of abuse were recorded. Ireland's religious division gave rise to further allegations of misconduct, and the commissioners also found in 1613 that 'There have been practices in divers place to hinder the election of Protestants is very clear, and that the priests have been persuaded in these practices, appears both by the confession of some persons whom they have examined and by other pregnant circumstances'.[32] Particularly significant was the selection of juries, which was largely in the power of the sheriff. In 1641 it was alleged that the sheriff had returned a packed jury in Galway. The sheriff was fined £1,000, which was approved by the King through Secretary Coke.[33]

The confusion surrounding the method of appointment of sheriffs, their tenure of office and accountability for their duties remained unresolved throughout the seventeenth and eighteenth centuries. By the nineteenth century in Ireland difficulties of effectively regulating the sheriff by statute remained and the appointment of sheriffs was as

[29] *C.S.P.I., 1586-1588*, 212.
[30] *C.S.P.I., 1603-1606*, 235.
[31] *C.S.P.I., 1606-1608*, 377-78.
[32] *C.S.P.I., 1611-1614*, 426-27.
[33] *C.S.P.I., 1633-1647*, xxv-xxvi.

controversial as before.

The earl of Mulgrave, the Irish Chief Secretary in 1838, explained to the House of Lords some of the significant differences between the practice of appointing sheriffs in Ireland compared to England.[34] According to his evidence in early times there were no meetings of the judges in Ireland analogous to the meetings of the judges in England to nominate sheriffs. In England judges were required to meet in the exchequer chamber with the treasurer of the Exchequer. In Ireland there were many instances where the King appointed the sheriffs of counties, not only for the year, but in some cases for up to eight or nine years. Clearly, Mulgrave's description of the Irish system differed from the English statute law which in theory applied to Ireland, and was contrary to the spirit in which the statutes were passed. Chief Baron Joy explained: 'The nomination of sheriffs both in England and Ireland is regularised by Statutes which were passed expressly for the purpose of correcting the abuses committed by Sheriffs, and ensuring the appointment of proper and sufficient persons to the office'.[35] Again, the interpretation of the early statutes was linked with the practical problems of the nineteenth century.

4

In 1826 the *Fifteenth Report of The Commissioners* on duties, salaries and emoluments in courts of justice found evidence of many of the abuses in the office of sheriff already mentioned in the sixteenth and seventeenth centuries still in existence in Ireland.[36] Their findings confirmed the inadequacy of statute law to regulate the sheriff effectively. Thus, it was said that the requirement that the sheriff ought to have land in his shire under 9 Edward II stat. 2. 'seems to have been forgotten or overlooked in the appointment of sheriffs'. Sheriffs were appointed in many instances for two or more years consecutively. The practice of sheriffs delegating their duties to their sub-sheriffs had also given rise to abuse and irregularities. Sub-sheriffs were solely appointed by the sheriff, and religious or political considerations had often influenced both their appointment and the carrying out of their duties. The commissioners reported that they

[34] Hansard, *Parliamentary Debates*, 3rd series xliii, cols. 1011-1012 (25 June 1838).

[35] Correspondence: H. Joy to T. Drummond, 14 June 1837.

[36] *Fifteenth Report of the Commissioners appointed to inquire into the Duties, Salaries and Emoluments . . . in all Temporal and Ecclesiastical Courts in Ireland*, Parliamentary Papers 1826, xvii, 29.

found evidence that there was systematic abuse of the legal process in the hands of the sub-sheriffs.

The appointment of sheriffs had also resisted statutory rules. It seems that from 1776 to 1816 in Ireland the executive appointed the sheriff without consulting the judges. This resulted in the exercise of considerable patronage by the government of the day and allowed political influence on the individual sheriffs. In 1816 Sir John Newport's motion on the State of Ireland drew attention to the potential abuses: 'The office of High Sheriff, here [England] accounted burthersom, is in Ireland a cause of political contest, and the appointment and means of attaching powerful individuals to the Government of the day'.[37] The practical result according to Newport's view was that 'justice is poisoned at its source'.

In reply Sir Robert Peel, then the Irish Chief Secretary, admitted that the evidence received from a recent select committee on grand jury presentments confirmed 'the existence of many evils'.[38] Peel promised that the existing system of the executive appointing sheriffs without consultation with the judges would cease, and shortly after the debate, on 1 May 1816, he honoured his promise to the House of Commons. The Lord Chancellor of Ireland received a letter from Dublin Castle setting out the Lord Lieutenant's desire to revert to the 'ancient practice of appointing sheriffs in Ireland'.[39]

The 'ancient practice' of appointment referred to the procedure of the judges of the assize receiving from the outgoing sheriff the names of three persons who were thought suitable to serve. The names were examined by all the judges who met in the Lord Chancellor's chamber in Michaelmas term and they selected names to be forwarded to the Lord Lieutenant. The judges were free to depart from the advice of the sheriffs and alter the names. In 1817 the judges were told 'to make inquiry on their respective circuits into the qualifications in point of character and property' of the nominees to be submitted to the Lord Lieutenant.[40] It soon became common procedure for the judges to submit three names to the Lord Lieutenant without first meeting, and the Lord Lieutenant normally appointed as sheriff the first name from each list. The names of the appointed sheriffs were published annually

[37] Hansard, *Parliamentary Debates*, xxxiv, cols. 11-74, quotation at 21 (26 April 1816).

[38] Hansard, *Parliamentary Debates*, xxxiv, col. 32 (26 April 1816). The select committee referred to by Peel in the House of Commons was: *Report from the Select Committee on Irish Grand Jury Presentments*, Parliamentary Papers 1816, ix, 1.

[39] Correspondence: W. Gregory to the Lord Chancellor, 10 May 1816.

[40] Correspondence: ibid.

in the Dublin Gazette, the warrant of appointment directed by the Lord Lieutenant.[41]

Peel's method of appointment was an attempt to restore what he assumed was the practice set out under 9 Edward II and applied in England. But the restoration was not intended to remove completely the Lord Lieutenant's powers. Before the House of Commons debate and his promise to restore 'the ancient practice of appointment', Peel confided in a letter to Attorney-General Saurin in April 1816:

> It is of the greatest importance to the administration of justice, I believe, that the Lord Lieutenant should have a very large discretion as to the appointment of Sheriff, but it is quite impossible to defend the exercise by the Sheriff of any power which gives to the party supporting Government undue preponderance in the County. That will, I am sure, be felt to be an abuse, and a great abuse of the authority of the Sheriff. The best plan probably of remedying the evil will be to curtail the power which makes his appointment political, and if there are any abuses in the office of sub-sheriff to correct them without delay . . .[42]

The restoration of the 'ancient practice' once more involved the judges in Ireland directly in the appointments of sheriffs. This may be seen as a clear attempt by Peel to give respectability to what otherwise had been seen as a crude political act of the executive in bestowing patronage by appointing sheriffs. Privately Peel had misgivings about giving the judges in Ireland complete power of nominating sheriffs.

> I cannot make Lord Liverpool understand why the judges in Ireland should not have the virtual nomination. If there were no Smith, and no Fletcher, and no Day, and no electioneering judges, I think the recommendation of the judge of assize might be safely attended to. But you will see at once the difficulty of making an objection to the application of the principle on account of the character or practices of individuals.[43]

Both the practice of the Lord Lieutenant directly appointing sheriffs and the restoration of the 'ancient practice' raised questions of legality. We have already seen that the judges' participation in the appointment process had evolved through custom rather than through clear statutory authority. The judges' practice of asking the

[41] A full description of the system may be found in Lord Lyndhurst's speech on the appointment of sheriffs in the House of Lords: Hansard, *Parliamentary Debates*, 3rd series xliv, cols. 1000–1001 (25 June 1838).

[42] Parker, 221-22: Peel to Attorney-General Saurin, 8 April 1816. See note 1 above.

[43] Parker, 221-22.

outgoing sheriff for names to be forwarded to the Lord Lieutenant is a case in point: there was no statute which authorised the practice of consulting the sheriffs. On such a flexible interpretation of the law, if the Lord Lieutenant wished there seemed little to prevent him from selecting a sheriff from names not nominated by the judges.

Privately Peel expressed doubt to Lord Whitworth of 'the legitimacy'[44] of the entire practice of the Lord Lieutenant appointing the sheriffs, and wrote: 'I really do not apprehend any, or at least very little, inconvenience from the abandonment of the present practice in any point of view, even in that of patronage. With a pure Bench – and time will, I hope purify it – the change would be an essential change for the better'.[45] Peel's decision to revert to the 'ancient practice' seemed calculated to meet the criticisms voiced in the House of Commons debate, and was also introduced to avoid legislation on appointments proposed by Sir John Newport. But it was seen by many in the Commons as an attempt to make the sheriff independent from the politics of the government of the day.

The legality of the restoration of the 'ancient practice of appointment' was left unresolved. It was assumed to be legal and the *Fifteenth Report of the Commissioners* in 1826 made only a passing reference to it: 'Of late years, however a marked improvement has been universally felt . . . owing perhaps partly to the restoration of the ancient mode of selection, and partly to the greater care and attention of the judges, in the first instance in preparing their returns'.[46]

In 1830 a committee of inquiry reported on the office of sheriff and called for continued vigilance by the proper authorities on the sheriff's work. Such vigilance was not confined to the public because Parliament continued to keep a scrutiny over the office. A return to the House of Lords in March 1836[47] examined to what extent consultation with the judges had been undertaken or the practice of consulting the judges had been applied. It found that only in one instance, in County Wexford in 1836, without the nominees' consent, a name had been passed over for the office of sheriff although returned by the judge.

[44] Parker, 222-23: Peel to Lord Whitworth, 8 April 1816.

[45] Parker, 224: Peel to Lord Whitworth, 10 April 1816.

[46] *Fifteenth Report*, 1826.

[47] *A Return of the several Persons Recommended by the Judges to fill the Office of High Sheriff in the respective Counties of Ireland, for the present Year and for the last Five Years, and also of those persons who have actually been Appointed* . . . Parliamentary Paper 1838, xlvii, 527.

On 4 December 1835 Francis Leigh was informed by the Lord Lieutenant that he was appointed sheriff of Wexford.[48] He awaited receipt of his warrant of appointment before formally taking up the office of sheriff. Soon after, in January 1836 he was told by letter from the Lord Lieutenant that he was not to be appointed sheriff and the warrant of appointment was not granted. The Lord Lieutenant had received information that Mr. Leigh was connected with an Orange Society and the Lord Lieutenant felt unable to appoint him sheriff. Some months later, when the entire affair came to be debated in the House of Lords new evidence was produced showing that Mr. Leigh was not a member of the Orange Society. Lord Mulgrave, then Irish Chief Secretary, admitted: 'his regret that he had been misinformed on the subject. If he had known at the time he rejected Mr. Leigh what he knew now, he should have acted differently . . .'[49] Political considerations had clearly effected the non-selection of Mr. Leigh and brought severe criticism in the House of Lords. An article in the *Dublin University Magazine* complained that the earl of Mulgrave: '. . . nominated sheriffs according to his own caprice or interest. His party applauded him loudly, little caring for the law or the constitution . . .'[50]

The return of 1836 found that no appointment of a sheriff from 1832 to 1835 had been made without recourse to the judges' opinion.[51] But in 1836, for eight counties the judges had not been consulted, which was a departure from the 'ancient practice' introduced by Peel. Once more the mode of appointing sheriffs in Ireland attracted controversy.[52]

Thomas Drummond in 1837 wrote to the Irish Chief Baron Henry Joy and pointed out that Peel's principle that the outgoing sheriffs should be consulted by the judges when considering nominees

[48] 'Letters from the Chief Secretary or Under Secretary for Ireland to Francis Leigh Esq., or others on his behalf. . .', House of Lords Sessional Papers 1836, lxxv, 635.

[49] Hansard, *Parliamentary Debates*, 3rd series xxxiii, col. 966. At cols. 963-64, Mulgrave suggested that Mr. Leigh had no property in the Courts (17 May 1836).

[50] Anon, 'Lord Mulgrave's appointment of the sheriffs in Ireland', *Dublin University Magazine* xi, 1838, 767-79.

[51] See: *Return of the Several Persons recommended by the Judges to fill the office of High Sheriff in the respective Counties of Ireland for the year 1836 and for the ten preceding years; and also of the persons actually appointed and of those passed over and whether any applications have been made without reference to the Judges.* House of Lords Sessional Papers 1836, xxv, 295 (not 301, as given in the catalogue).

[52] Several Select Committees provide evidence of controversy surrounding the appointment of sheriffs.

'should as little as possible be abandoned, without special cause';[53] it was the government's wish that the 'ancient practice' of selection should continue. In reply, Joy questioned whether Peel's interpretation of 'the ancient practice' was correct and raised the entire legality of the past practices of appointing sheriffs.[54]

Joy's interpretation of the early statutes was that three persons were to be nominated by the twelve judges and presented to the Lord Lieutenant, out of whom one was selected. The Lord Lieutenant was restricted to those names put forward by the judges, there was no power to dispense with statute and to the extent statute was violated the Lord Lieutenant acted illegally. He concluded:

> I am also of the opinion that by the statute law of Ireland and by 'ancient usage' the Right to nominate three persons to be presented to the Lord Lieutentant was absolutely and exclusively with the Judges, without any right in the Sheriff or any other person to interfere with them in that choice; and that the requiring them to receive and nominate such names as the Sheriff may think proper to return to them is an infringement of their right and a violation of the law . . .[55]

Joy's opinion was supported by his argument that the sheriff was an 'officer of the Judges' and it was wrong to give the sheriff the *de facto* power to appoint his successor. Many of Joy's arguments were taken up in the parliamentary debate which examined the entire question of the appointment of sheriffs in Ireland. The Chief Secretary of Ireland, Lord Mulgrave, was subjected to public condemnation for the practice which had resulted in the Crown effectively appointing sheriffs.[56] A select committee was moved in the House of Lords to inquire into the appointment of sheriffs in Ireland.[57]

On what was held to be the strict interpretation and application of the early statutes 9 Edward II stat. 1. and 14 Edward III c. 7 the appointment of sheriffs in Ireland rested on the nomination by the judges and on the selection by the Lord Lieutenant. Normally the Lord Lieutenant selected the first name appearing at the top of the list of nominees, usually three in number, received from the judges.

Such a strict application of the law was far removed from political

[53] Correspondence: T. Drummond to H. Joy, 20 May 1837.
[54] Correspondence: H. Joy to T. Drummond, 24 May 1837.
[55] Correspondence: ibid.
[56] See note 50 above.
[57] *Report from the Select Committee of the House of Lords on the manner in which Sheriffs have been appointed for Counties in Ireland.* House of Lords Sessional Papers 1838, xxi, 659.

reality in Ireland. The Irish Lord Lieutenant could frequently exercise a discretion to select a name other than one submitted by the judges. Names nominated by the judges could be rejected. Sheriffs were often consulted by the judges before making their list of nominations to be sent to the Lord Lieutentant. Accounts are available showing evidence for such practices throughout the nineteenth century.

Allegations of political bias and corruption were frequently made against the sheriff and in the method of appointment. One such example, where suspicion of political bias arose in 1836, has been discussed above,[58] and illustrates the problems caused by the wide discretion given to the Lord Lieutenant. There seemed no adequate form of accountability other than parliamentary debate and the occasional select committee report.[59] Both procedures inquired after the events were alleged to have taken place and the harm had already been done.

In Ireland, the office of sheriff remained as one of great importance throughout the nineteenth century. The eventual development of elected local government through the Local Government Board from 1872[60] and under the 1898 Act[61] brought a reduction in the influence of the grand jury and thereby that of the sheriff. But in the administration of justice the sheriff's influence, together with that of his sub-sheriff, in selecting jurors remained throughout the century. Accusations of political bias and jury packing were often made. *The McKenna Case*[62] was a good example of the practice of jury packing and of the difficulty experienced by the government when it wanted to dismiss the sheriff.

Medieval statutes were inherently difficult to enforce and apply according to the letter of the law. It is tempting to believe that the executive's failure to obey such an interpretation was deliberate. It allowed a wide and largely unfettered discretion over the appointment of sheriffs which was characteristic of successive governments' practice when dealing with Ireland.

A number of questions arise which remain unanswered. Why were the Irish judges willing to lend their name to the appointment of sheriffs when such appointments were so politically controversial and

[58] See notes 48 and 49 above.

[59] Hansard, *Parliamentary Debates*, 3rd series xxxiii, col. 956 (17 May 1836.)

[60] Local Government Board (Ireland) Act 1872, 35 and 36 Vict. c. 69.

[61] Local Government (Ireland) Act 1898, 61 and 62 Vict. c. 37.

[62] J. F. McEldowney, 'The Case of the Queen v. McKenna (1869) and Jury Packing in Ireland', *Irish Jurist* xii, 1977, 339-54.

sensitive? Still further, why were judges so keen to invite nomination from outgoing sheriffs to form the basis of their lists of nominees to be sent to the Lord Lieutenant? Very possibly the Irish judiciary offered an air of respectability to the appointment of the sheriff. They may have preferred to nominate names which they felt were 'dependable' as sheriff rather than have names imposed on them. The opportunity to exercise some degree of patronage was more accepted then than now. But given the number of complaints made about the sheriff and the way he carried out his duties the temptation is to see the judges as inept in their nominations to the Lord Lieutenant. Successive Lord Lieutenants were inadequate in ensuring effective control over a prominent local official. Throughout the nineteenth century the judges in Ireland continued to influence the selection of sheriffs thereby exercising an important influence over one of the most important, but sadly most neglected, officers in the administration of justice in Ireland.

10

Shooting the Elephant: Historians and the Problem of Frontier Lawlessness

Hamar Foster

To 'see the elephant' was a common expression in the United States before the Civil War. There is some disagreement as to what, exactly, it meant, but most used it to signify having suffered much in order to see or experience something extraordinary.[1] It is not surprising, therefore, that the expression was often used by those who crossed the continent to Oregon and California in the middle decades of the last century. Unfortunately, and to an extent that today is difficult to determine, too many of those who populated the American West during these years no sooner 'saw the elephant' than they began shooting at it. Law and order – whatever the true relationship between these two ideas may be – was slow in coming, and then as now many sought clues to America's national character in this fact.[2]

In the United States, the debate has tended to be between those who believe the American West was exceptionally lawless, and others who argue that Americans have been that way throughout their history and that the West was, if anything, not so bad.[3] Non-American historians, on the other hand, have tended to start from the proposition that the American frontier was the worst of the lot, and then have drawn favourable comparisons with their own national experiences.[4] On the periphery of this debate, Canadian historian

[1] One account of its origin is as follows: a farmer who had always wanted to see an elephant was overjoyed to learn that a circus was coming to town. Unfortunately, on his way to market one day, the circus passed him, and his horse was so frightened by the elephant and other animals that it bolted and upset his wagon, throwing the farmer in the ditch. Although his vegetables were ruined and he was bruised and dirty, he did not mind. 'I have seen the elephant,' he said. See R. May, *The Gold Rushes*, Sydney 1977, 30.

[2] One of the earliest and most interesting examples of this tradition is the philosopher Josiah Royce's book *California, From the Conquest in 1846 to the Second Vigilance Committee in San Francisco: A Study of American Character*, Boston 1886.

[3] A useful summary of this debate may be found in R. D. McGrath, *Gunfighters, Highwaymen and Vigilantes: Violence on the Frontier*, Berkeley 1984, 261-271.

[4] E.g., B. M. Gough, 'Keeping British Columbia British: The Law and Order Question on a Gold Mining Frontier', *Huntington Library Quarterly* xxxviii, 1975, 269-80. Gough is in fact the only Canadian scholar cited by John Phillip Reid as an example of this tendency in the introduction to his *Law for the Elephant: Property and Social Behaviour on the Overland Trail*, Huntington Library 1980.

Arthur S. Morton once remarked that 'the Anglo-Saxon, upholder of the law though he be, has never been its victim. When law fails him, and the public interest requires it, he feels free to act as the situation demands'.[5] Professor Morton might have been referring to the miners' courts of the California gold rush, or to any one of the many vigilance committees that are liberally sprinkled throughout American history, but he was not.[6] He was speaking instead of Governor James Douglas of British Columbia, a man whose name represents the antithesis of all movements associated with lawlessness of any kind. Moreover, it is an accurate statement: when the law failed him, Douglas was willing to act without it and even, occasionally, against it, if he conceived such action to be in the public interest.

Why, then, one wonders, has such a contrast been drawn between the lawless American West, on the one hand, and the law-abiding Canadian West, on the other? Is it, as one recent writer suggests, due mainly to American historians' traditional 'compulsion for national self-flagellation'? Or perhaps, as he also suggests, is it that the 'generally colorless history of Canada gains interest and significance from the mere assertion that Canadians settled their western provinces . . . with less loss of life than . . . the United States'?[7] While these accusations do sting just a little, they seem wide of the mark,[8] in part because the comparisons go well beyond Canada.

In New Zealand, for example, the gold rushes were less subject to violent disorders than in California. Asked why this was so, an American prospector who had tried his luck in both places replied that it might be 'something in the country and the people'. Somehow, he said, 'Law rules here [in New Zealand] and it don't there'.[9] Although

[5] A. S. Morton, *A History of the Canadian West*, 2nd ed., Toronto 1973, 769.

[6] The classic account of the frontier miners' courts is contained in Charles H. Shinn, *Mining Camps: A Study in American Frontier Government*, 1884. On vigilantism see the work of R. M. Brown, in particular 'The American Vigilante Tradition' in *The History of Violence in America*, ed. H. D. Graham and T. R. Gurr, New York 1969.

[7] Reid, 3.

[8] As for the history of Canada being 'generally colorless', I can say only that such a statement must proceed either from an ignorance of the subject (which in Reid's case I doubt) or from an equation of colour with the relatively bloody history of the American frontier – something I would have thought Professor Reid meant to avoid.

[9] Quoted in P. R. May, *The West Coast Gold Rushes*, rev. ed., Christchurch 1967, 282-3. Similar remarks about British Columbia abound. See, for example, the views of an old California miner named Downie in Antler, B.C., quoted in Judge Begbie's Report to the Colonial Secretary of 25 September 1861: *British Parliamentary Papers Relating to British Columbia*, vol. 24, 202-03. (This was probably the man for whom Downieville, California was named; it was the scene of a particularly 'disgraceful' lynching on 5 July 1851: see Royce, 290-95.)

mercifully brief, as an explanation this leaves something to be desired, and historians have been attempting to improve upon it and ones like it ever since. Not only is the saga of frontier law and order inherently interesting, it holds out the prospect of telling us something important about a legal culture and its ability to cope under stress. But the obstacles in the way of a more complete understanding are considerable.

The most obvious evidential obstacle is the lack of it. Court and police records often do not exist for the earliest phases of frontier development, and even when they do, they are difficult to interpret. Classification of offences tends to be eccentric, the keeping of records haphazard, and sometimes these combine to produce data that are internally inconsistent as well as merely opaque.[10] Beyond this, the interpretation of statistical evidence is controversial, even when it is current and properly gathered. Scholars who cannot agree about the extent and significance of crime and lawlessness in the 1980s certainly ought to feel a little of that old miner's hesitation in explaining the gold rushes of over 100 years ago.

Reliance upon contemporary accounts can also be precarious. It sometimes seems as though for every person who saw Placerville or Hokitika or Williams Creek as wild and woolly, another remarked upon its order and peace.[11] The writers of such memoirs cannot be cross-examined. If they could be, we might discover that things everywhere were much better than historical accounts that concentrate on the rougher aspects of frontier life would have us believe. In New Zealand, one of the principal reasons for British annexation was ostensibly the escalation of anarchy and lawlessness. Yet, when one of the witnesses before a parliamentary committee was asked whether a settlement he had described as being in a deplorable state was worse than any other British seaport town, he replied in the negative.[12] Whether annexation proceeded more in spite of than because of revelations such as this, is not clear.[13]

In this paper, however, I want to discuss not evidential problems,

[10] E.g., in R. C. Lundin Brown's *British Columbia. An Essay*, New Westminster 1863. Brown's text and his tables on criminal cases in the colony do not quite agree.

[11] These are in California, New Zealand and British Columbia, respectively. Other examples are easily found, e.g., in Australia and Klondike.

[12] Quoted by J. M. R. Owens, 'New Zealand Before Annexation', in *The Oxford History of New Zealand*, ed. W. H. Oliver, Oxford 1981, 49.

[13] See generally A. Ward, *A Show of Justice: Racial 'Amalgamation' in Nineteenth Century New Zealand*, Canberra 1974; and P. Adams, *Fatal Necessity: British Intervention in New Zealand 1830-1847*, Auckland 1977.

but problems with the term 'lawlessness' itself. If flows easily enough from the pen, but may carry any one of a number of different, though related, meanings. It seems important, therefore, to distinguish some of the ways in which it can be used.

In the earliest days of a frontier, when mining or trade has reached too far in advance of settlement, a land may be 'lawless' in a quite literal sense. Setting aside the possibility – as they nearly always did[14] – that Europeans should regard themselves as subject to the laws of the indigenous inhabitants,[15] these early adventurers found themselves in a realm beyond the law, subject only to their own consciences and their willingness to behave as if the legal institutions they had left behind had instead travelled with them.[16] When Britain found its nationals in this position – and it did so more often than any other imperial power in the nineteenth century – it usually passed a statute authorizing the trial of its wayward subjects in the nearest British colony with judicial institutions, and hoped for the best. The Canada Jurisdiction Act of 1803, for example, provided for the trial of serious offences committed in the Indian Territory in the courts of Lower Canada.[17] A little later, a series of imperial statutes passed

[14] Two interesting exceptions of which I am aware come from New Zealand and Australia. The colonial judges in New South Wales were asked in 1836 to hold that British settlers were bound to obey aboriginal laws, but they of course declined to do so. And in New Zealand in 1842, the Attorney-General advised the Governor that he had no authority to intervene in disputes between Maori *hapu* who had not signed the Treaty of Waitangi. This advice was promptly overruled by the Colonial Office, with a stiff reprimand to the man who gave it. See David Williams 'The Annexation of New Zealand to New South Wales: Where Did the Treaty of Waitangi Fit In?', Unpublished paper 1983, 76-84 and 92-94.

[15] And it seems pointless to deny, at least for the purposes of historical and comparative studies, that the pre-contact inhabitants of Australasia, North America and Africa had laws. See, for example, M. Gluckman, *Politics, Law and Ritual in Tribal Society*, Oxford 1965, 178-183.

[16] The classic statement of this view of the law is of course in Blackstone's *Commentaries on the Laws of England*, Oxford 1765-9; facsimile ed. Chicago 1979, vol. 1, 104-05. However, there are many ambiguities in this notion, one of which is whether settlement is required to attract the application of the law or simply trading in the territory is sufficient. This issue appears to have arisen in a Canadian case in 1867, where a court held that a 'marriage' between a fur trader and an Indian at Rat River in 1803 was valid for probate purposes because English law at that time did not apply: see *Connolly* v. *Woolrich* (1867), Lower Canada Jurist xi, 230, 248. Although this ruling was substantially undermined in a later case, it illustrates the problem. Certainly the overland emigrants to California in the 1840s and 1850s felt they had left the law behind: see Reid, 8-9.

[17] 43 Geo. III, c. 138 (U.K.). On the effectiveness of this statute, see Morton, ch. VII and D. H. Brown 'Unpredictable and Uncertain: Criminal Law in the Canadian Northwest Before 1886', *Alberta Law Review* xvii, 1979, 500-02.

between 1817 and 1828 authorized similar trials of New Zealand offenders in the courts of New South Wales.[18] At this stage of imperial expansion, law enforcement was rather more theoretical than real, and such solemn but largely futile gestures were often[19] accompanied by the appointment of an imperial representative to reside in the territory and impress everyone, European and native alike, with his helplessness.[20] Examples that immediately come to mind are William Busby in New Zealand, and even one colonial governor, Richard Blanshard of Vancouver's Island.[21] Self-help organizations (such as the Korororeka Association in New Zealand's Bay of Islands) were a natural response to these difficult situations. All this changes, however, once a decision to institute colonial or territorial government is made.

Typically, when Britain decided to colonize a territory, the sort of statute I mentioned earlier would be repealed and a local government established.[22] The question of the applicability of English law would

[18] 57 Geo. III, c. 53; 4 Geo. IV, c. 96, s. 3; 9 Geo. IV, c. 83, s. 4 (U.K.). The difference between the two situations is that the Indian Territory, although its boundaries were uncertain, was within British North America, whereas New Zealand prior to 1839-40 was not part of 'His Majesty's Dominions'. Often provision was also made for trying accused persons in England.

[19] But not always. One exception is 1 & 2 Geo. IV, c. 66 (U.K.). Passed in 1821 upon the amalgamation of the Northwest Company and the Hudson's Bay Company, this statute provided for the appointment of justices by His Majesty, but this was never done. The administration of justice was left, as was probably the intention from the beginning, in the hands of the new Hudson's Bay Company.

[20] Such policies were not confined to the Pacific Rim. In 1888 Lord Salisbury summed up the position of a consul despatched to the Nyasa District in Africa as follows: 'To please the missionaries, we send a representative of the Government; to spare the taxpayers we make him understand that he will in no case be supported by an armed force. The only weapon left him is bluster . . .'. Quoted in Adams, 71.

[21] Keith Sinclair's assessment of Busby is typical: 'No one took [Busby] seriously except Busby, a pompous young man . . . However, in view of the false position in which he had been placed by . . . the authorities, it is a mistake to attribute his failure chiefly to his personal faults. It was inconceivable that he should succeed', *A History of New Zealand*, Auckland 1984, 51.

Blanshard is not a true example because he was appointed after Britain officially founded the colony; nonetheless, for several years Vancouver's Island remained an outpost of the fur trade rather than a settlement colony, and the real power remained in the hands of the Hudson's Bay Company chief factor, James Douglas. As one historian has pointed out, when Blanshard arrived to take up his post, he 'soon found that there were no public affairs to administer, no judiciary, no legislature and no colonists; all the inhabitants being connected with the comapny', F. S. Howay, *British Columbia: The Making of a Province*, Toronto 1928, 105.

[22] For Vancouver's Island, see 12 & 13 Vict. c. 48 (U.K.); the equivalent statute for British Columbia is 21 & 22 Vict., c. 99 (U.K.).

sometimes be proclaimed by statute, as in British Columbia in 1858,[23] or simply assumed, as was the case with Vancouver's Island and New Zealand for their first two decades as colonies.[24] In the United States, the Northwest Ordinance of 1787 performed this function, imposing the Common Law and providing for territorial government until the population reached the number necessary to qualify for statehood.[25] It is in this second phase of frontier development, and during the transition to it, that the real issue of lawlessness arises. There are now local laws for the people to break, and local law enforcement procedures for them to ignore. In the first phase, 'lawlessness' is simply a convenient synonym for bad behaviour; in the second it refers to a much more sinister social phenomenon. And on this point, historians have tended to agree 'that democratic Americans of the nineteenth century . . . had much to learn about frontier government from the empire that had once ruled their country'.[26]

However, it is a mistake, I think, to draw a distinction solely in terms of law versus lawlessness. Americans, if anything, were and are far more obsessed with law than the British, whose instructions to their colonial governors spoke not of instituting peace, *law* and good government, but peace, *order* and good government. It is true that official communications from the Colonial Office stressed the need for strict observance of the law, but their men in the field – or at least those who had the most successful careers – knew that their first responsibility was to establish order. In British Columbia, first the Hudson's Bay Company and then a Hudson's Bay Company governor did this, with a little help from the Royal Navy and the

[23] Proclamation of 19 November 1858. See now the *Law and Equity Act*, R.S.B.C. 1979, c. 224, s. 2.

[24] New Zealand's first statute on the subject was passed in 1858, some eighteen years after the colony was established. Vancouver's Island also waited eighteen years, until amalgamation with the mainland colony of British Columbia: see *Laws of British Columbia*, 1871, No. 70. However, in 1861, Chief Justice Cameron had held that English statutes passed prior to the colony's establishment in 1849 applied, but those passed later did not: see *Bancroft Scraps*, Set W, Vol. 84, 124, Bancroft Library, University of California at Berkeley.

[25] L. M. Friedman *A History of American Law*, New York 1973, 96, 138-9.

[26] R. W. Paul, 'Old Californians in British Gold Fields' *Huntington Library Quarterly* xvii, 1984, 172. Another recent exponent of this view is Professor Howard Temperley in his 'Guns, Gold and Vigilantes: Government on the Montana and British Columbia Mining Frontiers', Inaugural Lecture at the University of Norwich, 8 February 1983. Perhaps a slightly different view is that of David Williams, 'The Administration of Criminal and Civil Justice in the Mining Camps and Frontier Communities of British Columbia', in *Law and Justice in a New Land: Essays in Western Canadian Legal History*, ed. L. Knafla, Toronto 1986, 215-32.

Royal Engineers. On the Canadian prairie, it was again the Hudson's Bay Company, and then the Northwest Mounted Police, who undertook this task. The result was that throughout the Canadian West a tradition of order was established before the frontiers of mining and settlement arrived. It was, however, not exactly a model of due process. As one Northwest Mounted Policeman put it, they were 'able to try any case and have only to wait for a *wink* from Ottawa to hang our man'.[27] He was, of course, speaking off the record.

As I suggested earlier, it was much the same in British Columbia. Governor Douglas was a man whose many years in the Hudson's Bay Company had impressed him with the importance of discipline and order, and while he had no particular wish to act without authority, he did not hesitate to do so when he deemed it necessary. Most of his excesses were probably due to lack of legal knowledge as much as anything else, although he does seem to have been unusually slow to mend his ways when problems were brought to his attention.[28] And on at least one occasion, he must have been quite aware that he was violating the law. In September of 1858 Douglas visited the mainland of British Columbia, where his authority was only that of a chief factor of the Hudson's Bay Company. The reason for the visit was the huge influx of American prospectors in search of gold, and the only law of the mainland was an imperial statute of 1821 which required the Company to send capital cases to Canada for trial.[29] In the course of this tour, Douglas commissioned a three-man tribunal to preside over the trial of an American miner for murder.[30] Although this was

[27] James F. Macleod to W. F. Sanders, 10 August 1877, quoted in P. F. Sharp, *Whoop-Up Country. The Canadian-American West*, Oklahama 1973, 110.

[28] When advised that he had to summon a representative assembly for Vancouver's Island in 1856, Douglas protested to the Secretary of State for the Colonies that he had 'a very slender knowledge of legislation' and that 'without legal advice or intelligent assistance of any kind' he approached the task 'with diffidence', *British Parliamentary Papers*, vol. 21, 392, Douglas to Labouchere. Diffidence, however, was not a quality that usually infused Douglas' actions; see, for example, the text following note 29, below, and L. H. Laing, 'An Unauthorized Admiralty Court in British Columbia', *The Washington Historical Quarterly* xxvi, 1935, 10-15.

[29] See note 19, above.

[30] See Private Papers of James Douglas, First Series at 103, Bancroft Library, and *British Parliamentary Papers*, vol. 22, Douglas to Lytton, 12 October 1858. It is possible, though unlikely, that Douglas was aware of a legal opinion by Adam Thom, the Hudson's Bay Company's recorder in Rupert's Land, that the 1821 statute did not apply west of the Rocky Mountains. However, this opinion was given years earlier in the context of the McLoughlin murder at Fort Stikine: see W. Kaye Lamb's introduction to *The Letters of John McLoughlin From Fort Vancouver to*

directly contrary to the existing law, Douglas went on to become governor of the mainland colony, and his actions were generally approved both at the time by the Colonial Office and subsequently by historians. Just to be on the safe side, however, an indemnity statute was passed: one never knew when someone less enamoured with imperial methods might want to challenge such things in the courts.[31]

None of this, I hasten to add, is intended to debunk the proposition that the British colonies on the Pacific Rim were more successful in their efforts to maintain law and order than were the Americans. Douglas and others like him moved quickly because he thought that swift and effective official (albeit illegal) action was to be preferred to vigilance committees and popular tribunals, and he was probably right. Once the initial crisis was over, and a colonial judiciary was established, British Columbia did not have to endure the outbreaks of vigilantism that periodically disrupted California, Idaho, Montana, and other American mining frontiers.[32] The explanation for this, however, is not to be found solely in British devotion to the rule of law. An older mining population, stricter gun control, fewer rogues, and a host of other factors all contributed to Britain's relative success in keeping the peace on its mining frontiers. But so, in the beginning, did a willingness to go beyond the law to maintain order rather than

the Governor and Committee, Second Series, 1839-44, Toronto 1943, xlvi. Moreover, it was almost certainly wrong, and the best evidence of that is the express repeal of the statute by 12 & 13 Vict. (1849), c. 48 (U.K.), which made new provision for the administration of justice in the colony of Vancouver's Island. The accused in this case was convicted of manslaughter and sentenced to transportation for life (an option probably not open at that time even to a legally constituted court). He escaped before sentence was executed.

[31] Proclamation of 19 November 1858. See Enclosure 2 in No. 22 (Despatch), *British Parliamentary Papers Relating to British Columbia*, vol. 22 at 79. Douglas' biographer, Walter N. Sage, notes that King's trial 'is usually considered to have been quite illegal': *Sir James Douglas and British Columbia*, Toronto 1930, 228. It certainly does not fall within the following advice passed on to Douglas by the Secretary of State for the Colonies on 2 September 1858. 'According to the opinion of lawyers in general,' he told Douglas, 'the Colonists of a territory circumstanced like British Columbia carry with them the law of England, so far as it is applicable to their circumstances. Acts, therefore, done in accordance with the law of England, will be substantially legal, although done before any regular authority was constituted there.' He then dealt with the question of the indemnity statute.

Sir George Grey, Governor of New Zealand, revealed a similar preference for order over strict legality when he incarcerated the Maori chief, Te Rauparaha, without trial in 1845: M. P. K. Sorenson, 'Maori and Pakeha', *Oxford History of New Zealand*, 179.

[32] On Montana see Temperley's paper at note 26, above, and W. J. Trimble, *The Mining Advance Into the Inland Empire*, Madison 1914.

wait for the population to do so. It may also be important that the appointed and autocratic British official was able to take this sort of stand without being subject to the electoral whirlwinds that always threatened his more democratic counterparts to the south.[33]

Recently the traditional dichotomy between the American experience and the Canadian has been subjected to criticism, most notably by Professor John Philip Reid in a book entitled *Law for the Elephant*. Reid argues, and he marshalls an impressive array of diaries and letters in support, that the overland immigrants to California were 'law minded' to an extraordinary degree, particularly when it came to rights of property. Further, he says that there is reason to believe that 'to a greater extent than has been thought, the . . . actions . . . of nineteenth-century American society were formed by a behaviourism based on law'.[34] If this is so, and I think it is, it is further evidence that comparing British and American frontiers in terms of 'lawlessness' misses the point, and that in the early stages of a frontier, competent officials committed to the maintenance of order are more important than popular commitment to a regime of legal rights. Indeed, instead of using Reid's findings to suggest (as he does) that the American mining frontier was much more peaceful than hitherto suspected, one might be prompted to ask a new question: how it is that, for all the obsession with law and property that his evidence reveals, the early years of the California gold rush remain remarkable not for their law and order, but for their vigilantism and violence?[35]

[33] As one American pioneer put it, he was not saying the popular thing in stating that the whites were more to blame than the Indians for the Washington Territory Wars, 'but I am not running for office'. Undated interview with Phillip Ritz of Walla Walla, Bancroft Library, P-C10, 18.

[34] Reid, 10-11.

[35] Temperley's view (above note 26, unpaginated) that the West was wild because the United States government permitted it to be seems correct for territories prior to statehood, but not after. Even Reid concedes that in California, 1852 was probably the year of greatest violence (Reid, 6); yet that was two years after statehood, when the excuse that there was a governmental vacuum no longer existed.

Indeed, one is even prompted to speculate whether there is not some sort of connection, at least in frontier communities, between an exaggerated and legalistic respect for property and a tendency to vigilantism and excess. Many contemporary commentators noted that in the American West severe punishments for theft often lived side by side with a high tolerance for acts of violence: see, for example, T. J. Dinsdale, *The Vigilantes of Montana*, 1865, University of Oklahoma Press ed. 1953, 14; *The Shirley Letters*, Layton 1983, 66, 83-90, 155-7. Indeed, in 1851 the California legislature made robbery and grand larceny punishable by death, and at least one jury, in its discretion, decided to hang a man for stealing $400 worth of supplies from Lowe and Bros. This law was repealed in 1856: see *A History of the Bench and Bar in California*, ed. O. T. Shuck, Los Angeles 1901, 75-77.

Perhaps George Orwell, who also wrote about law and elephants, should be permitted the last word. As much as he hated the British empire, he once wrote, it was a good deal better at some things than the younger empires that were going to replace it.[36]

[36] George Orwell, 'Shooting an Elephant' in *Inside the Whale and Other Essays* Harmondsworth 1966, 92.

11

*The Royal Prerogative or a Statutory Code? The War Office and Contingency Legal Planning, 1885-1914**

G. R. Rubin

On 30 June 1914, just one month before the outbreak of the First World War, a sub-committee of the Committee of Imperial Defence (CID), which was the Prime Minister's standing advisory committee on defence matters, met to discuss what emergency powers, if any, would need to be enacted in the event of war being declared.[1] The War Office representative at the meeting, Colonel G. M. W. MacDonogh,[2] produced a list of powers which the army believed should be made available to it by statute for implementation in wartime, or during the 'precautionary period' prior to the actual outbreak. This, suggested MacDonogh, might cover a period of 'imminent national danger or great emergency', the phrase used in the Reserve Forces Act 1882. Such emergency powers, which were to be exercised against or in relation to the civilian population, covered the provision of supplies to garrisons, arrest powers, the taking possession of property, transport and communications controls, censorship, controls over 'warlike stores' and many other categories. Finally, legislative powers were sought in order to 'take all measures necessary for the public safety'. But at this point in the Committee's discussion, the Attorney-General, Sir John Simon, expressed the

* The author wishes to express his gratitude to Professor G. J. Zellick who is not, of course, responsible for any views expressed herein. Crown copyright material in the Public Record Office is reproduced by kind permission of the Controller of H.M. Stationery Office.

[1] CAB16/31/EP1, 'Sub-Committee of the Committee of Imperial Defence. Emergency Powers in War. Minutes of the 1st Meeting held on 30 June 1914'. Until indicated otherwise, subsequent quotations in the text are from this source. The work of Dr. David French in drawing attention to some of the themes in this paper is acknowledged. See D. French, *British Economic and Strategic Planning, 1905-1915*, London 1982, 74-6.

[2] George Mark Watson MacDonogh (1865-1942). Joined army 1884; colonel 1912; lieutenant-general 1919; general staff officer 1912; adjutant-general 1916-18; director of Military Intelligence 1916-18. Barrister (Lincoln's Inn) 1897; Vice-President and member Executive Council, International Law Association; President, Federation of British Industries 1933-4. Photograph in J. H. Morgan, *Assize of Arms*, London 1945.

view that the last-named requirement,

> . . . covered all those that had preceded it, and was itself covered by the common law; for it was the duty of the military authorities in time of war to take such measures as might be necessary for the safety of the State.

His pointed remarks, however, drew no response as the committee members continued to discuss which novel powers ought to be enacted. Again, the Attorney-General intervened and insisted that,

> . . . it was important to consider without prejudice the main question before the Committee. This was whether it was expedient to pass legislation of the nature proposed or to trust to an act of indemnity.

This paper seeks to analyse briefly, for the period c.1885-1914, the conflicting legal viewpoints expressed by senior military officers on the one hand and government legal advisers on the other, over the *kind* of law deemed appropriate for use in relation to the domestic civilian population in wartime. The focus is on differing perspectives as to the appropriate *conceptual* structure of the legal proposals advanced to meet the contingencies of war, differences which cannot simply be attributed to conflicts over interpretations of existing law. The approach of the military authorities was to some extent grounded (perhaps not surprisingly) in the military preoccupation with precise forward planning, so that the supposed certainty of statute law, rather than the somewhat open-ended flexibility of the common law, as preferred by the lawyers, appealed to military planners anticipating operational needs, both in wartime and when armed conflict appeared imminent. What is proposed in this paper is neither a history of the doctrinal development of the relevant law, such as the nineteenth-century Defence Acts, nor an exploration of the doctrinal accuracy of legal arguments advanced at the time, such as the proper scope of alleged prerogative powers to take over land or property in appropriate circumstances.[3] Our concern, rather, is with military *perceptions* of existing law, not with whether the ensuing military criticisms were doctrinally sound.

A series of nineteenth-century statutes, known collectively as the

[3] Following the celebrated First World War case of *Attorney-General* v. *de Keyser's Royal Hotel Ltd.* (1920) A.C.508 (H.L.), two commentators concluded that, '. . . the Crown has no right by virtue of any prerogative to enter the land of the subject without consent, and that where an entry in the case of an instant danger is lawful, it is justified, not under any such prerogative but in accordance with the right, common both to the Crown and to its subjects, to take what steps are necessary at the moment to meet the emergency'. See L. Scott and A. Hildesley, *The Case of Requisition*, Oxford 1920, 72.

Defence Acts 1842-1873, made provision for the compulsory military take-over of land. Thus under section 9 of the principal 1842 Act, power was granted to the Secretary of State for War to lease or purchase lands for buildings 'for the Ordnance or Barrack Services or the Defence of the Realm', while section 16 authorized the military to enter on, survey or mark out lands 'for the service of the Ordnance Department or for the Defence of the Realm'. In such circumstances, they had power to treat and agree with the owners for the absolute purchase of the land or for the possession or use thereof during the exigencies of the public service. In default of agreement, section 19 provided that fourteen days after failure to treat, the Secretary of State could require two justices or three deputy lieutenants (one of whom had to be a magistrate) to put the Secretary of State or his nominee into immediate possession of the lands. Two warrants, one authorizing the military authorities to take possession, and the other requiring the sheriffs to summon a jury to assess compensation, were then to be issued by the justices.

Though exercised for the 'defence of the realm', such powers were assumed to be applicable in peacetime. This does, of course, partly explain why military acquisition was hedged around with limited procedural safeguards for landowners. Yet such peacetime powers were nonetheless considered sufficiently drastic to justify the Treasury Solicitor's observation that, '. . . the owner has really no voice in the matter at all'.[4] Even more draconian were the provisions in section 23. This granted power to the Lord Lieutenant or two deputies or to the governor of the county or two of his deputies to certify the necessity or expediency of a military take-over of land or buildings. A Treasury warrant authorising the take-over was also required. This procedure presumably would only occur in cases of emergency. Finally, section 23, not unexpectedly, dispensed with the need for a possession order under section 19 or a certificate under section 23 where the 'Enemy shall have actually invaded the United Kingdom'. Thus, the only circumstances envisaged when a military officer could take immediate possession of land on his own initiative appeared to be once the enemy had landed. Otherwise, bureaucratic procedures, perhaps not conducive to defence preparations, were to be followed. Indeed, under the Military Lands Act 1892,[5]

It frequently takes over a year from the time when it is decided to take

[4] TS 27/62 'Note on the Compulsory Procedures for taking land possessed by the Secretary of State for War, dated 1902.'

[5] TS 27/62.

the land before the Secretary of State for War is in a position to serve Notice to Treat.

Though the Defence Acts were not as dilatory, none of the statutory codes met all the contingency needs of the military authorities. For what was most desired was, first, the ability to offer an immediate and flexible response on the basis of their evaluation of the military situation, that is, whether or not war had been officially declared or whether or not an invasion had commenced. But secondly, the military wanted clear, statutory authority for such an instantaneous response. The varying procedural restrictions of the Defence Acts (apart from invasion)[6] were an impediment to speedy military reaction to enemy threats.

In 1885, for example, the Inspector-General of Fortifications had drawn attention to the fact that in the event of imminent danger of invasion, it would become necessary for the military to take certain defensive measures involving interference with private property. They might have to enter on lands, erect works, construct roads or demolish buildings. Given that the existing law, by which he presumably meant the Defence Acts, prescribed so many complicated formalities and imposed so many restrictions, he feared that the military authorities would, at a time of imminent danger, be seriously hampered in the performance of their obvious duties.[7] Moreover, international incidents, which might have given rise to mobilization, had drawn the attention of military commanders to what they believed were deficiences in their legal powers to deploy as they considered appropriate. Following the Fashoda incident, when Britain was on the verge of war with France in 1898, Lieutenant-General Sir Frederick Stopford minuted that the want of information as to what the military authorities might or might not do on mobilization had caused serious inconvenience. In one case, the General Officer Commanding (GOC) Home District had to

[6] There were also criticisms of the limited scope of the Defence Acts even in respect to peacetime usage. For example, the inability of the military authorities to divert carriage roads led to suggestions in 1889 to widen the military's peacetime powers. The Secretary of State at the time, Edward Stanhope, was decidedly unenthusiastic. 'I cannot imagine,' he minuted, 'any proposal more likely to provoke considerable opposition than this and I am inclined on the whole to leave the matter alone for the present.' See WO32/9269, 'As to the compulsory powers of the Secretary of State for War, for acquiring land etc,' minute of Secretary of State, 5 December 1889.

[7] CAB16/31/EP2, 'Memorandum by the General Staff of the Need for an Emergency Powers Bill', 1 May 1914, para. 1.

enquire whether he was authorized to arrange for the quartering of troops for whom no government quarters or camp equipment existed. As Stopford lamented, it was,[8]

> . . . very unsatisfactory in reply to all these questions to have to state that no definite instructions can be given them, but that the question is under consideration.

In effect, military commanders were simply told to rely on their own discretion as to whether they ought to infringe private property rights once a mobilization had been ordered. Thus in 1911 all GOC's Home Command had been instructed that in the event of mobilization, they:[9]

> . . . should take all such steps as you consider necessary to occupy, or make use of, such land as may be required for camping, training, artillery practice, or musketry of the troops under your Command by arrangement with the owners, or otherwise, in anticipation of subsequent indemnity, either by the existing Defence Acts, or by emergency legislation.

Of course, military commanders might reasonably doubt whether the Defence Acts *made* any provision for indemnities for illegal acts. They might also have preferred to see emergency legislation on the statute book, rather than being held out to them as an uncertain inducement. Yet the position was bound to be more obscure when a 'precautionary period', short of actual mobilization, was in existence. Major R. E. H. James told the CID sub-committee in June 1914 that a precautionary period would be initiated by means of a warning telegram from the War Office to GOC's, 'but there were no specific instructions as to how far the military authorities would be justified on receipt of it in disregarding private rights.'[10]

How might this state of uncertainty be resolved? The military authorities throughout the last two decades of the nineteenth century made various attempts to obtain a statute conferring on them extensive powers to take steps necessary for the defence and security of the realm, both in the critical period pending a major conflict and after the outbreak of war. Such a bill was drafted in 1888 on the suggestion of Colonel (later Major-General Sir John)

[8] CAB16/31/EP2, para. 14.

[9] WO32/7112, R. H. Brade to all GO's C in C at Home and GOC London District, 9 November 1911.

[10] CAB16/31/EP1, 'Sub-Committee etc . . .', p. 2.

Ardagh.[11] It included provisions for the immediate military take-over of land and roads. However, the bill was put aside on the understanding that it could be brought forward when the circumstances were ripe, the intention being that the bill would be passed rapidly through Parliament when the emergency existed.[12] This did not appear to satisfy the War Department. For the War Office subsequently wrote to the Treasury that Stanhope, the Secretary of State for War, had,[13]

> . . . had it impressed upon him by his military advisers that, for the safety of the country, it is essential that Her Majesty should possess in a time of great national emergency, powers over lands, property, and persons of Her subjects which are far in excess of those which the common law confers. At the same [time], it is necessary, both for securing prompt obedience to the mandates of military necessity and for assuring military commanders against actions for things illegal done in the execution of their duty, that these extraordinary powers at an extraordinary crisis should be sanctioned by the law.

It was at this point that the War Department came up against a powerful legal opponent in the shape of Mr. (later Sir) Courteney Ilbert, the parliamentary draughtsman. Ilbert,[14] before whom the measure was laid in 1891, intimated that he did not consider the bill was necessary. The War Department, however, remained undaunted, and despite the lack of support from Sir Henry Campbell-Bannerman, Secretary of State for War in 1895, it tried again. Ardagh redrafted his bill of 1888 and once more it went to Ilbert, again to receive the thumbs-down. On this occasion, Ilbert submitted a lengthy memorandum on the subject, dated August 1896, the essence of which was that the Crown already possessed, under common law, the necessary powers. He pointed out that in the event of an invasion of the realm or an imminent risk of invasion, it was the duty of the military authorities to take all steps necessary, in their opinion, for the defence of the realm; and that it would be the duty of the civil authorities and of every subject to aid and support the military authorities, compensation being payable to those suffering loss in such circumstances. Not only was this duty

[11] CAB16/31/EP2, 'Memorandum etc . . .' para. 8.

[12] WO32/7112, 'Martial Law in the United Kingdom. Case for the Opinion of the Law Officers of the Crown', c.April 1913.

[13] CAB16/31/EP2, 'Memorandum etc . . .' para. 9.

[14] For details of Ilbert's career, see *A Dictionary of Common Law Biography*, ed. A. W. B. Simpson, London 1984, 267-8. A photograph of Ilbert appears therein.

grounded in common law but,[15]

> . . . any attempt to specify in detail and to express in statutory language the powers exerciseable by the civil and military authorities under such circumstances might throw doubt on the prerogative powers of the Crown, and would probably involve the imposition of restrictions and limitations which would be inconvenient and misleading, and which in practice it would be necessary to disregard.

Thus Ilbert not only placed his faith on the generality of prerogative powers to act in cases of necessity. He also considered that a statute might be positively harmful if couched in specific terms, for it might then be construed as derogating from general powers under the 'ordinary' law, an unhelpful situation where 'difficulties arising in due course of war or of preparations for war cannot be foreseen'. Indeed, he warned,

> In the event of invasion or of imminent risk of invasion, it might, and probably would, be necessary to take much stronger steps than would be authorised by the War Office draft.

No doubt, if the Government insisted, he observed, a statute 'adequate to the necessities of the case' could be prepared within the hour and passed through Parliament in a single day. However, he dismissively concluded that,

> . . . the elaboration of a statutory 'emergency code' would appear to be an academic exercise on which a Government official would not be justified in spending his time unless he happened to be in the enjoyment of superabundant leisure.

Military criticism of Ilbert's opinion seems to have been informed by two related factors. First, as Ilbert himself acknowledged, the exercise of general powers at the discretion of military officers was to run the risk of exposing the latter to a continual danger of legal proceedings, as the boundaries of lawful action might not be capable of delineation with pinpoint accuracy in the event of tumult or disorder or chaos. The fate of Pinney, the Mayor of Bristol, tried for neglect of duty, and of Colonel Brereton who as commander of the troops during the Bristol Riots in 1831 was court-martialled; and the martial law controversy involving Governor Eyre's handling of the Jamaica rebellion in 1865, continually haunted the military

[15] WO32/7112, 'Emergency Powers. Memorandum by C. P. Ilbert, 5 August 1896', para. 2. Subsequent quotations in the text, until otherwise indicated, are from paras 12, 11, 27(5) and 28, respectively, of this memorandum.

authorities.[16] The CID sub-committee in 1914 were reminded of Lord Wolseley's remarks in 1887:

> To rely on General Officers taking all the necessary responsibility in an emergency would be the height of madness. The manner in which Government treated Governor Eyre is too fresh in the memory of the Army to admit of any reliance being placed on officers to break the law in a dire emergency. Some, doubtless, would do so deliberately, preferring to be treated as Governor Eyre was, to exposing the country to risk; but many law-abiding gentlemen would not have the moral courage to do so. It is not fair deliberately to place an officer in such a dilemma.[17]

As MacDonogh had pointed out to his superior, Sir Henry Wilson, in 1911, the common law, as described in the *Manual of Military Law*, permitted the taking of 'exceptional measures in time of invasion as may be necessary' for the restoration of order. However, such measures were limited by 'immediate necessity'. Therefore, he added,[18]

> It does not seem that anything beyond this is allowed, and in addition to the fact that, human nature being what it is, many officers and others will in time of emergency either do the wrong thing or fail to do the right one, there is the further difficulty of dealing with the Civil Power as represented by the Courts. In the absence of an Act of Parliament it is too much to expect that the Courts will not hamper the military powers.

Thus fears of exposure to legal proceedings might cause military officers to act indecisively, and the consequences might be military disaster. But, second, Ilbert's general approach was dubbed by the War Department as a policy of *laisser faire* which was in direct conflict with that being pursued by the CID itself, and its preoccupation with contingency wartime planning. Legal preparations were as valid, in the view of the military, as those concerned more directly with the fighting and security aspects. Indeed, since the law provided the framework for the latter activities, the law had to be got 'right'.

The difficulty was to persuade their political masters that the War Department's complaint of inadequate legal powers was real and not

[16] On these episodes, see Charles Townshend, 'Martial Law: Legal and Administrative Problems of Civil Emergency in Britain and the Empire, 1800-1940', *Historical Journal* xxv, 1982, 167.

[17] CAB16/31/EP2, 'Memorandum etc . . .', para. 22.

[18] WO32/7112, MacDonogh to Wilson, c. 27 May 1911.

imaginary. During the first few years of the twentieth century, the matter appeared to have been put to one side, perhaps because of the more immediate need to absorb the recruitment lessons of the Boer War. In particular, the political uproar caused by the revelations of the Inter-departmental Committee on Physical Deterioration in 1904 no doubt preoccupied the military authorities at the time. In 1911, however, attempts were made to interest the then Secretary of State Lord Haldane in the proposals. But to no avail, for Haldane, the future Lord Chancellor, was content to place reliance on the flexible qualities of the common law. Eventually, his successor, Colonel Seely, agreed to refer the question to the law officers in 1913. MacDonogh busied himself with drafting a memorandum for this purpose, calling attention to the fact that English law, unlike its counterparts abroad, knew no concept of *l'état de siège*. This was an interim situation between normality and emergency, during which time precautionary powers might be exercised before an immediate necessity had arisen. Yet the common law appeared to make no provision for such contingency. He ended by pouring scorn on Ilbert's advocacy of the sufficiency of prerogative powers, concluding that,[19]

> . . . the exercise of martial law [here meaning non-statutory emergency powers] being justified solely by necessity, which may have to be proved, the prerogative power is too doubtful to be relied on for practical service . . .

But yet again, the lawyers appeared to close ranks against the military. Once more the legal advisers came down on the side of the *status quo*; on this occasion, Rufus Isaacs, the Attorney-General, and Sir John Simon, Solicitor-General, expressing their agreement with the thrust of the Ilbert memorandum drafted seventeen years previously. Their brief one hundred and sixty-nine word opinion merely reiterated the malleability of the common law and the danger of enacting an exhaustive list of required powers. 'The great merit of the Common Law', they wrote,[20] 'is that it will justify even an unprecedented course of action if it is fairly covered by the maxim *salus respublicae suprema lex*'. For good measure, they added, a bill of indemnity could, if necessary, be passed. The apparent contradiction

[19] WO32/7112, 'Martial Law etc . . .' p. 5.

[20] WO32/7112, 'Martial Law in the United Kingdom. Opinion of the Law Officers of the Crown, 17 July 1913.' French, who cites the Opinion (which was reprinted in CAB16/31/EP2, Appendix 2 for the CID Sub-Committee), wrongly dates it to 1914. See French, 83 note 9.

appeared to cause the law officers no problems of self-doubt.

But MacDonogh was nothing if not persistent. Following the rebuff in July 1913, he tried once more, with the support of Henry Wilson and of Brigadier-General Henderson, Director of Military Training, to bring about a fundamental change of thinking on the part of the government.[21] By November 1913, there was light at the end of the tunnel. The Prime Minister, Asquith, eventually agreed to refer the whole matter to the CID sub-committee whose deliberations provided the point of departure for this paper. Though the sub-committee papers were prepared in March-April 1914, the actual meeting did not take place till 30 June. Two days earlier, the Archduke Franz Ferdinand had been assassinated, though the significance of this event had not yet been grasped. Perhaps this is one explanation why Sir John Simon, who was by now Attorney-General, continued to play a similar legal refrain before the sub-committee to that which had accompanied the previous enquiries into the nature and content of emergency powers. When the chairman of the sub-committee, the Home Secretary Reginald McKenna, enquired whether in the event of a 'precautionary period' being declared, the common law would not cover officers entering private property for the erection of necessary defensive works, the Attorney-General answered in the affirmative.[22] Yet at least he now recognized a difficulty facing the military. He acknowledged that, '. . . what the War Office wanted was some way of convincing officers', that their actions would be lawful where war had not yet broken out. A bill, he suggested, would merely discourage the executive from taking action while it was going through Parliament. But a proclamation, Simon considered, would be suitable. It would state that,

> . . . whereas certain conditions had arisen necessitating the adoption of precautionary measures for the defence of the country, the responsible authorities might be compelled to take certain steps which were justified by the common law . . . An advantage of the Proclamation would be that it would enlighten the public on the powers which it was lawful to exercise in time of emergency.

And, of course, Simon could thus maintain his consistent line that the common law was adequate to meet the necessity of the case.

[21] WO32/7112, MacDonogh to Wilson, 13 November 1913.

[22] CAB16/31/EP1, 'Sub-Committe etc . . .', pp. 3-4 for this and subsequent references.

Inasmuch as the object was to 'reassure a timid General Officer', the War Office representative at the meeting, Major James, declared himself satisfied.

But international events moved rapidly thereafter, especially from 24 July when Austria's ultimatum to Serbia was endorsed by Germany. A few days later, the British home fleet's orders to disperse after exercises were countermanded by Churchill. So *was* there a proclamation forthcoming, indicating the powers which it was lawful for the military authorities to exercise in an emergency prior to the actual declaration of war? Since the 'precautionary period' was instituted less than a month after the CID meeting, such a proclamation might have been expected. Instead, Maurice Hankey, the secretary of the CID, recalled that,[23]

> During the next few days I was extremely busy putting the finishing touches on the War Book – printing off copies of some belated instructions still in proof, working with MacDonogh and Parliamentary Counsel on the Defence of the Realm Regulations, and so forth.[24]

Thus within the space of five weeks, there appeared to have taken place a rapid about-turn in policy on the kind of legal framework required in wartime. The sub-committee had indeed been charged with considering what emergency legislation 'if any' was necessary or desirable during the precautionary period *and* in war. However, the actual discussions were, in the event, confined to a consideration of the legal framework only for the precautionary period. It therefore appears that the War Office's shopping list of emergency powers for use during wartime itself managed to be slipped through the committee undebated and without challenge.

A full explanation for this complete shift awaits further investigation. A proclamation *was* published in the *London Gazette* for 14 August 1914, but it merely incorporated the Regulations of 12 August issued under the authority of the first Defence of the Realm Act of 8 August, the statutory embodiment of that shopping list of emergency powers.

The Defence of the Realm Act itself, Sir John Simon noted in his autobiography, had passed through all its stages in Parliament, on the first day of the war, even before there was time to circulate it as a

[23] Lord Hankey, *The Supreme Command 1914-1918*, vol. 1, London 1961, 153-4.

[24] The War Book contained all approved defensive preparations of the state including necessary orders-in-council, regulations, telegrams and other communications. See Hankey, Ch. xii.

bill. Indeed far from bemoaning the failure to resort to a proclamation outlining the military authorities' common law powers, as Simon had recommended a month previously, he now remarked that the statute '. . . and much else beside, had been carefully prepared beforehand'.[25] His own ambiguous role in respect of such a general purpose defence statute passed without comment.

What is more intriguing, however, is the view expressed in January 1915 by Professor J. H. Morgan, then engaged as Home Office Commissioner with the British Expeditionary Force in France. In a legal treatise published jointly with Thomas Baty, an Oxford don, Morgan threw doubt on whether the two Defence of the Realm statutes of August 1914, which purported to make provision for the issue of Defence Regulations, did in fact confer legal authority on His Majesty in Council to do so.[26] The August 1914 measures declared that H.M. in Council 'has power during the continuance of the present war', to issue regulations as to the powers and duties of the Admiralty and Army Council 'for securing the safety and defence of the realm'. The scope of such regulations was left undefined. In view of the wording adopted, Morgan opined that the Acts appeared to confer no more power on the Privy Council to make regulations than already existed at common law (such common law powers being assumed) apart from the exceptions expressly listed in the last footnote. The power to issue regulations as to the 'powers' of the Army Council seemed simply to be declaratory of the *existing* powers of the Army Council. Morgan advanced two possible explanations for this obscure wording. First, the intention was to confer a power to suspend the common law at pleasure, but this intention had to be disguised, presumably for political reasons. Second, and more charitably, Morgan preferred to believe that no new powers were intended to be conferred apart from the limited exceptions noted above.

Now, if this second interpretation *was* the correct one, then the lawyers, Ilbert, Isaacs and Simon, would indeed have had the second-last (but not the last) laugh. For a statute which was substantially declaratory of common law powers was to some extent

[25] Viscount Simon, *Retrospect*, London 1952, 103–4.

[26] The doubts did not extend to the issue of regulations concerning communicating witht the enemy, spreading of alarmist reports, securing the safety of communications and, of relevance to matters discussed heretofore, the suspension of any restrictions on the acquisition or user of land under the Defence Acts. These were expressly listed in the first Defence of the Realm Act of 8 August.

a vindication of the stance which the government's legal advisers had consistently adopted. The anomalous legal position lasted, in fact, for four months during which time, Morgan argues, '. . . we have been living under decrees of the military and naval authorities which were absolutely illegal'.[27] Such regulations presumably asserted powers beyond that permitted by the common law requirement of 'necessity' in respect to measures for immediate national security. The firing line, where the claim of necessity would surely prevail, was, after all, on the other side of the Channel.[28]

To rectify the deficiency in the first two Defence of the Realm Acts, it was necessary merely to transpose some of the wording in the August statutes so that section 1 of the Consolidation Act of November 1914 now read,

> His Majesty in Council has power during the continuance of the present war to issue regulations for securing the public safety and defence of the realm, and as to the powers and duties for that purpose of the Admiralty and Army Council.

The result was that the Privy Council now had power under statute not merely to issue regulations as to the *existing* powers of the Army Council for the defence of the realm and for public safety, but to issue regulations independently of, and not constrained by, existing military powers.[29] In effect, the Crown now had a general *statutory* power to make regulations for the defence of the realm and for

[27] T. Baty and J. H. Morgan, *War: Its Conduct and Legal Results*, London 1915, 102. John Hartman Morgan (1876-1955). Q.C. 1926; Barrister; legal editor of *Encyclopaedia Britannica*; Emeritus Professor of Constitutional Law, University of London; member, Executive Council of International Law Association; Liberal candidate in both general elections of 1910; Assistant Advocate General, Military Section of Paris Peace Conference; Deputy Adjutant-General and GOC Effectives Sub-Committee on Inter-Allied Military Control Commission in Germany, 1919-23; Vice-Chairman, Government Committee of Enquiry into Breaches of Laws of War; Home Office Commissioner with British Expeditionary Force 1914-15; Staff Captain on Adjutant-General's staff; Publications included *The House of Lords and the Constitution*, 1910; *The German War Book*, 1915; and *Assize of Arms*, 1945.

[28] For the courts' approach to prerogative powers to meet the threat of Zeppelin raids, see *In re a Petition of Right* (1915) 3KB 649 (C.A.) on the take-over of Shoreham Aerodrome. The owners appealed to the House of Lords, and the government agreed to settle out of court. See *The Times*, 28 July 1916. The case, incidentally, was Dicey's last at the bar. Whether the War Office could have invoked the prerogative to take over de Keyser's Royal Hotel in the absence of statutory authority must surely be doubtful. The 'necessity' did not seem immediate. See also note 3, above.

[29] It would, perhaps, have been better to declare that, 'It shall be lawful for H.M. in Council to issue regulations etc . . .'

public safety, and to make provision for the punishment of offenders. This was, indeed, the prize for which the military authorities had been agitating for twenty years. Detailed regulations could now be issued thick and fast under lawful authority as the pattern of the war shifted. Subject only to such regulations being confirmed as being for the defence of the realm (a phrase employed, as we have noted, even in the peacetime Defence Acts 1842-1873), and therefore *intra vires*, a flexible legal response by the military could now be achieved.

Why did this change come about? Perhaps astute lawyers in the War Office noticed the deficiency. Perhaps even Morgan, who had observed that, 'It is extraordinary . . . that no one, so far as we know, has during those four months, pointed out these illegalities',[30] communicated with the Home Office, the sponsoring department, on the matter. But the broader explanation is surely that by the end of November 1914 even the most conservative of lawyers must have come to recognize that the nature of warfare had been transformed beyond recognition. Large, sweeping land battles began to give way to a war of attrition. A war of attrition demanded vast quantities of men and *matériel* beyond the wildest imagination of pre-war planners. A war being fought by British troops on the continent of Europe was, for the first time in history, one which involved directly the civilian population. Workers and employers were now part of the military struggle, albeit physically remote from the Front, thereby surely precluding any confident reliance on prerogative powers,. There *were*, it is true, vast problems surrounding the *vires* of many regulations throughout the war,[31] while on rare occasions prerogative powers were invoked by the military authorities only to lead them into embarrassing retreat.[32] Nonetheless, the principle of a statutory emergency code was no longer in question.

[30] Baty and Morgan, 104.

[31] For a glimpse of these legal difficulties, see E. M. H. Lloyd, *Experiments in State Control*, Oxford 1924, ch. v.

[32] See note 28, above. The decision in *In re a Petition of Right* was roundly condemned by Sir Frederick Pollock on the ground that, 'The dicta about lawful entry on a man's land to make a bulwark for the defence of the realm seem to us not to contemplate general military requisition, but the precise emergency of apprehended attack on the spot'. See *Law Quarterly Review* xxxii, 1916, 339. Also CAB16/31/EP4, 'The Power to Erect Defence Works in Time of War. Memorandum Prepared by Sir Edward Troup, Home Office, August 27, 1912'. This discussed principally the *King's Prerogative in Saltpetre* (1606) 12 Co.Rep. 12; 77 *ER* 1294.

12

The Origins of the Nolo *Plea*

A. D. E. Lewis

In what can now be seen as the waning years of Richard Nixon's Presidency of the United States, his Vice-President Spiro Agnew was charged with tax evasion. Compared with what was to come this seems a trivial matter. To political observers in the Old World not the least interesting aspect of the case was the fact that Agnew was able to enter a plea which, whilst it admitted his culpability quite sufficiently to ensure the termination of his political career, nevertheless seemed to salvage some pride. The Vice-President 'did not contest the charges' against him. Not all were fooled. *The Times*' leader-writer declared without qualification that Agnew was guilty though the news report of the front page had been careful to acknowledge that the Vice-President had entered a plea of 'no contest'.[1]

Readers of Megarry's *Miscellany-at-Law*[2] may recall encountering a reference to this so-called plea and it will, of course, be familiar to those with an acquaintance with American criminal procedure as well as those who specialise in anti-trust law, for reasons which will appear. The rest are entitled to feel puzzled. It is the purpose of this paper to explain the puzzle and point the way towards an historical explanation of its development.

We can begin with a case in 1702 *R.* v. *Templeman*[3] which is the focus of Megarry's attention as well as an authority cited in more recent American decisions. It has the dubious distinction of having been the last recorded instance of the use of the device in England.

[1] *The Times*, 11 October 1973, 1 and 11. The leader writer had some authority for his conclusion: eg. 'it is now settled by the Supreme Court that it [the plea of *nolo contendere*] is, in effect, a plea of guilty', *U.S.* v. *Food and Grocery Bureau* (1942: D.C.) 43 F. Supp. 974. For this and other discussion see the annotation by Dreschsler in 89 *A.L.R.* 2d, 545. There is, of course, a wealth of literature on the modern U.S. practice, little of it bearing directly on the historical and policy issues addressed here. See N. B. Lenvin and E. S. Meyers, 'Nolo Contendere: its Nature and Implications', *Yale Law Journal* li, 1942, 1255-68.

[2] R. M. Megarry, *Miscellany-at-Law*, rev. ed., London 1956, 190.

[3] *ER* 91, 54 (1 Salk., 55).

The report in Salkeld reads in full:

> Upon a motion to submit to a small fine, after a confession of the indictment which was for assault, Holt CJ took a difference where a man confesses an indictment and where he is found guilty; in the first case a man may produce affidavits to prove *son assault* upon the prosecutor in mitigation of the fine: otherwise where the defendant is found guilty: for the entry upon a confession is only *non vult contendere cum Domina Reginae et pon. se in gratiam curiae.*

Templeman, it would appear, was indicted for assault. He decided against pleading not guilty and going to the jury, probably because, like the unfortunate perpetrator of the running down accident case in *Gibbons* v. *Pepper*[4] he feared that the jury would be misled by his denial. Rather he wished to show that although he had struck the plaintiff, it was the latter who had started the affair (*son assault demesne*). He seems therefore to have admitted to the Court that he struck a blow – Holt says that he *confessed* – but was permitted to submit himself not to judgement for the assault but to make fine, as it were to compromise the matter.

This form of record is traceable back to the thirteenth century. In 1226 for example, Magnus Turgod was attached to answer an abbot concerning a disseisin.[5] The defendant acknowledged the abbot's right 'et ponit se in misericordiam et finem fecit pro misericordia.' Again in 1342[6] two hobelers – persons obliged to maintain a horse for military service – were presented for unlawfully detaining money. One was acquitted but the other convicted by a jury and remanded to the marshalcy. Afterwards he came and 'petit admitti ad finem faciendum cum domino rege occasione predicta' upon which he was released from custody. Here of course the defendant had been found guilty and in the 1226 case he had clearly admitted his wrong-doing. But elsewhere in the 1342 roll is a case where those who had plundered Flemish merchants at sea are indicted for piracy and are asked how they wish to acquit themselves.[7] They say that they cannot deny their involvement and 'ponunt se inde ad graciam domini regis et petunt quod possint admitti ad finem faciendum cum domino rege'. This seems more equivocal. Are we to say that they confessed or not?

[4] *ER* 87, 469 (4 Mod. Rep., 404).

[5] *Curia Regis Rolls xii, 1225-1226*, no. 2225.

[6] *Select Cases in the Court of King's Bench*, vol. 6, ed. G. O. Sayles, Selden Soc. lxxxii, 1965, 17.

[7] *Select Cases . . . King's Bench*, vol. 6, 14.

Year Book discussions follow. In a case in 1410 the defendant pleaded not guilty to a writ of trespass. The plaintiff objected that the defendant was barred from this plea because when earlier indicted before justices of the peace, he had first pleaded *son assault demesne* upon which a jury had been summoned and then, before the verdict was taken, had waived his plea and confessed the trespass 'soy mist en le grace le Roy et puis fist fine'. The court held that he could not be received to plead against his former confession which was of record.[8]

Conversely in 1431 a defendant in *debt sur obligation* said that he was lay and unlettered and that the deed had been read over to him in another sense and so *non est factum*.[9] The plaintiff objected that in an earlier proceeding for detinue the defendant had admitted that the deed had been delivered: could he now deny that it was his? By way of argument counsel raised a comparable case where one indicted for trespass gave himself up and made fine: could he be received thereafter to plead not guilty? Yes, said the court. Even where it were of record that he confessed? Babbington, J.: 'If that were the case then he would be estopped, but the entry is this: *posuit se in Gratiam Domini Regis et petit se admitti per finem.* So if one were indicted of felony and had a charter of pardon and pleaded it and prayed allowance of it this would not prove that he was guilty, but only that the King had excused him by the charter.'

A final variant is an earlier case from the *Liber Assisarum* probably from the reign of Edward III.[10] A man was presented at assizes for extortion: 'il se mist en le grace le Roy et fist fine.' Mainprised to answer a bill entered by the victim he pleaded not guilty, only to be met with: 'You cannot get to that because you have made fine to the King for the same extortion and therefore confessed the extortion'. Regrettably this issue was not addressed by the court since the parties went off on a debate as to whether the plaintiff could make use of the defendant's admission in a case to which he was not privy. It might be significant that the defendant did not care to fight on the issue of whether he had confessed or not. But a note in the account of the case in Brooke's Abridgement states that the entry on the record in such a case in Henry VIII's day would be *quod petit se admitti per finem* without any express confession.[11]

8 *Year Books* 11 Henry IV, 65.
9 *Year Books* 9 Henry VI, 60.
10 *Liber Assisarum*, London 1679, 27 plea 57.
11 R. Brooke, *La Graunde Abridgement*, London 1573, 161 (s.v. Confession).

The essential question whether in such cases the defendant is to be taken as having confessed or not is therefore variously answered. It seems also that what is crucial is not so much what actually happens at the time that the earlier case is compromised but what gets into the record. If it is of record that he confessed then he cannot afterwards be heard to deny. If he is not recorded as having confessed then it is open to him to do so. In *Templeman*, for example, Holt seems to say that the defendant has confessed but because it is not of record – the entry being *non vult contendere* – he is not bound by it.

If we turn to look at the criminal law writers we see an interesting division between those who discuss our device and those who ignore it altogether. The earliest discussion is in Lambarde where he distinguishes between free and forced confessions, dividing free confessions into absolute confessions and confessions 'after a manner'. Absolute confession is where the party admits the fault and submits to such pain as the court will inflict. Confession after a manner, however, 'is only a not denying, in which the partie doth cunningly . . . take the fault upon him without plainly confessing himselfe guiltie thereof: as where he putteth himself *in Gratiam Regis et petit admitti per finem*, without any more; sometimes (by protestation that he is not guiltie) pleadeth his pardon . . .' He cites the two Year Book discussions from Henry IV and Henry VI, noted above.[12] Later writers either follow Lambarde or simply ignore this variety of confession altogether. Hawkins, for example, divides confession into express and implied. Express is Lambarde's absolute. Implied is where 'a defendant doth not directly own himself Guilty but in a manner admits it by yielding to the King's mercy and desiring to submit to a small fine . . .'[13] Hale's *History of the Pleas of the Crown*, however, recognises only a distinction between simple confession (Hawkin's express and Lambarde's absolute) and confessions to some advantage, such as clergy or turning approver.[14] Blackstone's account follows Hale.[15]

Although it seemingly disappeared from practice after 1702 and failed to make the pages of the most important treatise on English law, knowledge of the device did not die out completely. Indeed it

[12] W. Lambarde, *Eirenarcha*, London 1581, iv, 9.
[13] W. Hawkins, *A Treatise of the Pleas of the Crown*, 2nd ed., London 1723, c. 31.
[14] M. Hale, *History of the Pleas of the Crown*, London 1736, II c. 29.
[15] W. Blackstone, *Commentaries on the Laws of England*, vol. 4, Oxford 1769, 324.

found in what was the standard English criminal procedure handbook up until the Second World War. The 28th edition of Archbold has:

> Where the defendant, upon indictment for misdemeanour, yields himself to the King's mercy and desires to submit to a small fine: the Court may accept such submission if they think fit without putting the defendant to a direct confession.[16]

Why would anyone have bothered? There are two possible advantages to be gained. One, as we have seen and which attracted the attentions of the authors of the Abridgements, is that where there was a possibility of subsequent civil proceedings such an initial result would not estop the defendant from subsequently pleading not guilty and putting the plaintiff to his proof. The second attraction is reflected by the word 'small' qualifying 'fine' in Archbold's account which comes straight from Hawkins (who offers no authority). In English practice the first advantage would appear to have been sidestepped by a line of decisions beginning with *Gibson* v. *McCarthy*[17] which held that no record of a criminal action can be given in evidence in a civil suit except to credit. This line of authority was brought to an end in 1911 *Crippen's Case* where the President accepted that a criminal conviction is not only receivable but presumptive evidence to establish the truth of the facts upon which it is based even in proceedings *inter alios acta*.[18] By 1942 the Lord Chief Justice (Goddard) could say: 'The real incentive for the observance by employers of their statutory duties under Railway Acts, Factory Acts, Dock Acts, and similar legislation is not their liability to substantial fine, but the possibility of heavy claims for damages.'[19] It may not be entirely coincidental that the edition of Archbold published the very next year was the first to suppress mention of the use of our device.[20]

There was never much in the second supported advantage, that of

[16] J. F. Archbold, *Pleading, Evidence and Practice in Criminal Cases*, 28th ed., ed. R. E. Ross and T. R. Butler, London 1931, 393.

[17] *ER* 95, 202 (Cas. Temp. Hard., 311) dated 1736.

[18] *In the estate of Cunigunda Crippen* (1911) P. 108. The President thus, perhaps unwittingly, answered the query raised but not resolved in the *Liber Assisarum*, above note 10.

[19] *Hutchinson* v. *L. and N. E. Railway* (1942) 1 K.B. 488.

[20] Archbold, 31st ed., ed. T. R. Butler and M. Garcia, London 1943. Subsequent decisions resulting from *Crippen*, notably *Hollington* v. *Hewthorn* (1943) 1 K.B. 587, have not, however, restored mention of the device. I am grateful to Professor Hamar Foster for drawing my attention to this.

a small fine. In origin, of course, there was no question of a fine being imposed by the court: in theory the parties, King and defendant, were reaching a compromise conclusion for the privilege of which the defendant would have to pay. It was always open to the King to refuse such an accommodation and drive the defendant to either a plea or a confession proper.

Matters took a different turn the other side of the Atlantic. The early development is, as yet, obscure to me but the existence of the tactic was recognised in Massachusetts in 1829 and from thence reports throughout the nineteenth century attest to its existence in most State jurisdictions as well as the Federal.[21] It would seem that the conclusive force of a prior confession was one reason for resort to the device but the notion that one could in this way escape corporal penalties was also a motivating factor. The history of the *nolo* plea – as it came most illegitimately to be called in the United States – is in fact a small chapter in the development of the practice of plea-bargaining. The prosecutor would accept the plea which guaranteed the defendant some punishment to avoid the difficulties of proof and a jury-verdict. The defendant gained the certainty of outcome with a reduced punishment. The *nolo* plea really came into its own, however, as a device whereby corporations could escape the consequences of the Clayton Act 1914 which provided that a final judgement in any proceedings for anti-trust violations brought by the State would be conclusive against the defendant in any subsequent proceedings. Guilty pleas were held covered by this provision but not *nolo* pleas. There was in consequence a vast upsurge in the number of such pleas. The leading case *Hudson* v. *U.S.* reinterpreted the device as a privileged plea of guilty by holding that there was nothing to prevent a court imposing a sentence of imprisonment on such a plea.[22] Although the basis for this ruling is as historic as the arguments of those who stress the use of the word fine in the older authorities, the result is justifiable on the ground that the present U.S. practice has left the origins of the compromise far behind and that it is better construed as a living reality than as a historical survival.

[21] *Commonwealth* v. *Horton* (1829) 9 Pick 206.

[22] The judgement in *Hudson* v. *U.S.* (1925) 272 U.S. 451, contains a useful survey of the historical background.